Kit Holden is a British-German author and journalist who lives and works in Berlin. He covers German news and sport for Agence France-Presse, *The Athletic, Die Zeit* and others. He writes regularly on Union Berlin for *Der Tagesspiegel.*

You can follow the author on Twitter, @KitHolden

'A wonderful journey into the heart of a unique club'

Raphael Honigstein, author of
Das Reboot and *Klopp: Bring the Noise*

'An engrossing portrait of a football club that carries with it the story of Berlin with all its appealing contradictions: a city with a radical counterculture guarded with conservative zeal, a global metropolis with a village mentality, a cultural niche that becomes cooler the harder it tries not to be'

Philip Oltermann, journalist and author of
Keeping Up With the Germans and *The Stasi Poetry Circle*

'From the very first page, *Scheisse!* grips you. And gradually, through the quality of Kit Holden's wry writing, and the rich good humour of the content, it takes you in a gentler embrace. The history and culture of a special football club deserve a special kind of chronicling – and Holden has executed it to perfection'

Patrick Barclay, award winning sportswriter
and author of *Football – Bloody Hell!*

'Holden delivers a beautifully crafted story that reveals a personal history of one of Germany's most special clubs and cities'

Jonathan Harding, author of *Mensch* and *Soul*

'A fascinating tale expertly told. By focusing on the figures behind the scenes, Kit Holden captures the social and cultural history of Union and in doing so does this special club justice'

Adam Bate, Football journalist for Sky Sports

'For the first time, *Scheisse* is a good thing! A captivating read on one of the most unique clubs in world football'

Archie Rhind-Tutt, Bundesliga touchline reporter for ESPN

'Kit Holden superbly portrays the fascinating and inspiring football club that is "Iron Union". He captures the myth, the history and the spirit that make Union so very special and beloved'

Andreas Michaelis, State Secretary, former Ambassador to the UK, to Israel and to Singapore and long-time Unioner

'Union Berlin is not just one of the great stories of German football but in all of sports. The commitment between supporters and club epitomizes the romanticism and universality that makes the beautiful game the world's most popular game, and Kit perfectly captures the ups and downs of the club's incredible journey back to Germany's top flight. A must-read for any football romantic, regardless of where you're from and what team you support'

Cristian Nyari, co-founder of the *Bundesliga Fanatic*

SCHEISSE!

WE'RE GOING UP!

THE UNEXPECTED RISE OF
BERLIN'S REBEL FOOTBALL CLUB

KIT HOLDEN

DUCKWORTH

First published in the United Kingdom by Duckworth,
an imprint of Duckworth Books Ltd, in 2022

Duckworth, an imprint of Duckworth Books Ltd
1 Golden Court, Richmond, TW9 1EU, United Kingdom
www.duckworthbooks.co.uk

For bulk and special sales please contact
info@duckworthbooks.com

A CIP catalogue record for this book
is available from the British Library

Text design and typesetting by Danny Lyle

Printed and bound in Great Britain by Clays

1 3 5 7 9 10 8 6 4 2

Hardback ISBN: 9780715654439
eISBN: 9780715654446

To Jim, who gave me football,
and to Josie, who gave me Berlin.

CONTENTS

ACKNOWLEDGEMENTS

Nobody writes alone and the stories in this book do not belong to me. I owe a huge debt of gratitude to everyone I interviewed for their time, their enthusiasm and their trust.

I received unflinching and gracious support from several people at 1. FC Union Berlin. Special thanks to Christian Arbeit for his help arranging interviews and to Gerald Karpa for his critical eye and the many hours he spent reading and fact-checking my work. His diligence and attention to detail are matched only by his generosity.

Thank you to Stefanie Vogler, Stefanie Fiebrig, Matthias Koch and Andora for providing the pictures for this book, and to Luke Bird for his brilliant cover.

Finding interviewees and source material would have been a lot harder without the kind help of Torsten Eisenbeiser, Andora and Julian Gräber. It was also a happy coincidence that I was able to cover Union as a reporter while working on this project. I am eternally grateful to Claus Vetter and all my colleagues at *Der Tagesspiegel* for their belief in me.

The book would be considerably poorer if I had not been able to consult the excellent works listed in the bibliography, and in particular those of Matthias Koch and Frank Willmann, whose German-language histories of Union are far more comprehensive than mine.

Thank you to my agent, Robert Dudley, and to my publisher, Duckworth, for believing in such a niche project. Special thanks to my editor Rob Wilding, whose tireless enthusiasm and professionalism have made this book far better than it otherwise would have been.

There is no point writing a book if nobody reads it, so I am indebted to all the friends, colleagues and strangers who have helped spread the word.

Finally, while nobody writes alone, writing can be very lonely. The book would not have been completed without the emotional and practical support of my friends and family. Jim Holden is still my idol, and Josie Le Blond is the finest editor I know.

INTRODUCTION
WE DON'T GO TO THE FOOTBALL.
WE GO TO UNION.

On a cold night in March 2017, Union Berlin's players lined up in their penalty area to applaud the fans. In front of them, the trees of the eastern district of Köpenick loomed over the little terraced stand. All around them, the Alte Försterei stadium was rocking, and to the right the little brick scoreboard showed why. Despite going down to ten men in the first half, Union had just scrapped to an unlikely 2–0 win over Würzburg, which put them just four points off the top of the second division and meant they were in with a real chance of reaching the Bundesliga, Germany's top flight. The fans were in dreamland. A win against the odds was always sweet. Under these circumstances, it was vertigo inducing. As they cheered the players, they struck up a new chant, the lyrics of which were raised on a home-made banner behind the goal.

'Shit…We're Going Up!'

It was a joke, of course. Promotion to the Bundesliga would be one of the greatest achievements in Union's history, and the fans were bouncing off the walls in excitement. But all the best jokes contain a hint of truth, and besides the elation, there was also genuine disquiet. Top-flight football had never been a real possibility before, and now it was, the Union fans had to ask themselves how much they really wanted it. When their promotion hopes faded towards the end of that season, there was a faint sense of relief amid the disappointment. For many Unioners, the second division felt high enough.

It wasn't that they didn't like winning; it was that they cared more about the spirit of the club. Right back to their roots behind the Iron Curtain, Union fans had always identified as underdogs. In socialist East Berlin, they had been a yo-yo team, forever in the shadow of their powerful, regime-backed rivals, BFC Dynamo. In modern, reunified Germany, they had become a cult club, known for their community spirit and raucous stadium atmosphere rather than their success on the pitch. In both the communist and the capitalist era, Union fans thought of themselves as different: footballing outlaws in a world where the wrong people always won.

But now they were winning, and that made them nervous. Union narrowly missed out on the Bundesliga in 2017, but it wasn't long before the next promotion charge. When they found themselves near the top of the table again in 2019, the same fears began to surface. What if too much money and success changed the club? What if they changed it for the worse? Opinions differed, but most agreed that no title in the world was worth losing what they already had. Because what they had was more than just a football club.

'We don't go to the football,' they say in Köpenick. 'We go to Union.'

So, what is Union? Firstly, it is just 'Union'. It is never 'the Union', because that is the German name for the centre-right political alliance once led by Angela Merkel. It is also not 'a Union'. There have been several Union Berlins in German football history, and the club's full name, 1. (1st) FC Union Berlin, is technically a misnomer. But only one of them has meant so much to so many people, and only one of them is known simply as 'Union'. Most importantly, the name is pronounced *oon-yawn*, rather than *yoo-nyun*, which is why this book will often refer to 'an Union fan' rather than 'a Union fan'. To write or read Union like the English word 'union' feels wrong, because that is not how Unioners themselves pronounce it. They always say *oon-yawn*. And when they say *oon-yawn*, they don't just mean the team or even the club; they mean the whole package, from the profound sense of a shared history and local identity to the traditional pre-match piss in the forest.

Union is also not a monolith. It means different things to different people, and its varied, overlapping identities have all emerged from different eras in Berlin's chequered history. The idea of the rebel club began in the Cold War, when East Germany was a satellite state of Soviet Russia, and Union existed in the shadow of the Berlin Wall. The German Democratic Republic (GDR), which described itself as socialist rather than communist, was an autocracy where all aspects of life were carefully monitored and micro-managed by the state. While their cross-town rivals BFC Dynamo were affiliated to the Stasi secret police, Union were the civilian club – a plucky David to the state-backed Goliath. Their fans played up to this idea, giving rise to the enduring (and largely false) myth that Union was a dissident club.

Once the Wall fell, Union took on a new significance in people's lives. The end of communism and the reunification of Germany brought not only democracy and hope to East Berlin, but also economic hardship and uncertainty. Like many former East German clubs, Union struggled to adapt to capitalism and were plagued by existential financial crises long into the 2000s. Very often, it was only the absurd commitment and solidarity of the fanbase which kept it from going under entirely. Between 1989 and 2009, the fans begged, borrowed, and stole on Union's behalf. They mobilised to save the club from bankruptcy, redesigned it in their own image, and even rebuilt their own stadium when nobody else would help them. In doing so, they brought new life to the Union myth: the rebel club had become a community club.

Eventually, that myth began to attract outsiders. As the twenty-first century ground into gear, Berlin began to shake off the damage and division which had defined its recent history. It became cooler and wealthier, attracting hipsters and partygoers from across the continent. In time, that coolness inevitably began to rub off on Union. For those who had grown tired of the slick, commercialised football of the English Premier League, the little Alte Försterei stadium was like a portal to a bygone world. For little more than ten euros, you could squeeze onto packed, standing-only terraces wherever you found space, and marvel as 20,000 people sang louder than 50,000 would in London or Liverpool. You could smoke and drink while you watched the game, nobody left early, and even when the team lost 4–0 the crowd kept singing long after the final whistle. For many newcomers, the club's appeal was similar to Berlin's. They had come for the romance, and stayed for the cheap, cheerful charm of the underdog.

Except, suddenly, Union were no longer the underdogs. Two years after the game against Würzburg, they really did go up. In May 2019, they beat five-time German champions Stuttgart in a promotion/relegation play-off, prompting one of the biggest parties the Alte Försterei had ever seen. As Union fans downed thousands of litres of beer and lit up the forests with fireworks, most of them believed it would never get better. But then it did.

In the years after promotion, Union continued to rise to ever more unexpected heights; they avoided relegation, qualified for Europe, and even began to dream of a place in the Champions League. Just like Berlin itself, Union seemed unable to stop their balloon from rising. And the higher it got the more it had people looking nervously over their shoulder. While the German capital struggled to contain rising living costs and an influx of new wealth, Union fans worried about what success would do to their identity. Through all of it – the Stasi, the Wall, the wild 1990s and the more recent gentrification of the inner city – the club had been the rock at the centre of people's lives. It was a rare constant amid all the upheaval, and a refuge from the outside world. Now it was threatening to change as quickly and dramatically as Berlin.

Union's story is the story of a football club which rose from the brink of oblivion to the very top of the German game. But it is not just about that. It is also a story about Berlin, a city which, after the chaos and tragedy of the twentieth century, is now finding that stability and success bring their own troubles. It is a story about history, the division of Germany, and the mutual suspicion which lingers between East and West even today. It is a story about the financial crash, the coronavirus pandemic, and the Berlin housing crisis. Most of all, it is about people and the stories they tell about themselves.

To tell the history of the club only through the neat results and numbers of football would be to miss the point. The only way to tell it is through the people. At Union, the most interesting people are not the players or the coaches but the fans and the figures in the background. They are the dissident pop artist who designed the club's corner flags; the woman who rallied a team of untrained volunteers to build a stadium; and the hundreds who donated their own blood to save the club from bankruptcy. All of them attach an inordinate amount of their identity to one football club. All of them have a story to tell.

Each of the following chapters is based on an interview with a different Unioner. The short, introductory scenes are based on subjective memories of particular games. In every case, I have sought to allow each Unioner to freely tell their own story, while also providing enough historical context to make sense of them. The stories are snapshots. They do not tell a comprehensive history of either the city or the club. But they should paint a picture of a unique community and its struggles with the questions facing modern Berlin. What happens when a place defined by hardship becomes prosperous? How does a chronic underdog deal with success? Who is really winning anyway?

Every one of the strange and enchanting characters I spoke to had their own take on these questions. Some already mourn for a lost age, while others see a golden future ahead. Many more are just enjoying the ride.

All of them, though, have one thing in common. They all woke up the morning after promotion night with a ferocious hangover and the same thought rattling around their heads.

Scheisse! We're going up.

PART ONE
EAST

CHAPTER 1
DISSIDENTS IN INVERTED COMMAS

UNION BERLIN 0–2 BFC DYNAMO – 14 APRIL 1973

At half-time, Andreas makes a dash for it. He leaps over the advertising hoarding and sprints towards the centre circle, his red-and-white flag held high above his head. The Union fans roar him on from the block around the halfway line. Their team are a goal down in the Berlin derby against BFC Dynamo, and they could do with a little divine intervention. In the middle of the pitch, Andreas plants his flag in the turf and drops to his knees to pray.

Union or BFC? Scarlet or claret? Civilians or secret police? For 14-year-old Andreas, it is a fundamental question of character. In the street, the wrong answer can be a one-way ticket to a beating, and if he is caught this time, he is risking more than just a punch in the face. Crowd trouble has become increasingly common at this fixture and there is a heightened security presence at the Alte Försterei. The place is swarming with men in claret tracksuits. 'Cops,' thinks Andreas. 'Every last one of them.'

Dynamo is the police sports club. Their president is the East German Minister for State Security, Erich Mielke, head of the notorious Stasi secret police and the de facto second-most powerful man in the ruling Socialist Unity Party. A passionate BFC fan, Mielke will soon see to it that his team overtake their sister club Dynamo Dresden as the country's strongest side. They are already the biggest club in Berlin, with better facilities than Union, better players, and the advantage of the odd controversial refereeing decision in their favour. They are fourth in the Oberliga table and pushing for European qualification. Union are bottom. They have won just one of the last nine derbies and are on course for another defeat today.

But Andreas has a plan. Reaching the centre circle, he turns to face the goal which Union will be attacking in the second half. With a flourish, he prostrates himself in front of it. It is more of a performance than a real prayer – a rallying dance for the rabble of long-haired Union fans in the block on the halfway line, and a middle finger to the Stasi pigs in their claret tracksuits. 'If I can do three bows without being caught, then we'll beat the bastards,' he thinks. 'We'll chase them out of the stadium and wipe the smile off Mielke's face.'

As he comes up from the third bow, he sees claret tracksuits streaming towards him from all corners of the pitch, shouting in outrage. Andreas's lip curls. He really hates those tracksuits. His school's headmaster, another Dynamo fan, wears one every day, and to see so many here at the Alte Försterei makes him feel sick. The vodka flowing through his veins gives him courage. For a second, he considers standing his ground and swinging his fists. But he knows it would be better to run. When they've got you boxed in, there's no shame in running.

Andreas grabs his flag and dodges the first tackle. He has played football since he was 5 years old, and he is quick on his feet and strong on the ball. When he turned up uninvited for trials at Union the previous year they called him 'butterfly', because he ran with his elbows out to ward off the heavy challenges. Now, as he races back towards the block, the claret tracksuits bounce off his outstretched arms.

The Alte Försterei is at full capacity: 18,000 pairs of eyes are on him as he sprints towards the crowd. In the block on the halfway line, the Union fans cheer him on in delight, reaching out their arms as he gets closer and closer. On the crowded terraces, even the police struggle to maintain control. They line the steps with their German shepherds and batons, but they rarely breach the line themselves. The crowd is too wild, too confident, and to charge it would risk a full-scale confrontation. Andreas knows that if he can just get back into that block, he should be safe.

With a last burst of adrenaline, he leaps over the advertising board and is bundled into the throng of supporters. Within seconds, the police have lost sight of him. The fans bray in delight. Someone thrusts a bottle into his hands, and the triumphant swigs burn his throat. It is a year since his official Jugendweihe, but this feels like a more meaningful coming-of-age ceremony. As far as the Unioners are concerned, the boy Andreas is now a man. Drunk on adrenaline and alcohol, he doesn't even make it home. He sleeps in the forest. Underneath the canopy of trees, just like in the block on the halfway line, he is safe.

✻   ✻   ✻

At school on Monday morning, a flag ceremony is called. The students line up in the courtyard before the headmaster in his claret Dynamo tracksuit, and this time there is nowhere to escape. While others are praised for their good work and commitment, Andreas is called to the front for self-criticism. He mumbles a few words of remorse before the headmaster delivers a clean, hard blow to his left cheek. Andreas is buzzing. This time he has really pissed them off.

But that is also the extent of his triumph. Union lose the game 2–0 and are relegated later that season. Future derbies are moved to a larger, more accessible neutral stadium in the city centre, and it is fifteen years before the Stasi club return to the Alte Försterei.

By that time, Andreas is on the other side of the Wall.

Old grudges die hard, and Andreas Hoge still refuses to speak the name of BFC Dynamo. Like many Union fans of his generation, he refers to them only by euphemisms: *Biffzen, Befies, The Unspeakables, The Three Letters.* Though the two sides have not played a league game against each other since 2006, the once fierce rivalry is still a defining feature of Union's identity. The old dividing lines of police and civilian, regime and people still run deep, and Hoge is not the only one with a tall tale of how he personally stuck it to the Stasi club. 'You know the old adage,' he says. 'Not every Union fan was a dissident, but every dissident was an Union fan.'

He is in his sixties now, and he goes by his artist's name: *Andora*. His nose – wide and flat with a bump in the middle of it – still bears the marks of his early teenage rebellion at the Alte Försterei. 'My girlfriends used to want me to fix it, but I'd say no,' he cackles. 'This nose is protection! I look like a boxer, and it makes people shit themselves.'

It's not just people. It is a baking hot day in August when he first meets me, and we are drinking Bavarian wheat beer at eleven a.m. The wasps, a constant irritation of the Berlin summer, swarm over my glass but ignore Andora. When one of them has the temerity to land on his arm, he breaks off mid-sentence and glares at it. 'No, no, no, Mr Wasp,' he growls in a thick Berlin accent. 'Don't you even think about messing with me, because I'm telling you now, you will regret it.'

The wasp flies away.

Andora is around two metres tall with piercing grey eyes, long silver hair and a bushy, black-and-white goatee. In every other respect, he is an explosion of colour. He is wearing paint-splattered white overalls, a pair of red Converse trainers and a sleeveless denim jacket which reveals the tattoos snaking up his arms. One of them, which stretches from the inside of his elbow down to his wrist, shows the long, rectangular emblem of his football club. The word 'Union' has been replaced with '*Kunst*': the German word for art.

In the four decades since he left East Berlin, Andora has become one of Germany's most renowned pop artists. He began under the wing of the West German neo-expressionists and made a name for himself daubing wild and colourful motifs on everyday objects. His canvases have included shoes, electric guitars, boxing robes and Formula One cars. In 1992, he trained as a cosmonaut while painting a proton rocket for the Russian Space Agency. He insists that, to this day, he is the only artist in the world whose work has orbited the planet.

Over the past fifteen years, his favoured muse has been Union. From watering cans to anti-Stasi footballs, he has put together a small gallery's worth of works dedicated to the spirit of the football club which defined his adolescence. The most famous of them is exhibited on the pitch at the Alte Försterei. On the corner flags, where most clubs just have their emblem or plain block colours, Union have a face. The top half of each flag is red, and the bottom half is white. At the furthest edge, the line separating the two colours splits to reveal a snarling mouth full of razor-sharp teeth. The upper lip curls upwards around a mischievous, glinting eye towards the top corner, where it meets a flat nose with a bump in the middle of it. At first glance, the flag looks like a shark. At second glance, you realise it is also Andora's self-portrait.

'I am the human corner flag of 1. FC Union Berlin,' he beams. 'I am the only human corner flag in German professional football, and probably the only one in the whole world.' It is an unpaid role, but one which Andora takes seriously. He even has an official employee ID card. He acts as a kind of official club artist, there to entertain the fans and, as he puts it, draw the boundaries of what it is to be an Unioner. 'To be the human corner flag of a club like this is even bigger than my rocket,' he says.

Union is Andora's founding myth. 'It was my adolescent home, my temporary home and, as it turns out, my lifelong home,' he says; adolescent, because he was just 17 years old when he was banned from attending Union games; temporary, because it was only a decade after first going to the Alte Försterei that he left East Germany for good in the back of a police bus; and lifelong, because after a career which took him from Hamburg to New York via Moscow and Vienna, he eventually returned home to offer the club his services as an artist.

Andora's generation is also a core part of Union's founding myth. It was fans like him who forged the idea of Union as a rebel club, using the safety of the football crowd as a stage to mock the state and even cast themselves as dissidents in an oppressive regime. In the decades that followed, the idea took hold and Union's supposed 'resistance' to Mielke and the Stasi became established German football mythology. As with most of the identities football fans carve out for themselves, it is more than a little exaggerated. Even Andora admits that most Union fans were, at best, 'dissidents in inverted commas'.

But Union, like Andora, clung on to their reputation long after East Germany ceased to exist. The spirit of rebellion, however nebulous, has lingered on in the tall tales they tell about themselves, and which others tell about them. Andora's stories are as colourful as his paintings, and none of them would make sense without his football club. Even the snarling corner flag is a strange amalgam of the two biographies, as much a portrait of Union as one of himself.

'It is called *Der kleine Biss* (*The Little Bite*),' he explains. 'And it represents the bite we Unioners have always had, ever since the beginning.'

* * *

When exactly the beginning was is hard to say. In its current form, the club has only been around since 1966. But its roots go far deeper, stretching from the German Empire to the building of the Berlin Wall, via a revolution and two world wars. Like Germany itself, the club which eventually became Union Berlin was born and reborn countless times in the first half of the twentieth century. 'We are the only club in Germany which has existed in all the Germanies,' says Andora.

Union's earliest ancestor, SC Olympia Oberschöneweide, were founded in 1906 when Kaiser Wilhelm II was still on the throne. Oberschöneweide (meaning 'upper pretty meadow') was an industrial district in the south-east which was not yet officially part of Berlin, and football – an English import – was still in its infancy in Germany. So, it did not make headlines when a small group of students got together in the pub to form SC Olympia. Nonetheless, the young footballers had chosen a fateful year to found their club. For just a few months later in neighbouring Köpenick, confidence trickster Wilhelm Voigt made the local area famous with one of the most celebrated criminal acts in Berlin's history.

Posing as an army captain, Voigt convinced a group of soldiers to help him storm the Köpenick town hall, arrest the mayor and confiscate 4,000 marks from public coffers. The story is sometimes held up as a parable about slavish Prussian obedience, a warning tale of soldiers so in awe of the chain of command that they will follow even the most obvious charlatan. Another way of looking at it is that Voigt kickstarted a long Köpenick tradition of thumbing one's nose at authority – one which local football fans would later gladly latch on to. A popular matchday pub near the train station is still named after the notorious 'Captain of Köpenick'.

SC Union Oberschöneweide, as the club later became, did not move to Köpenick until 1920. By that time, Germany had been defeated in the First World War, a violent revolution had overthrown the monarchy, and the Kaiser had fled. The punishing war reparations helped fuel devastating hyperinflation in the fledgling Weimar Republic, and when SC Union played Hamburger SV in the final of the German Championship in June 1923 the cost of a kilo of rye bread was in the hundreds of billions of marks.

The next time they made it to the national play-offs, the Wall
Street Crash had turned the world on its head and Germany
had long since descended into fascism. In 1940, a year after
Nazi expansionism had unleashed the Second World War,
Union were beaten in the German Championship quarter-
finals by Rapid Vienna, who had become a German club with
the annexation of Austria two years earlier. That one failed title
bid remains the only notable episode of the club's story in the
twelve darkest years of German history. If Union's legendary
'bite' was around at this point, it did not show itself against the
horrors of Nazism.

In the Cold War, however, a first seed was sown for the rebel
myth. After the defeat of Nazism in 1945, the Allies divided
both Germany and its capital into four sectors, leaving West
Berlin as an island of western influence in a sea of communist-
controlled territory. Tensions between the USSR and the
western powers began to simmer almost immediately, and in
1948 the Soviets escalated a dispute over competing currencies
by blockading West Berlin. The crisis lasted well into 1949 and
led to the founding of two separate German states: the capitalist,
democratic Federal Republic of Germany in the West, and
the German Democratic Republic under one-party, socialist
rule in the East. But the tensions between them did not end
with the blockade. Between 1949 and the construction of the
Berlin Wall in 1961, more than two million East Germans are
estimated to have moved west through West Berlin in search of
either freedom or simply greater prosperity. Among them were
a handful of footballers from Union Oberschöneweide.

In 1950, the borders between the two states were yet to
harden and the structure of German football was still in flux.
Union had come second in the Berlin championship, making
them the only team from the East to qualify for the national
play-offs that summer. That was a problem for the East German

authorities, who were already pushing their own separate national league in the GDR. Union were forbidden from taking part, prompting a number of their players and directors to move permanently to the West, taking their families and lorries full of belongings with them across the border. By the time they played their first play-off match against Hamburg in the West German city of Kiel, they had already re-formed in West Berlin as SC Union 06.

It is tempting to see this episode as Union's original sin under socialism, the first of many occasions on which they bravely defied socialist rule in the name of freedom and individuality. The reality is less romantic: even before the introduction of professionalism, there was still more money to be earned as a footballer in the West, and most of those who joined the break-away club probably did so for financial reasons. Others simply returned to East Berlin after the play-offs. From now on, there were two clubs who could claim to be the heirs of the old Union Oberschöneweide: the new breakaway club in the West, and the old club at the Alte Försterei, which would soon drop the name Union altogether. In 1951, a year after the split, they were merged with a neighbouring club, taking on both their red-and-white colours and their more socialist-sounding name: BSG Motor.

When the name Union finally returned to the Alte Försterei in 1966, it returned not to a rebel club, but to a member of the new elite. In the mid-1960s, spooked by the GDR's decline on the world stage, the authorities set about a drastic reform of East German football. Ten of the country's best teams were reorganised into specialist centres of football development, each sponsored by a state organisation. BFC kept the name of the police's Dynamo sports association, while FC Vorwärts Berlin remained affiliated to the army sports club ASK. But there was also a third Berlin club, sponsored by the local metal and electrical industry, and named by the readers of the local newspapers. 1. FC Union Berlin, as they would henceforth be known, were the civilian club.

'A civilian club in a dictatorship. Whoever it was who let that happen, Mielke should have had them shot,' says Andora with a laugh. In reality, though, Union were as much a product of the establishment as any of the others. They may not have been affiliated to an organ of state security, but they were still an organisation created by the state. Their official founding in January 1966 took place in the clubhouse of a factory named after socialist revolutionary Karl Liebknecht, and included a speech by Paul Verner, a high-ranking member of the Politbüro. Like BFC, Union also had friends in high places well into the 1970s. The head of the state trade union, Herbert Warnke, had been a keen supporter of their predecessor clubs, and he regularly turned up to watch first-team and youth games at the Alte Försterei.

But for Andora, it wasn't about the suits at the top. Purely by virtue of not being the police or the army club, Union were a natural choice for the misfits of East Berlin. That included him, a youth growing up on Friedrichshain's Marchlewskistraße, which today runs behind the famous Berghain nightclub. Back then, it was a residential street which housed both an enormous police station and, as Andora tells it, some of the less well-adjusted members of socialist society. 'The only people who lived there were trash,' he says. 'Drunks, whores' kids, junkies.' Andora himself left home at 15, agreeing with his dad that, if he needed him, he would find him in the pub.

It was Andora's dad who had got him hooked on Union, taking his son to the 1968 East German Cup final against FC Carl Zeiss Jena on his tenth birthday. 'I was too short to see anything, but I could tell I had witnessed something special just by the looks on other people's faces,' he says. Underdogs Union battled to a sensational 2–1 victory to win their first and only piece of major silverware. Catching glimpses from behind the sea of legs, a 10-year-old Andora fell in love with his first footballing idol: a free-spirited, talismanic winger named Günter 'Jimmy' Hoge.

Hoge was Union's first cult hero. A short, slightly hunched man with beady eyes and bowed legs, his awkward physique belied his speed and grace on the ball. Union fans of a certain age go misty-eyed when they talk about him and point to an endorsement from one of the greatest ever to play the game. 'That number seven must have a motor on his back,' the Brazilian legend Pelé is said to have remarked when he saw Hoge play at an exhibition tournament in South America in 1968. The Union fans loved him because he was one of them. For Andora, who shared his surname, he was both a rebel icon and a footballing father figure.

'A lot of people thought I actually was Jimmy Hoge's son,' he says. And while he never pretended he was, he liked the comparison. Hoge, after all, was both an artist on the pitch and a troublemaker off it. In 1961, just weeks before construction work started on the Berlin Wall, he made his first two international appearances for the GDR. Despite playing well, he was not picked for another six years after falling out of favour with the authorities. Having left army club Vorwärts under a cloud in 1962, he was transferred to a team two divisions below them and only returned to the top flight with Union in 1966. At the Alte Försterei, he developed a reputation for drinking and was twice suspended internally for disciplinary reasons. In an interview with author and seasoned Union reporter Matthias Koch in 2011, he claimed that, on at least one occasion, he had been punished on trumped-up accusations for skiving political education sessions. 'I wasn't swimming in the direction the state wanted me to,' he said.

Hoge's reputation had a lasting impression on Andora. 'When your favourite players have that kind of attitude as a young man, it's a formative thing,' he says. But if Hoge was a rebel, his cause was a losing one. In 1970, his career ended prematurely after one indiscretion too many. Having gone to the pub with former coach Werner Schwenzfeier to watch West Germany play Italy at the 1970 World Cup, he was denounced to the authorities for drunkenly singing the West German national anthem. Although he once again denied the accusation, Günter 'Jimmy' Hoge was effectively banned for good from all forms of elite football. He was 29 years old.

It is easy to see why Union fans came to lionise Jimmy Hoge. He could be held up as footballing proof of both the injustice of the system and the righteousness of the underdog. Like many East German men of that age, says Andora, he cut a tragic figure. 'That generation was full of drunks because of what they lived through: the building of the Wall and everything else. You have to understand that,' he says. 'That's why I never blamed my own father. I just told him I wasn't going to live like him.'

East Germany still holds a reputation for having been a hard-drinking society, and both beer and spirits have always played a prominent role in fan culture at Union. But Andora, himself a formidable drinker, insists that his generation was different to that of his parents. He and his peers came of age in the shadow of 1968, the summer in which student uprisings swept across Europe and Union won the cup. 'We were the gold dust generation, the first ones to really take charge of our lives,' he says. 'I was the first person in my family who was truly autonomous. I left home at fifteen and I was able to do that because of the armour Union gave me – the ability to craft my own character as an individual.' Perhaps that is why he is so averse to the fatalism of his father's generation. Years later, he says, he found himself chatting to the real Jimmy Hoge.

'*Meister*, I wish you really were my son,' Jimmy said.

'Well Jimmy,' Andora replied. 'You should have shagged my mum then, shouldn't you?'

✳   ✳   ✳

It was in 1970, the year Jimmy Hoge was banned, that Andora first made the trip out to the Alte Försterei. The football he saw there was nothing to get excited about. Only once in the following five years did Union finish in the top half of the first-tier Oberliga. But like everyone else, he didn't care. 'We didn't go for the football, we went for the social environment,' he says. He remembers a sense of feeling 'protected' when he walked through the woods with his friends before a game. 'And then in those two hours in the stadium, there was this incredible strength, energy and feeling of resistance.'

Resistance is a strong word. It conjures images of covert meetings, daring escape attempts and epic space battles above the Death Star. This is the romantic view of Union: that they were the footballing Rebel Alliance, a rallying point for dissidents of all stripes; that from the safety of the crowd at the Alte Försterei, people could shout things they would never dare to say elsewhere; that when their team got a free-kick and the opposition lined up to defend it, the fans would chant 'down with the wall!' and everyone would know which Wall they meant; that to be an Union fan was inherently political.

The idea is not entirely apocryphal. When Union fans talk about the 1970s and 1980s, they almost always recall a similar feeling to Andora. Only a few remember shouting 'down with the wall', but most agree that the stadium was a place where the norms and niceties of socialist society no longer applied. And while that is arguably true of football stadiums in any political system, drunken rowdiness can perhaps seem more subversive in a police state. For his part, Andora insists it was political: 'We were in Berlin, on the front line of the Cold War. You can't see it without politics,' he says. But he also makes an important distinction: 'The politics we had on the terraces were different to the politics of the club itself.'

The club itself was anything but anti-regime. Generally, anti-regime clubs do not exist in one-party dictatorships, and they certainly don't compete regularly on national television. In the GDR, the party didn't just run society through force and surveillance, it also managed it on more mundane levels. Like any formal organisation, Union were a product of the system and they could not exist outside of it. The players were employed by state-owned companies, and the chairmen were invariably party members. If there was a whiff of rebellion on the terraces, it was never officially endorsed. Andora recalls regular messages from the club urging 'football rowdies' to stay away from the stadium. 'They meant people like me, and everyone else who saw the club as more than just a sports club,' he says.

But even those like him were hardly dissidents in any meaningful sense of the word. Union fans may have clashed with police and drawn attention from the Stasi, but they were small fry compared to the regime's real critics. For the most part, football fans were a headache not because they were plotting to overthrow the system, but because they drank, fought and dressed differently to ordinary socialist citizens. Union, like punk rock, was non-conformity which could masquerade as political activism.

'We were dissidents in inverted commas,' says Andora. Revolutionaries in style if not necessarily in substance. The typical Union 'look' – a green shell-parka, blue jeans and sometimes sandals – was borrowed from the *Bluesers* or *Trampers*, a loose counterculture of musicians and hitchhikers who were equally irritating for the authorities. As the name suggests, the *Bluesers* started out as blues-rock fans, but were also inspired by the hippies and student revolutionaries making waves in the West. 'We wore the parkas because the 1968ers in the West were the first people to do so: people like

Rudi Dutschke, although I'm not sure he ever wore one,' says Andora. Because western goods were scarce and few were lucky enough to have a source of Levi's and genuine US army parkas, they improvised instead. 'I had no relatives in the West, so I cut out the Union badge from a pendant and stuck it on my Polish denim jacket,' says Andora. 'I looked like an idiot, but it was a way of showing your colours on the street.'

Union may not have been dissidents, but they were cool. Despite their comparatively miserable results on the pitch, they consistently drew higher attendances than BFC in the 1970s. In fact, Dynamo's success may even have made Union more popular. Even political conformists had no love for the Stasi, and it was clear to everyone that Mielke's patronage rigged the system in BFC's favour. It wasn't just that they won more games; it wasn't just that refereeing decisions tended to go their way. It was also that Dynamo had more than six times as many youth academies from which they were able to recruit talent.

Union, meanwhile, never seemed to hold on to their best players. In the same year Jimmy Hoge was banned, his team-mate Klaus Korn's career was also forcibly ended after he allegedly called several BFC players 'Stasi pigs' in a particularly heated derby match. Others were not banned, but simply transferred from Union to BFC. The most famous case was Reinhard 'Mecky' Lauck, a hero of the 1968 cup win who was transferred to BFC after Union were relegated in 1973. Andora, then just 15, was part of a several-hundred-strong delegation of Union fans who marched on Lauck's flat near Alexanderplatz in a bid to convince him to stay. Lauck pretended not to be home; it was not up to him which club he played for. 'The Lauck transfer was torture for my soul,' says Andora. 'It was the first moment that it really hit me: everything is regulated here; everything is decided by some unknown people, and there is nothing I can do or say about it.'

That was a reality which extended beyond football. A year earlier, Andora had celebrated his *Jugendweihe*, a secular coming-of-age ceremony after which East German teenagers received their first ID document. Andora, who was already on the Stasi's books by that point, was handed only a 'provisional ID'. The dreaded two-page document, which also went by the more Orwellian name of PM12, was the regime's bureaucratic naughty step. It effectively made the holder a second-class citizen, unable to travel abroad and obliged to report to a police station at regular intervals. 'It said provisional on it, but you knew it would be for life. You knew you would never get a real one,' he says. 'When I asked them why, they told me I wasn't worthy to represent the Republic in our socialist brotherlands.'

The PM12 meant that, at 14, Andora's prospects in the GDR were dwindling fast. His teenage misdemeanours at school and at Union had made him *persona non grata* within the country of his birth. And that pushed him closer to the real dissidents.

* * *

When Andora starts talking, he can talk for hours. His anecdotes are like his paintings, full of exclamations, constantly charging from one idea to the next. There is rarely a pause for breath, rarely a moment of reflection, and almost never a sad note. Even when he is talking about the worst aspects of East German socialism – repression, imprisonment, state violence – his tone is relentlessly energetic. If he is haunted by the things he experienced, he chooses not to show it. He tells the stories as if it all bounced off him. As if, ultimately, he was always winning the battle. And perhaps he was.

Even the party couldn't control everything, and for both Andora and Union, there were victories as well as defeats. In

1976, Union were promoted back into the Oberliga after three years in the second division. That meant that they were once again in the same league as BFC, though the derbies were now to be played on neutral ground at the Stadion der Weltjugend. The official line was that the stadium in the city centre would allow more fans from both sides to attend. Union fans suspected it was a ruse to rob them of home advantage. But if it was, it backfired. Thanks to heroics from goalkeeper Wolfgang 'Potti' Matthies, Union won both derbies there in the 1976/77 season.

Andora missed the games because he was in prison. 'I only knew Union had won because the guard brought me a newspaper the next day with a hole in the page where the match report would have been,' he beams. He had been arrested earlier that year, he explains, on suspicion of being involved in a plot to escape the GDR in the back of a lorry.

Perhaps the most damning indictment of the East German state was the lengths to which they would go to prevent their own citizens from leaving. At least 140 people are estimated to have been killed at the Berlin Wall alone, and tens if not hundreds of thousands were arrested for attempting to flee to the West. In some cases, the Stasi are believed to have pursued people even after they made it out. In 1979, BFC's star midfielder Lutz Eigendorf absconded while on a trip to play Kaiserslautern in West Germany. Four years later, he died in a car accident. It was widely speculated, though never proven, that the Stasi had a hand in his death.

For those who did not want to risk illegal escape, another option was to be deported. Throughout the Cold War, the West German government would regularly buy the freedom of East German political prisoners, paying the socialist regime to expatriate them and deliver them over the border. A money-spinner for the perennially broke GDR state and a humanitarian coup for the West, it was a dirty deal which suited all sides, not least the prisoners themselves. To Andora, it seemed like the best way of getting out. For that to happen, he needed to be recognised by the West as a political prisoner worth freeing, and then get arrested.

A few years after being blackmarked with a 'provisional ID', Andora was banned from the Alte Försterei. Initially, he claims, he kept going to Union anyway, shaking off his Stasi shadow in the gridded streets of Friedrichshain before hopping unnoticed onto the train. But slowly, he drifted away from football towards the nightclubs and the writers' circles in other parts of East Berlin, and began to restyle himself as a more serious critic of the regime. 'I went to Prenzlauer Berg, and started to work against the GDR politically,' he says.

Prenzlauer Berg, a district just north of Friedrichshain, was at that time the epicentre of a budding underground literary scene in East Berlin. After a brief period of cultural liberalisation under new party leader Erich Honecker in the early 1970s, the state took a harder line with the forced expatriation of singer Wolf Biermann in 1976. The move sparked widespread protests, with high-profile cultural and literary figures at the heart of them. Andora says he was on the fringes of the movement, networking with well-known dissidents and western journalists. 'Was I a dissident?' he asks himself. 'You're only really a dissident when you get recognised as a dissident and thrown out of the country.'

By 1980, he was convinced that he had done enough groundwork to achieve that aim. He had grabbed the attention of the West; now he just needed to get arrested, and this part was easy. He decided to go to the border crossing at Friedrichstraße and ask to cross without permission, an offence which could land you eight years behind bars. At the border, he waited in line in front of a West German school group who had come over on a day trip. Just before he reached the first checkpoint, he turned to the first pupil behind him. 'My name is Andreas

Georg Hoge, and I was born on the 7th of June 1958,' he told him. 'Memorise that information, and when you are through, go straight to the *Springer* newspaper offices on Kochstraße and tell them who I am and what you have seen here.' Then he walked up to the guard and asked for a one-way ticket to West Berlin. Within seconds, he was surrounded by armed soldiers and taken away.

In detention the following day, Andora saw that his Stasi interrogator had a West German newspaper under his documents, and he reasoned that his gamble had paid off. With his name in the press, the West German government was more likely to buy his freedom. He was right. He was sentenced to six years in prison without trial but served only a few months before being deported to the West. Later, when he gained access to his Stasi file, he looked up how much they had paid for him. 'It interested me to see how much I was worth to them,' he says. '40,000 marks!' He seems happy with that. If it was 40,000 marks, he was a bargain. According to the German government, that figure was indeed the going rate for political prisoners, but only until 1977. When Andora was freed three years later, it was already more than 90,000.

But as with all the stories of Union and the Stasi, the details can get muddled in the telling. Whatever the exact circumstances, by 1980 Andora was in the West – a political refugee but a free man. 'I don't know how or why, because it was the same sky on either side of the border,' he says. 'But the grass was genuinely greener on the other side.'

* * *

The second time I meet Andora, shortly after Euro 2020, he tells me to bring 'a very good bottle of gin' with me. I order one from a distillery in Herefordshire, and the bottle comes adorned with a gaudy, elasticated Union Jack bow tie attached to the neck. Upon seeing it, he cackles and begins to hold forth on the subject of what Germans call 'the island'. He says unprintable things about the Queen, hails the Irish and the Welsh, and eventually works himself into a rage about English football fans.

'All I can say to the fans in England is "Look at our club, and you will see something incredible,"' he says. '"Something you will never see again at your clubs, because they all belong to some rich wanker. You're not watching football anymore; you're watching the stock market. And if you keep watching, you are worshipping the very people who exploit you, and anyone who does that must be stupid."' He switches from German into English to deliver the final, crushing blow: 'Football is never coming home!'

Andora can find only one good thing to say about English supporters. A few months earlier, fans of the Premier League's six biggest teams had staged unprecedented protests over the attempt to form a breakaway European Super League. On 2 May 2021, Manchester United fans stormed the pitch at Old Trafford, forcing the postponement of a game against Liverpool. To the surprise of world football, the clubs backed down. Fan power worked. 'That,' he says approvingly, 'is the spirit of Union'.

At Union, of course, it would never have got that far in the first place. German football's so-called '50+1' rule means that most clubs are democratically accountable to their own fans, and even the country's biggest teams didn't dare sign up to a project as unpopular as the Super League in the spring of 2021. Union, meanwhile, have developed a reputation for being a particularly supporter-friendly club, even by German standards. Andora believes that the club stands for a different kind of football, one which is fundamentally suspicious of power. The rebel spirit of his adolescence is still there; the difference is that now, the fans and the board are on the same page. 'In the context of everything that happened in the seventies, what is happening now is basically a biblical resurrection,' he says.

He has witnessed that resurrection first-hand. For a quarter of a century, Andora had given up on Union, consigning it along with everything else in the GDR to the dustbin of his own, personal, history. Then, at the turn of the millennium, something stirred within him once more. On 21 August 2005 he returned to the Alte Försterei for the first time in almost three decades to witness what would be one of the most famous victories in Union's history: an 8–0 thrashing of the old enemy BFC Dynamo. By then, both clubs were in the fourth division of a reunified Germany, but the win still felt like a final reckoning.

In the years that followed, BFC continued to struggle, while Union began an inexorable rise towards the Bundesliga, which Andora has documented with his paintbrush. One of his first works about Union, commissioned for the club's fortieth anniversary in 2006, is a footballing Madonna. While the infant messiah is wrapped in the red-and-white stripes of 1. FC Union, the Mother of God herself is in the blue shirt of Union Oberschöneweide. Around their heads like a halo run the words 'Semel Unionus, Semper Unionus': Once an Unioner, always an Unioner. Whether as a dissident or a dissident in inverted commas, Andora without Union does not make sense. 'Since 2005, Union has been one of the strongest, most reliable cornerstones of my existence,' he says. 'And it has closed the circle of my life.'

But Union is changing. The club have never been as successful as they are now, in capitalist, reunified Germany. The empty stadiums of the coronavirus pandemic aside, the terraces have never been so consistently packed as they are in the modern era, and the club have never looked so stable, both financially and on the pitch. The stories and myths which surround Union have drawn new fans from across the globe, and Andora's generation are now a minority on the terraces. Even he speaks frankly about a changing of the guard. 'We sing about living forever, but, in truth, everything must end,' he says. 'It is up to the younger generations now.'

CHAPTER 2
RED BRICKS

FC KARL-MARX-STADT 2–3 UNION BERLIN – 28 MAY 1988

It is a Saturday afternoon, and all Frank wants is to be at the football. A few hundred kilometres away, several thousand Union fans have arrived in Karl-Marx-Stadt to support their team on the last day of the Oberliga season. Frank is also miles from home, but he is not at the match, and he can't even watch it on TV. The only thing he can look at when the game kicks off at three o'clock is the afternoon sun, streaming through the window of his prison cell.

For Union, the outlook is anything but sunny. They haven't won in Karl-Marx-Stadt for twenty years, and if they don't break the curse today, they will be relegated from the Oberliga for the third time in a decade. At half-time, the scores are level at 1–1 thanks to a fluky equaliser from their captain, Olaf Seier. But they still need another to save their skins. Right now, there seems to be more chance of Frank busting out of prison.

At least the news filtering through to the terraces via the radios is good. Elsewhere in the country, Lok Leipzig are beating Rot-Weiß Erfurt and BFC Dynamo are 1–0 up at home to Vorwärts Frankfurt. The other results are going Union's way, and in the stands the travelling Berliners remain unbowed. They make up almost half of the 7,000-strong crowd, and they have been drowning out the home fans for much of the game. Even as Union fall behind for a second time after the break, the fans from the capital mercilessly bait their provincial southern hosts: 'You're from Saxony! Losers from Saxony! You sleep under bridges and in the homeless shelter...'

With a quarter of an hour to go, there is a fresh flash of hope. An acrobatic cross from Frank Placzek finds Michael Weinrich at the far post, and Union are level. They need just one goal now, and as adrenaline surges around the ground the fans switch from abuse to defiance. 'Eisern Union! Eisern Union!'

Eisern – Iron. They have used that rallying cry for as long as there have been metalworkers in Oberschöneweide. In moments like this, it is a reminder that at this club you never give up, however hopeless the battle seems to be. But as the clock ticks down, Union's iron will starts to weaken. Long-range efforts are sliced wide and promising breaks end with wasteful, looping crosses. In the stands, radio commentator Wolfgang Hempel tells his listeners that he can't see Union snatching a winner. For all their fight, there is little sign of a last-minute miracle.

Then, one minute into injury time, they get a free-kick on the right wing. This time, the cross fizzes, and Seier sends a glancing header onto the far post. The ball falls to Mario Maek who scuffs it over the line. The red-and-white mass on the terraces swarms in all directions, unable to contain its violent delight. Now it's Vorwärts who are going down. Union have saved themselves with almost the very last kick of the game.

'The football god is an Unioner!' writes Andreas Baingo, a journalist and former Union player, in his report for the Deutsches Sportecho. As the delirious away fans storm the pitch, even Karl-Marx-Stadt coach Heinz Werner gets a hug. Having spent six years at the Alte Försterei a decade ago, he is still an honorary Unioner. 'The Kurt-Fischer-Stadion is a madhouse!' screams Hempel from the gantry.

Back in prison, Frank hears nothing of the miracle. There is no radio in his cell, and he has not been allowed contact with his family in Berlin for weeks. The only person who can tell him whether Union have stayed up is Vodka, the guard with booze on his breath, and he won't come around until five a.m. the next morning. By the time he hears footsteps in the corridor,

Frank can also hear his jangling nerves echoing against the concrete. 'What about the football, Vodka? What happened to Union?' he babbles when the guard barks at him to report.

'Your lot went down,' says Vodka with a dismissive wave of his hand, his Saxon accent rubbing salt in the wound. Frank's nerves disappear through his feet, and he slumps back down onto the bed. The guard begins to cackle. 'Only messing with you, they got a last-minute winner and stayed up.'

A second later, Frank is charging around the cell, his fists clenched and the veins throbbing from his neck as he bellows in furious delight at the walls. Alarmed, Vodka stops laughing and takes a step back.

'Prisoner Seifert! Control yourself!'

Many of the terrace chants at the *Alte Försterei* have remained unchanged since the days of the dictatorship. Union fans still sing 'Fuck Dynamo' as they walk from the station to the stadium. They still shout 'Eisern Union!', and they still hurl abuse at visitors from Saxony. Sometimes, though, the memory of the former East Germany is a little more poetic. One song, which goes to the tune of 'Oh My Darling, Clementine', laments a youth spent behind bars:

> It was by the train station near Dessau,
> In a house of red bricks.
> That's where I spent my youth,
> Without light or sunshine.
>
> One day, the guard came,
> And he told me: you are free!
> A thousand tears in my eyes,
> My jail time was over.

The house of red bricks is a real place, and it stands for one of the darkest chapters of GDR history. In its bid to form 'socialist personalities', the regime frequently sought to break those it could not win over by persuasion. As well as political dissidents, that included children and young adults who had either broken the law or were otherwise deemed 'difficult to educate'. Young offenders were put in juvenile detention centres like the Jugendhaus Dessau, while countless others were sent for 're-education' in so-called youth workhouses. Both types of institution were notorious for their horrendous conditions and callous mistreatment of inmates. The routine physical and psychological abuse of young people in youth workhouses like the notorious GWJH Torgau is well documented, and ranged from brutal military drills to violent beatings.

'We sing the song because all of that is part of Union's history,' says Frank Seifert, a towering pub landlord with a low, gruff voice. He spent a year behind bars in the late 1980s after an altercation with police at an Union game, and he is not the only fan of his generation who had first-hand experience of the East German correctional system. 'I would say about thirty per cent of the guys who were going to Union back then had either been in a youth workhouse or a prison or something similar,' he says. 'They really experienced those red bricks.'

Now in his fifties, Seifert runs the Tanke, a popular beer garden halfway between the stadium and Köpenick train station. The place is a matchday institution, and its charm lies in the lack of frills. Drinkers sit on long wooden benches, or else simply stand in whatever space there is available. There is one bar and one sausage stand, both of which serve both inwards to the drinkers on the premises, and outwards to those on the pavement. Both sides of the fence are invariably packed on matchday, but there is rarely any grumbling about lack of space. 'It's the only fan beer garden where there hasn't been a fight in the last twenty-one years,' says Seifert proudly, and it is not hard to see why; his size alone is enough to put off any potential troublemakers. On matchdays, he keeps a watchful eye on proceedings from a barstool by the gate.

From that vantage point, he has seen the Union fanbase change dramatically since he opened the beer garden at the turn of the millennium. They may still sing about the red bricks, but many Union fans are now too young to have had any first-hand experience of them. The ultras, who lead the song, are largely in their twenties and thirties, and were either not yet born or in nappies when the Berlin Wall fell. Not only that, but there is also an increasing number of fans who come from somewhere else entirely. Around ten years ago, Seifert says, the Tanke started to attract a new wave of international fans – stag parties and father-son duos from England, Sweden, the Netherlands and western Germany. 'It's a completely different crowd at Union these days,' he says.

For many of these new fans, the stories of resistance and repression are part of Union's appeal, and the old-world feel of the Tanke is their window into that lost world. But the relative peace of a spit-and-sawdust beer garden is a different beast to the football Seifert remembers from his youth in East Germany. When he started going to Union as a 7-year-old in the 1970s, skipping school and abseiling out of his bedroom window to get to the Alte Försterei, the rowdy fans of Andora's generation were already drawing the attention of the authorities. By the time he hit adolescence, a more developed culture of violence was sweeping through football stadiums across Europe.

The term 'hooligan' did not become established in Germany until later, but in East Berlin too, disaffected young fans expressed their frustration, boredom and discontent through violence and vandalism at the football. They often clashed with the state, and as Seifert himself attests, the state's response was often brutal. But despite it all, there is a certain nostalgia in his voice when he talks about the 1970s and 1980s. 'Nobody cared back then if you had a proper scrap with other fans. The police would come in and split you up, but there would be no charges or damages claimed. If you snatched somebody's scarf in a fight, then you had a trophy, and he didn't have a scarf anymore. That was it. These days, that would be aggravated robbery.'

The world is different now. East Germany no longer exists, and the worst elements of dictatorship have long been consigned to history. To feel nostalgic about it may seem strange. But as Seifert says, the violence and oppression are still part of Union's story, and one which shines a light on the complexities behind the resistance club myth. Many Union fans suffered under the socialist regime, but the GDR was also a country full of contradictions, paradoxes, and inconsistencies. The restrictive society had its own freedoms, and the victims of oppression were not always angels. There were grey areas among the red bricks.

*   *   *

Seifert has a clear memory of shouting 'down with the Wall!' The neutral Stadion der Weltjugend, where Union and BFC were forced to play each other from 1976 onwards, was right up against the Wall in a spot which is now home to Germany's Federal Intelligence Service. To get there, Union fans would get off at the divided Friedrichstraße station and walk almost alongside the Wall through an area which was home to various western embassies. 'When we passed the West German representation, we would always shout "down with the Wall" as loud as we could,' he remembers.

It was less a serious demand and more a simple provocation, a chance to vent some frustration after yet another defeat to the Stasi club. 'We knew Union were a different kind of club, and that they were put at a disadvantage. But it was mainly about confrontation, and being against it all,' he says. 'The hardcore Union fans weren't politicised; they were just antisocial fuck-ups who smashed up everything they could.'

Football hooliganism is sometimes called 'the English disease', and by the 1980s, it had spread from British stadiums across Europe, paying no heed to the Iron Curtain. In East Berlin, it fed into an already heated relationship between Union and BFC Dynamo. 'There were parts of town which you had to avoid. Union fans wouldn't go to Alexanderplatz because that was BFC territory, and you'd get beaten up,' says Seifert. The derbies at Stadion der Weltjugend – supposedly held on neutral ground to help keep the peace – also became natural flashpoints, with Union and Dynamo fans frequently clashing on the walk back towards Friedrichstraße. 'Quite a few people got thrown in the river around there,' he says.

If the authorities turned one blind eye to the violence, the other eye remained watchful. Seifert may remember there being less danger of litigation in the GDR, but the Stasi were still an ever-present threat. The 'company', as they were euphemistically referred to, had always kept tabs on football violence across the country, and in the late 1970s, they set up a small working group in Berlin to monitor the 'rowdy behaviour' which had become increasingly noticeable at Union.

In October 1977, the Stasi published a report on 'negative-decadent' youths who had drawn attention to themselves at Union games by engaging in vandalism, violence and aggression towards police officers. It noted with some horror that 'these youths do not go to the stadium to watch sport or even cheer on their team' but simply to indulge in 'wild bawling and boorish behaviour'. They were, it concluded, a threat to public security and society at large.

Union fans were also implicated in incidents away from the stadium. Another Stasi report from the same day recorded the unrest at a rock concert at Alexanderplatz on 7 October 1977, the 28th anniversary of the GDR. The concert had been cancelled at short notice after a fatal accident in the crowd, which prompted rioting in the heart of the capital and led to dozens of arrests. In public, the authorities sought to play down the incident and suppress western reporting. (One Reuters journalist was even hauled into the foreign ministry for a dressing down after the agency reported that two police officers had been killed.) Internally, however, the Stasi documented the events with their usual meticulous attention to detail. As well as shouts of 'Russians out' and demands to repatriate dissident singer Wolf Biermann, they noted, there had also been football chants from among the rioters: 'A large number of youths attempted to unsettle the People's Police by loudly singing songs which glorified 1. FC Union Berlin and disparaged BFC Dynamo.'

The role of Union fans in those clashes has since been over-exaggerated. It is often said that many of the protesters had come to the concert on their way back from a match, but records show Union did not play until the following day. This was not a football riot, and for some Unioners, the fact that they were implicated was more proof that the state had it in for them.

Erich Mielke's love for rivals BFC was hardly a secret, after all, and the Stasi club's advantages on the pitch were undeniable. They won ten titles in a row from 1979 to 1988 while Union suffered multiple relegations. Off the pitch too, it seemed there was one rule for Union, and another for BFC. According to Seifert, BFC fans were treated more leniently by law enforcement. 'Their parents were high-ranking Stasi or state officials, so they thought of themselves as the elite. They could get away with more than your average yob.' That is a claim backed up by other accounts. In an interview in Stadionpartisanen, the seminal book on East

German hooliganism, former Stasi official Harald Wittstock also described BFC fans being bailed out of trouble by their influential parents. 'If [the authorities] didn't want something to be happening, they preferred not to see it and tended to deny it,' he told authors Anne Hahn and Frank Willmann.

But it wasn't just with the BFC fans that the state pulled the wool over its own eyes. Even the violence at other clubs was considered incompatible with socialist society, and therefore had to be blamed on external factors. In the report on rioting Union fans from 1977, the Stasi concluded that 'ideological diversion' from outside influences was to blame. 'Their behaviour is exclusively the result of stupid glorification of Western-influenced idols and behaviours,' it read. Blaming the hated imperialist West was also convenient because it contained a grain of truth. Most youth subcultures did flirt with the West, in part because it was simply provocative to do so. Union fans were no different. Some adopted the English chant 'United!' while others developed a long-distance fan friendship with Hertha BSC, the biggest club in West Berlin.

Seifert was one of many Unioners who wore a badge with the words 'friends behind barbed wire' next to the two clubs' emblems and a map of divided Berlin. Hertha fans, meanwhile, allegedly smuggled Western fanzines and other paraphernalia across the Wall on day trips to East Berlin. Some Union fans also travelled to Hertha's rare away games in Eastern Bloc cities like Prague and Dresden. 'Almost nobody remembers it now, but there was one song we used to sing once or twice at pretty much every game. "We stick together like the wind and the sea, blue-and-white Hertha and FC Union..."' says Seifert. 'That was definitely not something the state approved of.'

How political it really was is another question. The relationship between Hertha and Union fans is another thing which tends to be exaggerated, in part because it is so surprising given their modern-day rivalry. The state may not have smiled upon fraternisation with the class enemy, and there were cases in which it cracked down on it. In the mid-1980s, a pub landlord was reportedly sent to prison for two years for hosting illicit Christmas meetups between Union and Hertha fans. But direct contact between Union and Hertha fans was hardly widespread or commonplace, and there is little evidence to suggest that it was seen as an imminent political threat.

Many of the pro-Hertha chants at Union seem to have more of a political edge now than they did at the time. 'Only two champions on the Spree – FC Union and Hertha BSC' carries the implicit suggestion that BFC's domestic titles were illegitimate. 'Hertha and Union: One Nation' seems now to be a direct call for a united Germany. But hindsight has its own biases. The fall of the Wall and the reunification of Germany seem inevitable from today's perspective, but even in the late 1980s, they did not seem like a real possibility to most people.

The chants were not revolutionary slogans, and those chanting them were not political visionaries. At most, they were highly skilled trolls, raging against the walls which kept them imprisoned. 'It was all about provocation,' says Seifert. 'The more you could provoke, the better you felt.'

*　　*　　*

If it was all about provocation, and the fans themselves admit as much, then why does the resistance club myth persist? Perhaps it is simply the better story: a plucky, righteous underdog against a morally corrupt and dictatorial state. But the reality is more complex. Union fans were subject to repressive measures, and they may have been given a tougher ride than their counterparts at BFC. But they were also no angels, and their provocations were not directed solely at the regime. Even in an unjust system, hooliganism is still hooliganism.

As they followed their team around the country, hardcore Union fans delighted in the same kind of aimless aggression which football fans delight in across the world. They vandalised state property on public transport and tormented ordinary, law-abiding citizens in smaller, provincial cities. Trips to Dresden, Leipzig and Karl-Marx-Stadt (now Chemnitz), were particularly heated. The animosity between Berlin and the eastern region of Saxony goes back centuries, and the inequalities of the socialist system only made it worse. Dresden and the surrounding area was mockingly referred to as the 'valley of the clueless' because it was one of the only places in the country where the signal was too weak to watch western TV. In an economy of scarcity, the provincial regions also had less access to luxury goods than those in the capital. At some away games, fans from Berlin would allegedly taunt their rivals with oranges and bananas. 'We were privileged in Berlin because we were the bit of the country which was presented to the rest of the world. That meant we got better food; stuff like fresh fruit and vegetables which they never had down there,' says Seifert. 'You can understand why they hated us.'

Regional rivalries were just one of the less savoury aspects of fan provocations. As well as mocking the Saxons, Seifert also remembers terrace chants which gleefully evoked the Holocaust. They do not bear repeating in print and would be almost unthinkable in most German football stadiums today. But as he tells it, anti-Semitism and other forms of racism were not uncommon in the 1980s. 'It had nothing to do with ideology – language like that was a normal part of everyday speech,' he says. 'There was a general antipathy towards foreigners because we were never taught how to get on with other people. If all the foreigners are being locked away and you're being told that any contact with them is bad unless they are from the Soviet Union, what do you expect to happen?'

The extent to which racism and xenophobia were systemic in the GDR is a question far beyond the scope of this book. It is true that the lived reality for foreigners was vastly different to the propaganda, which portrayed racism, including anti-semitism, as anathema to the socialist system. Guest workers from communist countries like Cuba, Mozambique and Vietnam were usually housed in separate blocks and integration was made deliberately difficult. Foreign workers who fell pregnant were frequently given the choice between deportation and abortion. But even if, as Seifert says, the anti-Semitism on the terraces was borne out of ignorance, that does not make it any less horrifying. And it also doesn't mean that it was always devoid of ideology. As in other countries both east and west of the Iron Curtain, there was also organised right-wing extremism in East German stadiums, and the boundaries between football fans, skinheads and neo-Nazis could be porous.

Some of the most notorious acts of far-right violence in 1980s East Berlin were attributed to football fans. In 1987, BFC hooligans were convicted over a neo-Nazi attack on a punk concert at the Zionskirche church in Prenzlauer Berg, a watershed moment in a growing radicalisation of their fanbase. 'In the late 1980s, the BFC fans started to change their clothes and actually call themselves hooligans,' says Seifert. 'They were less drunk, and they were real athletes, training all week so they could keep fighting for a few more minutes at the weekend. We never had anything like that at Union. Some Unioners switched to BFC at that point because they were bored of the fuck-ups and they wanted to fight properly.'

Increasingly, these were problems which even the most wilfully ignorant state could not overlook. The Stasi kept a closer eye on BFC fans from the mid-1980s onwards and continued to monitor 'rowdy' supporters from other clubs like Union. Their approach was not always heavy-handed. In Stadionpartisanen, Frank Willmann's book on football hooliganism in the GDR, one Stasi official describes it as social work, and there were also efforts to bring the organisation of away trips and supporter liaison under the auspices of the party youth organisation, the Free German Youth. Where the good cop routine came up short, however, the state could always fall back on more repressive means. Some fans, like Andora, were blackmarked with the dreaded PM12; others were given the so-called 'Berlin ban', a measure in the East German penal code which restricted movement and residence rights within certain areas of the country. The state was also happy to issue premature call-ups for military service and, in some cases, to simply throw people in jail.

As he tells it, Seifert was always going to end up behind bars one way or another. When he was called up for his eighteen-month stint in the army at the age of 21, he decided to refuse and face the consequences. 'I had made my peace with the idea of going to prison,' he says. He ended up there sooner than he expected. Three weeks before he was due to report for duty in 1988, he joined his usual group of Union fans on an away trip to Aue near the Czech border and only made it as far as the town square. 'Too much booze, too much adrenaline, two cops start hassling me, and I lash out. When I wake up the next morning, I have no idea where I am, and they tell me I am going to be here for a while yet,' he says. He had woken up behind the red bricks.

Seifert says he was kept for six months in pre-trial detention, hundreds of miles from home and without any means of contacting his family. 'All they knew was that it was to do with the police, because a friend of mine went back and told my mum I had been arrested,' he says. Eventually, he was sentenced to a year in prison, and sat out his full term in the Maxhütte steelworks in Unterwellenborn, near the Bavarian border.

The GDR may not have had gulags like Soviet Russia, but it did use prisoners as cheap labour. Hundreds and thousands worked in appalling conditions at various locations across the country, many of them producing consumer and industrial goods which were then sold to western companies. At Maxhütte, Seifert says inmates were forced to work three shifts a day at blast furnaces, often without proper equipment or protection. 'Prisoners were quite literally burned out there,' says Seifert. 'They faced death every day.'

Seifert refused to work, forgoing privileges and payment which were indispensable to other inmates. He says he got by with the help of his family in Berlin. His grandmother would buy exotic fruit on her trips to the West, which his wife would then bring to him on the rare occasions she was allowed to visit. In poorly stocked southern Thuringia, that gave him a highly valued currency. 'I remember one guy. He had pulled down a GDR flag and pissed on it because he wanted to get put in prison so he would be deported. I sold him a couple of bananas and he said, "If it wasn't so sad, it would be funny. I haven't had a banana in five years, and now I get one in prison."'

But for all the black humour (and presumably black bananas), prison was a harrowing experience. 'We had forty guys in our cell, sharing one toilet,' says Seifert. 'I was the only Berliner among 700 inmates, and that made it difficult at the start. It's a good job I was an Unioner, though, because if I had been a BFC fan, they would have killed me. As an Unioner, you were just about OK.' He says he came out a changed man. 'I didn't admit it to myself, but my wife said I was different afterwards: more introverted. I wasn't an easy-peasy kind of guy anymore.'

Seifert was released in the autumn of 1989, just weeks before the Berlin Wall came down. In the year that followed, everything changed. The state that had imprisoned him began to fall apart, and football became almost an irrelevance. 'You could do anything you wanted at that time,' he says. 'The East German cops didn't know what they were allowed to do anymore, and the West German ones weren't in charge yet. Football became completely crazy.'

Attendances, which had been in steady decline for much of the 1980s, fell away almost completely between the fall of the Wall in 1989 and official reunification in 1990. Some Union fans, who had dreamed for decades of being able to cross the border and watch Hertha in the Olympiastadion, now switched allegiances to the West Berlin club. Seifert stayed, even as the crowds reduced to just a few hundred familiar faces. 'For me,' he says, 'there was only ever Union.'

* * *

On 9 November 1989 – the night the Wall fell – Seifert picked up his wife from work so they could cross the border together. Like so many East Berliners, they headed straight for the shopping boulevard of Kurfürstendamm, with West Germans happily banging on the bonnet of their Trabant as they crawled through the crowds.

Western understanding of communism and the end of the Cold War is heavily informed by these kinds of scenes: delirious East Berliners sitting triumphant atop the Wall, the cars rumbling through Checkpoint Charlie, and David Hasselhoff singing *Looking For Freedom* at the Brandenburg Gate on New Year's Eve. The fall of the Berlin Wall was, undoubtedly, a moment of joy and celebration for those on both sides of the Iron Curtain. But the famous images of 9 November only tell a part of the story. History did not end in 1989.

Reunification did not put an end to violence or right-wing extremism on either side of the former East-West German border. The process of reunification may have overshadowed everything, but much of what was already happening in East and West Germany in the 1980s continued in the reunified country of the 1990s. Without the Stasi behind them, BFC plummeted into ignominy, but the skinhead scene which had developed around them did not simply dissolve with the GDR, and the club continued to fight a reputation for having far-right support well into the twenty-first century. As late as 2021, regional federation NOFV fined BFC 10,000 euros for 'racist insults and anti-Semitic chants' during a game against Chemie Leipzig. Racism has also not entirely disappeared from the terraces at Union, with individual incidents of anti-Semitic abuse making headlines in both 2019 and 2021.

Likewise, those who had suffered under the regime in the GDR did not always live happily ever after in modern Germany. As the lyrics of Hasselhoff's song repeatedly point out, freedom is also a hard thing to find in open, capitalist societies. With time, the euphoria of reunification gave way to frustration at the practical problems posed by establishing the new country it created, and in particular the enduring economic imbalance between the two former states. Even in 2020, average wages in the former East were still only around eighty-five per cent of those in the West. Given the benefit of hindsight, many Germans have come to see the narrative of a liberated East and triumphant West as over-simplistic, even problematic.

Seifert was one of many who made the most of his new-found liberty to travel when the Wall came down. After a brief spell abroad, he came home to, as he puts it, 'make do with smaller fry and stay near Union'. South-eastern Berlin remains his home, and with the distance of a few decades, his view of life in the GDR has softened. 'I would never swap my youth with the youth of someone today, because in hindsight it was amazing. We could go camping on our own on the Baltic Sea coast at the age of ten. It was cheap enough, and because there was surveillance everywhere, it wasn't dangerous. Beer was cheap; food was cheap; cigarettes were cheap. You never had to worry about money, and you never went hungry. So, if you look at it like that, it puts some of the stuff which pissed us off back then into perspective.'

With the GDR, everything depends on perspective. Those who suffered more under the brutality of the regime may be less inclined to relativise than those who lived comfortably. Those who struggled after the Wall fell may yearn more for the security of socialism than those who were successful. In recent decades, Germany has fiercely debated the idea of *Ostalgie*, a cultural nostalgia for the GDR among some people from the former East. Many consider it problematic, but you don't have to be a committed Marxist-Leninist to feel nostalgic for your youth. Thirty years on, the question of how to remember East Germany is still more than just a theoretical debate between historians. It is about real experience within living memory, and the loss of an entire society as well as an unpopular form of government.

As well as running the Tanke, Seifert also organises the occasional, nostalgic away trip for fans of his generation. Through friends at a local steam engine association, he arranges trips to away games on old-fashioned, GDR-era trains. The low speeds and specific infrastructure requirements mean the trains can generally only run within former East Germany, meaning passengers can travel on the same lines and carriages that many of them used to delight in smashing to pieces when they were teenagers. 'It's pretty cool, having the old carriages where you piss directly onto the track and everything,' he says, grinning. 'It's about upholding traditions.'

It is also, perhaps, a question of identity. In recent years, says Seifert, gentrification has had a profound effect on

Friedrichshagen, the area where he now runs his other pub. Many of the traditional working-class residents with whom he grew up have long been priced out, replaced by a more affluent, younger generation moving out from the inner city. 'The high-earners are coming in and it's nice for them because we're near the lake and everything is green,' he says. 'But it's difficult to get on with those people because none of them are ordinary workers. We all have trades, and they have jobs we have never even heard of. They have a completely different view of society.'

In many ways, it is the same in the Tanke. The new generation of drinkers have a fundamentally different experience of Union, one which in the last ten years has been marked more by victories than defeats. Seifert won't go so far as to say that he is not enjoying Union's recent success, but there is a sense that he finds it a little alienating. 'In sporting and economic terms, we've only been going upwards for a long time now, and sometimes I have to check myself. When you've gone through so much shit with Union in the past, sometimes you wonder whether it can still be your club. My Union was always a yo-yo club, always on the breadline, and more bad than good. And nowadays everything is always just better, better, better.'

Even in the good times, Unioners never stopped singing about the red bricks. But as the GDR drifts further into history and ever more perspectives flood into Union, the memory of those early decades could well become a battleground in years to come. There may be no fights when new and old fans drink alongside each other at the Tanke, but different people project different things onto their football club. Seifert admits that he sometimes gets annoyed about people who only want to see an idealised version of Union, and don't want to engage with the uglier sides of the history.

'There are people who just want to have the good things from the last ten years and to ignore the rest. They don't want to hear that there were Union fans who were homophobic, racist fuck-ups and liked to smash things up,' he says. 'But if you want to be part of the community, you have to talk to the older guys and be willing to take on the history in its entirety. The good bits and the bad bits.'

CHAPTER 3
BOUGHT BY THE WEST

HERTHA BERLIN 2–1 UNION BERLIN – 27 JANUARY 1990

When Axel Kruse gets the party started, even the away fans cheer. A quarter of an hour in, Union keeper Henryk Lihsa fumbles a low free-kick, and Kruse pounces in the six-yard box. Six months after fleeing East Germany to join Hertha, the 23-year-old striker has finally got his first goal in the West. The whole of Berlin is here to celebrate with him.

The world has turned upside down since Kruse arrived in West Berlin in July 1989, having fled the GDR on a trip to Copenhagen with his previous club, Hansa Rostock. He was the seventeenth footballer to flee East Germany on foreign duty, and as it turns out, he will also be the last. As he later admits to Der Spiegel, it pissed him off watching the Wall go down on TV. If he had known he only had to wait a few months to cross the border freely, he might not have gone to all the trouble of escaping illegally. Suspended by FIFA until Hertha agreed terms with Rostock, he has had to wait patiently to make his debut while everyone else celebrates. For him, the dreamy autumn of 1989 has been a professional nightmare.

Yet now here he is, an East German in a Hertha shirt, finally making his debut in front of a crowd of Berliners from both sides of the Wall. More than 50,000 have braved the cold January rain to watch this game, a historic and until recently unthinkable first meeting between Hertha and Union. Just twenty-five kilometres apart, the two clubs still officially belong to two different nations, so this is still a cross-border local derby. It is a friendly in the truest sense of the word: a match to unite a divided city.

Outside the Olympiastadion, the heavy rain of the last few days has turned the ground to sludge, and the West Berlin air is thick with the distinctive smell of East German Trabant fumes. Inside, blue and red embrace like long-lost cousins. Though separated by forty-three kilometres of steel and stone for twenty-eight years, the two sets of fans have been on friendly terms. Friends behind barbed wire, they called each other; but the barbed wire is gone now. At the crossing point at Friedrichstraße station, the warren of walls and tunnels which once kept passengers apart are being dismantled. The Union fans can travel freely into the western half of the city, and the Hertha fans can pick up cheap alcohol at the East German shops before the game.

It is not just the booze which is cheap. The West German postal service, soon to be fused with its East German counterpart, is sponsoring this game and the price of the ticket has been fixed across the two currencies. Five Deutschmarks, or five GDR marks – whichever you have in your pocket. The real exchange rate is more like five to one, but money is flexible now. When you are trying to merge a whole country into a completely new economic system, different rules apply. On the pitch, Union captain Olaf Seier and his team-mates have the name of a local drainage firm plastered across their chests. They are the first East German team ever to wear a sponsored shirt.

Seier and his Hertha counterpart Dirk Greiser are grinning as they emerge from the tunnel, and when the game kicks off, so is everyone else in the stadium. Blue and red flags wave side by side in the freezing winter wind, and the TV cameras pick up one banner in particular: 'Union and Hertha play each other, and the whole of Germany celebrates.'

Just a few minutes after Kruse's opener, the party briefly grinds to a halt. High up in a corner of the western side of the stadium, near the marathon gate where the Nazis once lit the Olympic flame, a hundred or so BFC Dynamo skinheads have appeared in search of a scuffle. As the gatecrashers are escorted out by police, the stadium roars its approval: 'Stasi out! Stasi out!'

When Andre Sirocks blasts in an equaliser ten minutes later, the enormous arena erupts in joy once again. Union flags have been hung in the Olympiastadion before, but the idea that an Union player might one day actually score here has always been little more than a pipe dream. Now, like so many other dreams in the winter of 1989–90, it has become reality.

Most of the crowd barely notice when Greiser knocks in a late winner for Hertha. They are too busy singing, swapping scarves, and dancing for the TV cameras. 'Only winners at Berlin's football party,' reads the headline in West Berlin's Der Tagesspiegel *the next morning. The party is still going on when the paper goes to print, as both teams settle in for a night of drinking at Brauhaus Rixdorf, a stone's throw from where the now toppled Wall once divided Neukölln from Treptow.*

But the fun can't last forever. In the coming months and years, the two clubs' fortunes will diverge considerably. While Axel Kruse fires Hertha back into the Bundesliga in his first half season, Union face an uphill fight to establish themselves in the new, unified Germany. As they wander back into East Berlin in the warm glow of that night in the Olympiastadion, the Unioners barely feel the cold. But very soon, reality will begin to bite.

Two days before the friendly at the Olympiastadion, Gerald Karpa was freed from the army. A year into his military service, he was called into the commander's offices with the other company reps for a surprise meeting. Still hungover from a heavy night out drinking in Berlin, he listened agog as the commander told them about a wide-reaching programme of reforms under the new defence minister. The political structures of the army were being completely overhauled, the word 'comrade' was no longer obligatory and, most importantly, military service was to be shortened. In a euphoric daze, Karpa returned to his comrades to tell them the good news. They were getting out four months early.

'Making me serve in the army was the only thing I really begrudged the GDR,' he says, three decades later. His voice, soft and measured, certainly doesn't sound like a soldier's. It is also not the voice of a rebel: unlike Andora and Frank Seifert, this Unioner rarely clashed with the authorities. His attitude towards the East German state seems to have been one of pragmatic ambivalence. He endured military service because refusing to do so would have meant losing his job at a national broadcaster. He thought about attempting to move to the West, but with no family and few job prospects over there, it didn't seem worth it. Karpa does not deny the horror stories of the dictatorship, but he equally has none to tell himself. 'I can't say I wasn't comfortable in the GDR, because I was,' he says.

Karpa is Union's club historian, though he stresses that his official job title is 'club chronicler'. He claims he is not qualified enough to call himself a historian, but he brings the same conscientious rigour to his job that Germans always seem to bring to their history. Karpa can talk for hours about Union, but there is no hyperbole, no shortcuts, and no gloss. He is constantly weighing up all sides, casting doubt on the myths, pointing to where there is evidence and where there is not. In his office, a little room overlooking the car park at the Alte Försterei, source material takes up every inch of free space. On the floor, there are boxes filled with stacks of old match programmes, on the walls there are pendants and newspaper clippings. On top of a stack of books on the desk, there is a large steel drinking bowl from the East Berlin zoo, where Union have recently adopted a red panda. It is one of many trinkets which Karpa has collected for an official club museum which the club plans to open in the coming years.

For now, the museum is still just a plan. Most of Karpa's job involves long hours in the libraries and state archives of Berlin, and the occasional interview with journalists, authors, and researchers about Union's history. Those who come in search of the Hollywood version – the resistance club fighting the Stasi in an unjust system – are invariably disappointed. Karpa tends to pour cold water on the myths: 'Nobody fought against the Stasi, because the Stasi wouldn't have allowed that to happen. They might have smacked someone in the face because they thought he was a Stasi informant, but they didn't fight against the Stasi. It just sounds cooler to say it like that.' It is not just the media, he says, who tend to exaggerate Union's rebellion. It is also the Union fans themselves. 'Everyone feels better about being against something. Being for something is boring,' he says.

That is as true today as it was in the 1980s. But when the Wall fell, much of what Union fans had once known – and loathed – simply faded away. With no barbed wire dividing them, the friendship with Hertha dissipated. Without the Stasi to sponsor them, BFC stopped winning titles left, right and centre. Union fans who had grown accustomed to thinking of themselves as disadvantaged had plenty of reasons to uphold that belief even after the GDR disappeared, but now they had a new bogeyman. For it wasn't the politically favoured clubs who now had the upper hand, but the wealthier ones, most of whom came from the former West Germany. Union and other former GDR clubs, meanwhile, continued to struggle on and off the pitch. If the 1980s were the era of oppression, the 1990s were a time of charlatans, chancers, and chaos which nearly killed the club.

As the world was transformed, Union too had to reimagine themselves in a new reality, and they had a new elite to rail against. When the club released a new official anthem in 1998, the lyrics hammed up their East German identity and played on bitterness towards the prosperous West. 'We from the East march onward forever,' goes the song, which is still sung before every single home game at the Alte Försterei. It continues in a similar vein until the climactic punchline:

'Who will never be bought by the West?'

*   *   *

Reunification may have been welcomed in East Germany, but it was a long and often arduous process, which many still believe to be incomplete. In theory, the process saw the creation of an entirely new Germany, often referred to as the 'Berlin Republic', to reflect the fact that the national government relocated to Berlin from its previous, West German, home in Bonn. But in political and structural terms, the new Federal Republic was a continuation of the former West Germany. A cultural imbalance was inevitable, and the complex issues facing German society were often reduced to toxic clichés of *Ossis* and *Wessis* – Easterners and Westerners. In the former West, they rolled their eyes at 'moaning *Ossis*', and huffed about the amount of public money that was being pumped into the new eastern regions. In the former East, people felt that 'know-it-all *Wessis*' were either patronising them or ignoring their concerns. For many, the 1990s were a decade of false dawns and festering acrimony.

One such false dawn came in the form of the currency union. In the summer of 1990, the former GDR Mark was replaced by the Deutschmark – a symbol of western wealth and prosperity. Initially, this was cause for wild celebration, but it also had negative impacts. The favourable exchange rate meant people could afford much-coveted western consumer goods, but that in turn caused East German manufacturers trouble as demand for their products plummeted. Food prices, which had previously been subsidised, also soared. In July 1990, *Spiegel* magazine reported that the price of a kilogram of potatoes had gone from one mark to five marks in some East German supermarkets.

Even bigger trouble was to come as largely state-owned East German industries were stuffed clumsily and quickly into a completely new economic system. It was the East German government who set up the Treuhand – the agency which transitioned the GDR's state-owned enterprises into capitalism. The name literally means 'trust', but it is now shorthand for what many East Germans consider an economic betrayal. 'The Treuhand privatised more enterprises in one year than Maggie Thatcher managed in a decade... to put it bluntly, it turned East Germany into a poundshop,' said Dietmar Bartsch, leader of the hard-left Linke party, in 2019. The Linke are left-wing populists, and they are perhaps inclined to overlook the subtleties: significant parts of the East German economy could never have survived the transition, and the Treuhand's record is coloured in part by its overly optimistic aims. But the fact remains that a huge proportion of public enterprises privatised in East Germany in the early 1990s ended up in the hands of western investors, and that process led to deindustrialisation and mass unemployment. Karpa lost his job almost immediately, in 1990. He had been working at *Radio Berlin International*, East Germany's international broadcaster. When it was merged with its western equivalent, *Deutsche Welle*, he was one of many who got laid off. That had nothing to do with the Treuhand, however, and typically, he is reluctant to cast himself in the historical drama. As a 25-year-old, he notes, he was reasonably well-placed to start again. 'It was more of a time of upheaval for the guys who lost their jobs and were, say, fifty-five.'

In football too, the euphoria quickly crashed into a cold economic reality. In 1990, West Germany coach Franz Beckenbauer infamously predicted that the newly unified German national team would be 'unbeatable for years to come'. But just as with the economy, this was not two powers pooling their combined forces, but one country being clumsily grafted onto another. In the GDR, players were officially amateurs and earned little compared to western counterparts, and in the years after reunification, scouts and sporting directors from western clubs immediately swarmed into the former East, luring the best players away with contracts much bigger than anything the local clubs could offer. The likes of Matthias Sammer and Michael Ballack, for instance, made their names at western clubs.

The old East German clubs, meanwhile, struggled to establish themselves in the new system. After their sponsor organisations were privatised and many of the old party officials in the board-rooms stepped back, Karpa suggests many lacked either the money or the know-how to be successful under capitalism. 'They had to find people who knew how to run a club. But running a club was suddenly no longer about having good contacts among local party officials. It was about knowing how to get commercial partners.'

There are some who argue the German Football Association – the Deutscher Fußball-Bund (DFB) – could have done more to help ease the transition, but Karpa is sceptical. 'There was a lack of guidance,' he says, but he also thinks many of the East German clubs would not have been open to help had the DFB offered it. This was the paradox of reunification in a nutshell. On the one hand, East Germans were understandably wary of being told how to do things. On the other hand, they were at an inherent structural disadvantage because it was their society, not the West's, that was having to change.

Amid violence on the terraces and an exodus of the best players, even grand footballing cities like Leipzig, Dresden and Berlin struggled to attract spectators. The only apparent solution was to get a place in one of the top two divisions of the reunified German Football League, and places there were strictly limited. As the eastern and western leagues merged, the Bundesliga and second division were expanded by two and six spots respectively to accommodate the eastern clubs. The thorny question of which eight clubs would get the golden ticket was hashed out in a complicated system of promotions and play-offs.

The Oberliga had already started its annual cycle when reunification was signed and sealed in October 1990, and so it remained separate until the following season in 1991. Champions Hansa Rostock and Dynamo Dresden bagged the two spots in the new top flight, and the best of the rest scrapped it out for the second division spots in a mini tournament. As one of two second-tier champions in the final season of East German football, Union qualified for the play-offs, but finished a disappointing third behind FC Berlin (previously BFC) and Stahl Brandenburg in a four-team round-robin. They would spend the next decade trying to get into the second division and failing so consistently that they soon earned the nickname 'The Unpromotables'.

If it wasn't failure on the pitch which scuppered their promotion dreams over the next decade, it was money trouble. To be granted a licence to play, German clubs must show that they meet the financial requirements of their league. Throughout the 1990s, Union's applications for a second division licence were repeatedly rejected.

The most famous rejection remains one of the great unsolved whodunnits of German football history. In June 1993, Union beat Bischofswerda in the third-tier play-offs to finally seal promotion after several failed attempts. As they celebrated in front of 17,000 jubilant fans, it seemed like the dawning of a new era. But the festivities were cut short a few weeks later when the DFB discovered a problem with Union's licence application. A crucial bank guarantee of one million marks was, it transpired, a complete forgery. 'We had a sponsor who had promised to invest the million, and his bank was supposed to take over the guarantee,' Karpa explains. 'But they didn't do that. There was no guarantor, and he didn't have the money. So, someone decided to draw up a guarantee themselves.'

To this day, nobody has claimed responsibility for the forgery. 'There are various accounts, and they are all contradictory,' shrugs Karpa. Union's sporting director at the time, Pedro Brombacher, was handed a suspended sentence for having forwarded the forged documents to the DFB, and he stepped down shortly afterwards with a reputation in tatters. But there is no conclusive proof that he created the fake document himself. Karpa insists Brombacher is one of the good guys, who helped Union both as a high-ranking party official in the GDR and as a hard-headed director in the early years of capitalism.

The attempted fraud meant that Union were denied the promotion they had earned with their success on the pitch. That fostered an understandable sense of betrayal among the fans, which was partly aimed at directors like Brombacher, but also at a vague idea of western power. The DFB, who had refused the licence, was a former West German institution based in Frankfurt. Worse still, they had apparently been tipped off about the forgery by Tennis Borussia, a club from former West Berlin who ended up being promoted instead of Union. If the Union fans already felt they were being punished for something over which they had no control, the fact that a West Berlin club profited from their misery only fuelled the sense of victimhood. Though as Karpa points out, Union would probably not have acted differently had the roles been reversed. 'It's not as if we were walking around with a halo on our heads,' he says.

It was not the last time that money trouble left a bitter political aftertaste at Union. The forgery affair led to a change in leadership, but the new brooms would oversee yet another scandal. As they bid to stave off bankruptcy in the mid-1990s, one of Union's biggest sponsors was Manfred Albrecht, a western German property developer who was already involved in various developments in Köpenick. In 1995, Albrecht signed a lease agreement with the Berlin Senate to build a sport and entertainment complex just over the road from the Alte Försterei. The so-called *Sportpark* was intended as a long-term asset for Union, to help the club pay off its mountain of debt and stabilise financially. The Senate, perhaps spying an opportunity to help bail out a popular East Berlin institution, poured twelve million marks of public money into it. But the cash disappeared into Union's black hole of debt, and the *Sportpark* was never built. In 1997, both Albrecht and Union president Horst Kahstein were grilled by a city parliamentary committee. By that time, Albrecht, whom Karpa somewhat charitably describes as 'dubious', had already parted ways with Union.

Controversial private development contracts were nothing unusual in post-reunification Berlin. Once the Wall fell, the newly reunified city became a blank canvas for visionaries and dreamers of all stripes. New spaces emerged in the underpopulated areas where the Wall had once stood. Some were filled by the artists, anarchists and ravers who founded countless squats and unleashed Berlin's world-famous techno scene from venues like Tresor, WMF and E-Werk. Others were pounced upon by architects and property developers, keen to exploit both the prime real estate and a unique historic moment. But their grand designs often faltered on an underwhelming reality. Initial expectations of a return to Berlin's pre-war population of more than four million proved wildly optimistic. Instead, the number of Berliners decreased over the course of the 1990s to around 3.3 million, and only began to rise again in the mid-2000s. Many of the grand architectural visions for the city proved to be a little premature.

The most famous example is Potsdamer Platz. A once bustling central hub of pre-war Berlin, it became a divided wasteland during the Cold War, with the Wall cutting directly through it at the spot where three of the four Allied sectors met. When the Wall came down, the Senate sold it off in large chunks to major multinationals like Daimler and Sony to build commercial skyscrapers. In the words of one Daimler executive, that made it 'the most hated construction project in Berlin', as various groups squabbled over competing visions for the city's future. Nowadays, it is an eyesore: an underwhelming jumble of awkward high-rises under which confused tourists search in vain for something interesting to do or see. It was supposed to be the beating heart of modern Berlin. Instead, it is a monument to the discord between expectation and reality.

The unbuilt *Sportpark* was a significantly more dubious project than Potsdamer Platz. Yet both speak of a certain naive optimism with which Berlin farmed out its open spaces to private developers, eroding trust between the city's various interest groups. The *Sportpark* debacle was not the only time the Berlin taxpayer would foot the bill for a grand design which backfired, and it understandably did long-term damage to the club's reputation. The Union fans, meanwhile, could feel left in the lurch once again by politicians and western investors. Despite having significantly reduced their debt, the club were still broke by the end of the *Sportpark* saga, and were ready to file for bankruptcy in 1997.

This time, it was the fans themselves who stepped up.

* * *

The Alte Försterei is on the urban edges of the forests and lakes which surround Berlin. To the north-west of the stadium is the Wuhlheide, a sprawling woodland park which stretches across the south-east of the city, from Köpenick to Karlshorst. The club's main offices are in the Old Forester's House which gives the stadium its name. On matchday, fans walk down a street from the station which crosses over a stream before turning off into the woods. They then follow a narrow, muddy path flanked by birches and oaks, with bin bags hung on the branches and lampposts nestled in the trees. As the stadium has expanded over the years, it has slowly cleared ever more space for itself. But in a country full of forest stadiums, the Alte Försterei is still one of the most magical.

The forest is deeply embedded in the German collective consciousness. In the year 9 CE, a Cherusci tribesman and former Roman soldier by the name of Arminius (or Hermann) led an alliance of Germanic tribes in the Battle of Teutoburg Forest, hiding in the trees to ambush a legion of 20,000 soldiers and push the Romans back across the Rhine for good. Centuries later, the triumph would be picked up as a founding myth by nineteenth century nationalists as they started to construct a common German identity. The forest took up a special place in the national psyche, and the oak became a national symbol. Germany without the forest is like Britain without the sea: it doesn't make sense.

Unioners are no exception. They still sing romantic songs about their 'wonderful, evergreen Alte Försterei' and the 'forests, valleys and lakes' of Köpenick. The trees are part of the club's soul and, just as they did for Hermann the German, they can also offer a strategic advantage. When spectators were banished from stadiums during the pandemic, many Union fans simply climbed the trees to watch and cheer on their team from outside. And, when the bailiffs came knocking in the 1990s, it was the trees which saved Union from bankruptcy.

One of the trinkets which Karpa is saving for his future museum is a flower vase. It is around half a metre tall, cheaply made and entirely innocuous. The perfect place, in other words, to store something you don't want to draw attention to. For several years in the 1990s, the vase served as Union's clandestine bank account, keeping an illicit cash flow running even as all the official income flooded directly to the club's creditors. The club kept it full by selling their matchday tickets on the forest path rather than at the gate. Having secured the day's income, the 'flying ticket-sellers' would then melt into the woods to shake off any official observers and return a few days later with cash for the vase. The trees helped Union cheat the bailiffs and keep themselves afloat. 'Someone once told me that whenever the bailiffs came, it was always a very bad day... for the bailiffs,' grins Karpa.

Stories like this quickly became part of the club mythology, part of a wider tale about the community rallying to save the club in its hour of need. It is true that many ordinary people gave up their free time, got by without wages and even bent the law to help Union in the 1990s. The club may only have been drawing crowds of a few thousand, but those who were there were fanatical in their support, and not just on matchday itself. In the romantic telling of Union's history, this was the period in which fans became activists.

But Unioners are pragmatists as well as romantics, and even the most committed fan knew that the club could not survive on the goodwill of its employees and fans alone. As the financial problems became ever more acute, a small group of fans headed by former board member Tino Czerwinski became more organised in their efforts, setting up a new 'fan council' and monthly 'fan meetings'. In February 1997, with the club ready to declare insolvency, Czerwinski and others mobilised 3,000 supporters to march from Alexanderplatz through the Brandenburg Gate to raise awareness of Union's plight.

'Nowadays, the story goes that new investors heard about the demo and rang up to offer money,' says Karpa, raising his myth-busting eyebrow. 'I'm not sure it was quite like that.' The fan mobilisation did prompt widespread reporting, however, and it did at least coincide with fresh interest from new financiers. In early 1997, US sports giant Nike signed a sponsorship deal which saved Union from bankruptcy. Though it was quietly wound down a few years later, the Nike partnership ushered in a new era for Union after the *Sportpark* affair. New president Heiner Bertram had experience revitalising failing businesses for Nike, and he immediately started casting around for new sources of income for Union.

To begin with, Bertram channelled the fire in the fans' bellies. A fundraising campaign under the slogan 'Union must live!' was launched in a bid to pay off around a million marks worth of debt and brought in around 200,000 marks worth of donations. As well as simply donating spare change, the fans also came up with creative ways to raise both money and attention. In February 1998, they organised a symbolic demonstration at an away game against Tennis Borussia, turning up to the game without buying tickets, and donating the money they would have spent to Union. At one point, Czerwinski even wrote to Mohamed Al-Fayed, owner of Harrods and Fulham FC, asking for a cash injection. He received a polite rejection from the marketing department at Fulham and a report in the *Guardian* for his troubles. The unofficial Union history podcast 'Und niemals vergessen' has since speculated that it may have been more of a publicity stunt than a genuine request. The death of Diana, Princess of Wales had been keenly followed by German media, and Al-Fayed, whose son Dodi also died in the crash, was regularly in the news around 1997.

At the same time, the new president also started sounding out more serious investors. Just a few months after launching the fundraising campaign, Bertram appeared in front of the press and declared: 'Union is saved, Union will live on!' In the end, it was not Al-Fayed who had saved the day but Michael Kölmel, a multi-millionaire cinema magnate from western

Germany. Kölmel lent money to several high-profile German football clubs in the 1990s, including Fortuna Düsseldorf, Dynamo Dresden and his hometown club Karlsruhe, but it was with Union that he built his strongest relationship. He loaned the club several million marks over the next few years, and at a time when the club was struggling to pay even the most basic bills, that was a godsend. 'He literally said: "How much do you need? Do you need it in cash? Do you need it now or next week?"' says Karpa.

In the following years, Kölmel's cash propelled Union back into professional football and brought the drama and intrigue of the 1990s to a welcome end. In 2001, the club hit dizzying new heights as they finally made it to the second division and shook off the 'Unpromotables' tag. In the same season, they made it to the German Cup final, playing in the Olympiastadion for the first time since their friendly against Hertha eleven years earlier. Finally, it seemed, they had broken the glass ceiling which loomed above the clubs of the former GDR.

There is a certain irony here: Kölmel was from the former West. But unlike other western investors, he was welcomed with open arms. While his ventures with other clubs were not always so successful, he remains highly regarded at Union even today. That is partly because he saved the club, but it is also perhaps because of the way he saved them. He didn't sell Union fans a grand vision of the future, and he didn't tell them they were doing everything wrong. As Karpa points out, he has been a reliable and engaged long-term investor, not just a white knight with a messiah complex: 'It's not like he has just sat there waiting to get his money back. He's continued to invest in the stadium and things like that.' Many Unioners also note approvingly that he still tends to avoid the limelight. 'He's been made an honorary member, which I guess is a political decision. But I think it's also a very reasonable one,' says Karpa.

Kölmel's light touch has also allowed the story of the fans to take centre stage in the telling of Union's resurgence. It is no secret that it was his money, far more than the flying ticket-sellers or the fan demonstrations, which saved Union from bankruptcy. But he has always spoken highly of the fans and has never sought to play down their contribution. His investment and influence did not dent the romantic notion of an East German tribe taking on the world from their fortress in the forest. If anything, it only made it stronger.

∗   ∗   ∗

It was Michael Kölmel who commissioned Union's new club anthem in 1998, and it was he who managed to persuade Nina Hagen, Germany's 'Godmother of Punk', to come and sing it. 'Hello, I'm Nina and I grew up around the corner from here,' Hagen told a bewildered pack of reporters when she turned up at the Alte Försterei to release the single. They knew exactly who she was. With her immaculate make-up, angular features and flared, outer-space-themed tights, she was one of the most instantly recognisable people in Germany. The question was more: what on earth was she doing in a run-down old football stadium?

Hagen had never shown any interest in the game before. But her biological father had been an Union fan, and in many ways, her biography suited Union. A product of both the former East and the former West, she had grown up in the same area of East Berlin as Andora, as the stepdaughter of dissident musician Wolf Biermann. Her early hopes of an acting career were dashed by Stasi interference, and after Biermann was expatriated in 1976, the fledgling pop star and her mother also emigrated to the West. Once there, she ditched her oompah pop for operatic punk, and became the *enfante terrible* of German rock'n'roll. In 1979, Hagen provided a fully clothed but vivid demonstration of female masturbation techniques on a live talk show broadcast by Austrian public broadcaster ORF. The talk show's host later resigned. In an interview with *Playboy*, Red Hot Chili Peppers frontman Anthony Kiedis later described her as his 'sexual and spiritual mentor'.

With a CV like that, a cheesy football anthem was never going to be Hagen's magnum opus. As it turned out, she only ever sang it live on two occasions. The first time was in the autumn of 1998, when she unveiled it in front of just 3,000 fans at a game against Chemnitz. The second was at the German Cup final, three years later. This time more than 20,000 Union fans were there, and most of them seemed surer of the words than Hagen herself. For more than two decades since, Union fans have belted it out before every single home game. Every time, the line about never being bought by the West is bellowed with particular gusto.

It is, by any measure, an absurd notion. The song was commissioned by an investor from south-western Germany, composed by musicians from Munich and recorded in a studio in Frankfurt. Even Hagen, the only bona fide East German in the entire process, had left the GDR more than a decade before the Wall came down and spent a good deal of her career in Los Angeles. But perhaps the line is a little more tongue-in-cheek than it is often given credit for. In another verse, it strikes a more conciliatory note: 'East and West/Our Berlin together/ For Eisern Union.'

The song's euphoric anger and schizophrenia about the West are a product of their time. In the same year it was released, Helmut Kohl, the Chancellor who had overseen reunification, finally left office after sixteen years. A year later, the German government and parliament completed their move from Bonn to Berlin. The political process of uniting the two Germanies was coming to a symbolic close, but the cement was not even beginning to dry on the so-called 'Wall in the minds'. Even in the 2020s, modern Germany has still not completely shaken off the idea of *Ossis* and *Wessis*.

There are good reasons to maintain the distinction. Voting trends and cultural references still differ hugely across the old divide. The regions of the former GDR (still referred to as 'the new states') continue to lag economically. Cities like Dresden, Leipzig and even Berlin remain far less populated than they were before the division, and their football teams still struggle in the reunified league system. Other than RB Leipzig, who were founded by Austrian drinks company Red Bull in 2009, Union are the only eastern club currently in the Bundesliga. When they were promoted in 2019, they were the first former GDR club to reach the Bundesliga since Energie Cottbus's relegation a decade earlier.

Karpa has little time for the victim complex, and he is adamant that former East German clubs like Union cannot blame their failures entirely on rivals and institutions from the former West. 'It should be clear to everyone that the people making the decisions in the 1990s were the people in charge of the club,' he says. 'We weren't being guided by any kind of evil outside forces.'

But the experience of reunification did differ from east to west, and the troubles and uncertainties of the 1990s did produce a distinct sense of modern East German identity. In Union's case, it was ultimately built less on resentment and more on community and solidarity. If you ask Union fans about the 1990s today, they are less likely to come up with conspiracy theories about the DFB, and more likely to talk about the achievements of their own fans: the Brandenburg Gate demo, the fan meetings, and the flying ticket-sellers. Perhaps a more fitting motto for Union's post-reunification identity is another line from the Hagen song: 'Shoulder to shoulder for Eisern Union.'

'Shoulder to shoulder' is now also the name of Union's club foundation, and it is regularly used as a slogan when the club or its fans organise community projects. It was the culture of supporter activism which arose in the years after the Wall fell which would set the tone for the next turbulent decade in the club's history. Having survived the wild years of the 1990s, Union were about to wholly embrace fan power.

PART TWO
IRON

CHAPTER 4
FAN POWER

UNION BERLIN 2–2 BORUSSIA MÖNCHENGLADBACH (4–2 ON PENALTIES) – 6 FEBRUARY 2001

The snow is thick from the day before, and it has frozen in the sub-zero temperatures overnight. If you step onto the pitch, your foot cracks the thin layer of ice into shards and sinks into the soft powder below. From the touchline in front of the main stand to the corner flags over by the terraces, there is not a blade of green grass to be seen. The hallowed turf of the Alte Försterei is completely white.

'We may as well bring our ice skates and play in them,' grumbles Borussia Mönchengladbach boss Hans Meyer to the RBB television reporters. The 58-year-old served as Union coach a few years ago, but he is not enjoying this return to his old stomping ground. Union are a nuisance, a banana skin in a cup semi-final that his team are expected to win. A division above the Berliners in the league pyramid and a world apart in terms of fame and financial clout, Gladbach fear slipping up. The ice is not going to make it easier for them.

It is already proving a rough ride. With every available football pitch in the capital covered in snow, the visitors have been forced to hold their final training session inside a hangar at Tempelhof airport. They know that the poor conditions will help the underdog and increase the chances of an upset. If it were up to Meyer, the game would be cancelled and postponed to a later, warmer date.

SCHEISSE! WE'RE GOING UP!

As they stand and look glumly over the gleaming white pitch, Union president Heiner Bertram and his right-hand man Bernd Hofmann are desperate not to postpone. The game against Gladbach tomorrow night is no ordinary cup tie. It is a chance for third division Union to reach the final and potentially qualify for Europe. Six million viewers are set to tune in to watch on television, and a further 18,000 Köpenickers will cram onto the terraces – the highest attendance that the Alte Försterei has seen since the fall of the Wall. With the mayor and his entourage expected in the stadium, Union have expanded their VIP tent to three times its usual size. And most importantly, they are confident of an upset. If the game goes ahead, Union can make history on the pitch and earn a much-needed dollar off it.

But first they have to clear the ice. With a thaw scheduled to set in during the day, the melting snow will almost certainly waterlog the grass and create a mudbath. After the financial turmoil of the last ten years, the Alte Försterei is hardly state of the art. Even the floodlights are only a few weeks old, and undersoil heating is still a fantastical notion.

What Union lack in facilities, though, they can more than make up for in support. After a three-hour crisis meeting, Bertram and Hofmann decide to turn to the faithful. 'We need all Union fans to come and help clear the stadium of snow,' declares fan liaison officer Sven Schlensog on the radio. By three o'clock, dozens of fans have arrived, and are happily chipping ice from the terraces and shovelling snow off the pitch with enormous metal spades. The club have promised mulled wine, sausages, and beer, but most need no encouragement. 'The snow must go, it must go, it must go,' one Unioner babbles into the TV cameras. 'We're going to smash Gladbach tomorrow.'

When referee Helmut Fleischer strides out the next morning to inspect the pitch, his feet squelch on the surface, and the grass looks, in the words of the sceptical groundsman, 'like you could plant potatoes in it'. Fleischer, a medical doctor in the German military, is unfazed. There has been no more snow, no more torrential rain, and the pitch is at the very least not entirely underwater. After a brief splash in the mud, the referee gives his thumbs up. The game can go ahead. 'The weather god is an Unioner,' writes a jubilant journalist at the Berliner Kurier.

But it is the mere mortals who have saved the game for Union, and it is they who cook up a hellish atmosphere in the mud and cold that night. They roar through the smoke of the flares when Bozidar Djurkovic rounds the Gladbach keeper to put Union in front in the 27th minute and wheels away across the boggy pitch, flapping his arms like a swan in celebration. Gladbach fight back to take a 2–1 lead, but as the pitch crumbles beneath their feet so does their resolve. Union snatch a late equaliser, and when the shootout begins, their goalkeeper Sven Beuckert is already so drenched in mud that he has no qualms about hurling himself into the dirt to save the first two penalties.

By the time Union's Ronny Nikol steps up to take the decisive spot kick, the mud is so thick that he can't find the penalty spot. With a little help from referee Fleischer, he sets the ball down, and looks almost amused to see himself thump it down the middle. As the fans stream onto the pitch, stadium announcer Andre Rolle makes one last desperate attempt to stop the invasion and salvage what is left of the grass. 'Let's not ruin the hallowed turf even more!' he begs over the PA system. Yet there is little chance of that. Down below, the fans are celebrating as if they have already won the cup. Their efforts shovelling snow the day before have paid off: Union are in the cup final. They are also the first third division team ever to qualify for the UEFA Cup. The world suddenly looks as bright as the winter snow, and a new millennium can begin.

The snow melted and spring passed like a dream. The victory over Gladbach in the cup set Union off on an astonishing promotion charge in the league, and they stormed their way to promotion with an unbeaten run of fourteen games. After a decade of disappointment, the 'Unpromotables' had finally reached the second division. Even better, their cup run meant they had a season finale against Bundesliga giants Schalke to celebrate it all. As they flooded into the Olympiastadion wearing curly red wigs on 26 May 2001, Unioners felt their luck had changed. Veteran fan Sven Mühle grins as he remembers it. 'None of it felt real,' he says.

As it turned out, the hope of a new dawn proved illusory. Union spent only three years in the second division, and they were soon staring into the financial abyss once again. But the brief renaissance around the turn of millennium sparked a change in culture which would define the next two decades. In the GDR, Union fans had been a loud but loose rabble, frequently at odds with the state and the club bosses and often out only to provoke. In the 1990s, they had channelled their energy into protest, mobilising to drum up financial and political support for their ailing club. That spark of activism soon blossomed into a full-blown movement. By the mid-2000s, the supporters were organised and powerful in a way they had never been before.

Mühle is a case in point. On that cold February afternoon in 2001, he was one of the dozens of fans who picked up a spade and shovelled snow off the pitch in an act of spontaneous solidarity. Back then, helping the club was just a hobby. He was still making his living as a professional chef, and that meant maintaining a delicate work-Union balance. On the day of the cup final itself, he persuaded his boss to give him a few hours off in the middle of his shift, went to the stadium to watch the game, and returned to his kitchen in a cab immediately after the final whistle. Nowadays, it is different: Union is his job.

For almost two decades now, Mühle has been chairman of the *Eiserner V.I.R.U.S.*, one of the most influential fan organisations at Union. Founded shortly after the 2001 cup final, the *V.I.R.U.S.* (which stands for Club of Infected Red-and-White Union Supporters) started as an attempt to better organise a keen but disorderly active fanbase. From the street protests to the production of novelty red wigs for the cup final, Union fans had developed a taste for collective stunts, and the *V.I.R.U.S.* sought to channel those efforts. It has since become a fundamental pillar of the Union community, representing fans at club and national level, organising raucous away trips and helping to run various social and charity projects, such as soup kitchens and donations to local care homes. If Union is a more tightly knit footballing family than most, the *V.I.R.U.S.* is what keeps it together.

Not that its current chairman would put it in quite such grand terms. Mühle is an unassuming, slightly taciturn Berliner in his late forties, and our conversation takes a little while to warm up. 'I don't like being centre stage; other people are better at presenting themselves,' he mutters. He is more of an organiser than a frontman, a pragmatist rather than a theorist, and his organisation also favours substance over style. The *V.I.R.U.S.* has a minimalist approach to public relations – its website appears to have remained unchanged since 2001. Looking good, says Mühle, is not the point. 'The fundamental principle is always the same: don't just think of yourself, and don't judge everything you do on how many likes it gets on Facebook or Instagram or whatever other rubbish. The question is whether it has put something in motion. Whether it has helped someone.'

When they cleared the snow ahead of the Gladbach game, none of the Union fans were thinking of what they would get in return, he says. That unquestioning willingness to contribute would soon come to define Union, as the fans put one mad idea after another into practice over the course of the 2000s. It was they who began to shape the club in their own image and build its reputation as a bastion of fan power and community spirit.

The *V.I.R.U.S.* has been a driving force behind that process, and it is now almost impossible to imagine Union without it. But like the club itself, the fan organisation has been on quite a journey since the dreamy summer of 2001. And that journey began with two drunken, ill-fated trips to the furthest reaches of Europe.

* * *

I meet Mühle in an old supermarket building just a stone's throw from the Alte Försterei. The shelves and checkouts have long been cleared, and the space is being converted into Union's new *Fanhaus*, a central hub providing services, social endeavours and events for supporters. The project, which Mühle oversees, is still far from complete, but the location is already very much in use. There is a Covid testing centre in the car park, which has also played host to a food bank and various *V.I.R.U.S.*-organised events. From his office in a side wing, Mühle is busy making travel arrangements. Union have recently qualified for the UEFA Europa Conference League, and the *V.I.R.U.S.* is putting on package trips to away games in Rotterdam and Haifa. As we speak, his phone rings constantly, and a steady stream of people poke their head through the door to ask him questions. His eyes drift regularly to his emails.

The last time Union qualified for Europe, the *V.I.R.U.S.* was still in its infancy. Much has changed since then, but Union are still small enough to make international competition both a novelty and a logistical nightmare. Because the Alte Försterei doesn't comply with UEFA regulations, Union must play at Hertha's Olympiastadion – the only stadium in the city big enough for European football. A few hours after our interview, a bus will leave the *Fanhaus* to take a few dozen Unioners to the other side of Berlin. 'It's a bitter pill to swallow having to play there, but it's still a highlight playing in Europe,' says Mühle. The Olympiastadion is the least of his worries. Organising away trips abroad is difficult at the best of times, and it has become even harder during the pandemic. With a game against Maccabi Haifa on the horizon, Israel's strict entry requirements are proving to be a particular headache.

But then again, Union's adventures in Europe have always been cursed. This is the third time in their history that they have qualified for a major European competition, and each occasion has been overshadowed by international catastrophe. When Union qualified for the European Cup Winners' Cup in 1968, their dreams of travelling the continent were immediately dashed by an escalation of the Cold War. In the fallout from the Soviets' brutal suppression of the Prague Spring, several Eastern Bloc countries, including East Germany, decided to boycott UEFA competition in the 1968/69 season, denying Union their shot at European glory.

Thirty-three years later, it was an international terrorist incident. In 2001, Union's UEFA Cup first-round tie against Finnish side Haka Valkeakoski was originally scheduled for 13 September but was one of dozens of games postponed after the 9/11 attacks in New York. The players found out after landing in Finland and flew back home almost immediately. For the fans, some of whom had taken the cheaper option of going by ferry, it was more complicated. When the postponement was announced, they were still at sea, in the middle of a thirty-hour journey from Travemünde to Helsinki. Their miserable, seasick return trip was later immortalised in a stage play about Union, which is performed every year at a theatre in Köpenick.

'If we had organised a trip for that game, the *V.I.R.U.S.* would probably have gone bankrupt reimbursing people,' chuckles Mühle. Luckily, the organisation had not quite got off the ground by the time the ferry left for Finland, and it wasn't until the second-round tie against Bulgarian side Litex Lovech that they organised their first trip abroad. Even without a geopolitical incident, this trip also proved something of a disaster. A thirty-seven-hour bus journey from Berlin and a hold-up at the Romanian border meant that one group of fans only set foot on Bulgarian soil just as the game was kicking off, and they arrived at their hotel long after full time. By that time, Union had been held to a 0–0 draw and were out of the competition. In the context of that long history of misfortune, navigating a global pandemic is child's play.

Nowadays, away trips are more smoothly run operations, with Mühle carefully coordinating with police, travel agents and hotel managers. The *V.I.R.U.S.* now have many years of experience putting on travel arrangements for fans. They are most famous for their 'party trains' which would run to most league away games until the pandemic put a stop to it in 2020. The trains do exactly what they say on the tin, transporting hundreds of Union fans to away games in carriages complete with a bar, a dance floor and a disco ball. As recently as 2010, there were occasions when the players joined the fans on the return journey, pouring pints behind the bar as they celebrated a successful away result.

But that intimacy, says Mühle, is one of many joys which have been sacrificed at the altar of sporting success. With a wistful twinkle in his eye, he recalls fans and players partying side by side just hours after the team had been relegated for the second year in a row in 2005, and one player having to be carried off the train after trying alcohol for the first time. 'Good memories,' he says. 'I understand why that sort of thing doesn't happen anymore, because we have a different level of athlete these days. But it's still a shame because it was something which brought people together.'

Bringing people together is Mühle's thing. As well as the away trips, the *V.I.R.U.S.* also organises annual events like tenpin bowling competitions, indoor football tournaments and an annual dragon boat race on the Dahme river in south-eastern

Berlin. They are all raucous social events, open to any Union fan who wishes to turn up, regardless of how active a member they are. The effect can be somewhat disorienting. Union are a professional team playing at the highest level of German football in the third-biggest city in continental Europe. But outside of the stadium, they often have the air of a beloved village cricket club.

That also means helping people outside the fanbase. As the club has stabilised in the last few decades, they have slowly expanded their community and social projects, and the *V.I.R.U.S.* has led the charge. It has helped set up the club's official foundation; it still helps to fund and run a soup kitchen at the *Fanhaus*; it has a long-standing relationship with a local community centre providing advice and assistance for homeless people; and has also taken part in nationwide campaigns. In 2015, the *V.I.R.U.S.* also played a tiny role in one of the biggest challenges modern Germany had ever faced. Conflicts like the Syrian civil war were pushing more people to seek refuge in Europe than ever before, and, according to government figures, just under a million asylum seekers arrived in Germany between January and December 2015. The crisis prompted an astonishing mobilisation in all corners of German civil society, with sports halls, airports and hotels quickly repurposed into temporary shelters. Union also did their bit, delaying the *Fanhaus* project to house 112 refugees in the building throughout the winter.

As Mühle tells it, it was a spontaneous decision made in a face-to-face conversation between himself and club president, Dirk Zingler, and a move which was emblematic of the club's wider approach. 'There's a link between business and social responsibility. Dirk and the board have a very clear position: for years, we weren't able to keep ourselves afloat financially. Now we can, we have to give something back,' he says.

It is a curious thing: the people who organised the party train are also the ones who house refugees and feed the homeless; the same man who was chuckling about binge-drinking footballers a moment ago is now talking about a fierce sense of social responsibility. But Mühle insists that it is all part of the same philosophy. 'It's about helping your neighbour, whether that means taking him to an away game, sorting him out if he loses his flat, or getting someone you don't know a bowl of soup,' he says.

'For me that is the most important thing in the life of a club – to get that social idea across to people. What is a football club? Why am I part of a football club? What does it mean to be part of it? Those are the questions people have to ask themselves.'

* * *

What is a football club? Are modern football clubs even clubs in any real sense? A Premier League fan may feel an emotional attachment to their team, but unless they are an employee, they are unlikely to be a part of it in the same way they would be part of a local association or a university society. Most of the grand old 'clubs' of European football are now little more than multi-million-dollar companies which trade on the pageantry of a bygone era. Football is a nostalgia business, and it was so long before the game was flooded with money at the end of the last century.

Fan power, meanwhile, has become a buzzword in modern football. In an era where many elite clubs are backed either directly or indirectly by multinational corporations and oil-rich Gulf states, there is a broad consensus that the world's game has become detached from its roots. Many see empowering supporters as part of the solution, and German football is frequently held up as a model to follow. When supporter discontent boiled over after the attempted Super League breakaway in the summer of 2021, Manchester United fans held up a banner outside Old Trafford calling for the 50+1 rule to be introduced in England.

You could see their logic. The 50+1 rule theoretically gives German fans more of a say in how their club is run. At clubs like United, Liverpool and Chelsea, whose owners had unilaterally decided to join the Super League against the wishes of the supporters, that seemed like an enticing prospect to the protesters.

In England, most football clubs have been private companies for decades. In Germany, the majority were still non-profit registered associations by the end of the twentieth century. The fans didn't just support the team and pay for their tickets, they also paid annual subs and were able to vote at the annual general meeting (AGM), just as they would at a local tiddlywinks club. But football's financial boom had begun to muddy the waters. Clubs were now expanding into larger commercial groups, which encompassed both the traditional members' association, and new, more dynamic commercial operations which could float on the stock market and be run as private, profit-making companies. Increasingly, that meant the fans were losing influence over the big decisions. So the football authorities hit the brakes.

Introduced in 1998, the 50+1 rule stipulates that the members' association must maintain a majority of voting shares (fifty per cent plus one share) in the entire football club. At Borussia Dortmund, for example, the members technically have a less than six per cent stake in the club. But the 50+1 rule ensures that they still have the most voting shares. However, contrary to popular belief, the rule does not enforce fan ownership of football clubs per se. It simply stops any single investor exercising direct control over the club. A wealthy investor could still buy a majority stake and technically become the club's owner, but they could never treat it as their personal plaything.

In many ways, it is a very parochial rule. In a world of individuals and corporations, Germany remains a country with a deeply ingrained cultural affection for registered societies. According to one old joke, if three Germans meet in one place, they will immediately form a club. Though the numbers have long been in steady decline, more than half of Germans are still members of some kind of third-sector organisation, ranging from carnival associations to clubs for computer hackers. The 50+1 rule, which was implemented by an ageing football establishment, was not a revolutionary act of fan power. It was a way of protecting tradition against the vulgarity of the free market.

But it also does empower fans. At a club like Union, which is still a pure, non-profit registered association, the club hierarchy is elected almost directly by the supporters. Members vote for the supervisory board, which in turn votes for the executive board, meaning fans theoretically have the power to vote their leaders out of power. In 2003, they did just that.

As the glow of the 2001 successes started to fade, familiar problems began to creep back in at Union. Financial trouble for Bundesliga broadcaster KirchMedia and Union benefactor Michael Kölmel meant that, two years after promotion to the second tier, the club once again found themselves strapped for cash. President Heiner Bertram, meanwhile, was proving to be increasingly divisive. His approach to the question of a stadium renovation had angered the fans, and he had become embroiled in a series of power struggles, first with coach Georgi Vasilev and later with his own supervisory board. Opposition to Bertram's leadership began to brew within the club, including at the still fledgling *V.I.R.U.S.*, and he was effectively removed from power by the supervisory board in October 2003. The following month, a last-ditch attempt to regain control failed at an embittered AGM, as the members ultimately sided against him.

After a brief period of financial chaos, Union moved quickly towards what some have described as a 'fan takeover' in 2004. A new leadership was elected, largely made up of people who already knew the club and the community from the inside. 'It was more the wealthy fans than the ones who were starting work at six a.m. on the factory floor. But they were fans, so you can call it a fan takeover,' says Mühle. 'They weren't people who were completely emotionless and saw the club only as a way of printing money.'

Dirk Zingler, who became president in the summer of 2004, was definitely not that. The then 39-year-old was a lifelong Union fan who had stood on the terraces with his grandfather as a boy. His rise to power coincided with a more pluralistic structuring of the club, which empowered fans in ways that went far beyond the 50+1 rule.

When his construction logistics company had become a sponsor the previous year, Zingler founded an independent 'economic council' to represent sponsor interests at Union. Under his presidency, the *V.I.R.U.S.* came to take on a similar consultation role on fan issues. At the same time Zingler joined the board, Union also founded the *FuMA* – or fan and member's department – an internal committee to ensure supporter representation, which also has a permanent seat on the supervisory board. All of this created an environment in which the members not only had electoral power via the 50+1 rule, but also direct representation in the club hierarchy. 'For that to work, you have to have someone at the top who is there with his heart and soul,' says Mühle. 'It wouldn't work with a Sheikh.'

'Sheikh', in this case, is shorthand for any wealthy football club owner, whether it is Sheikh Mansour at Manchester City, Russian billionaire and long-time Chelsea owner Roman Abramovich, or the Saudi Arabian public investment fund which now controls Newcastle United. English club owners are, by definition, accountable to their shareholders, and without the 50+1 rule, that does not include the fans. Their money may have made the Premier League the richest and most competitive league in the world, but it has also further disenfranchised supporters on the ground. Mühle, like most Union fans, would not want that for all the money and success in the world.

As well as the traditional affection for club culture, there are flashes here of another typically German trait: allergy to debt. Historical traumas such as hyperinflation in the Weimar Republic and, to a lesser extent, the economic collapse of the GDR, still inform German political culture. The battle for supporter rights and the soul of football are likewise infused with a kind of economic moralism and exceptionalism. When Zingler founded the economic council at Union, notes Mühle, it operated on the premise that it was better for the club to spend their own money than somebody else's. In German football media, there is often a general tone of disapproval about the big spending of clubs like Paris Saint-Germain, Manchester City and Barcelona. 'Some big clubs in other leagues spend more on superstars, because they have a very different approach to money. But our German virtues have served us well,' Bundesliga CEO Donata Hopfen told *Bild* newspaper in 2022.

At clubs like Union, those virtues go beyond the basic rules about club ownership. The 50+1 rule has become the byword for the 'German model', but in fact, it is just one aspect of a wider culture of engagement and compromise between fans and directors, which extends from the shareholder structure to the daily work on the ground done by people like Sven Mühle. For Mühle, groups and structures like the *V.I.R.U.S.* and the *FuMA* are to Union what the opposition benches in parliament are to a functioning democracy. 'We provide the idealism. But it is also important that there is the marketing department that does the capitalist bit, and it's the job of the board to bring all the different things together,' he says.

As always in politics, the day-to-day is a lot less sexy than the headlines. Fan power is often reduced to dramatic images, such as Manchester United fans storming Old Trafford or German ultras staging street demos in defence of 50+1. But the real work to protect fan interests is more mundane and less choreographed. 'It's about working in many small steps. Nobody is going to thank you for it, often nobody will see you, and sometimes someone else will even take the credit,' says Mühle. It is less about revolutions and rules, he argues, and more about upholding the sense of genuine community which has long been expunged from most professional football clubs. 'It's about keeping something alive in the way you want it, so that other people can experience what you have experienced. So that it can continue.'

*   *   *

Mühle may be fighting a losing battle. Union remain an unusually community-minded club, but will that last? The huge sums of money needed to stay afloat in top-flight football mean that the capitalist arm of the club, as Mühle puts it, will arguably become more and more important in the years to come. What bearing that will have on the other side, the idealists, remains to be seen. 'We try to keep one eye on the future,' he says. 'Will we always have representatives on the board? How high are the hurdles to stop things like that being reversed? What happens when we are all no longer here, what influence will fans have then?'

He is not entirely optimistic: 'To be honest, I think it's mainly the older fans who think like I do now. Unless we get more young people on board with the values of the club, we could very quickly lose it all once we're gone.' Mühle has been working in and around Union for almost two decades, and he is convinced that it is getting harder to find people who will commit to the club in the same way he has. 'Often people ask me: "what do I get if I become a member?" That question is horrifying to me, because it reflects a society which is more interested in individual gain than the common good. You become a member of something out of conviction, not because you get something in return.'

He doesn't think it is a generational difference per se. There are plenty of younger people who do want to help the community, he argues, just not as many as he would like there to be. When I suggest that might be something to do with socialisation, he hesitates, perhaps sensing a slightly leading question. 'I don't necessarily want to open up the whole East versus West thing,' he says. 'But there were different living standards in the East and the West, and I do think it's generally the case that there is more solidarity among people in poor countries than in richer societies. In the East, we were more reliant on the people around us than we were after the Wall fell.'

That thought should not be mistaken for a glowing endorsement of East German socialism. 'We weren't living in a progressive, socialist community of values,' he chuckles. Mühle also suffered under the vindictiveness of the socialist state. A passionate boxer as a young man, he found himself unable to box competitively after his brother fled to the West in the 1980s. 'I suddenly failed a medical exam which I had passed without any trouble before,' he explains, adding that it was a 'liberation' when the Wall fell. 'You had the feeling of being free to do things you wanted to do, without being punished, without being ratted on and without being shot on the border.'

But every society has its flaws, and Mühle wonders openly about how modern consumerism has reshaped the way people think about community. He grumbles that the rise of social media has left people more self-interested, shallower and with shorter attention spans. 'It's a general development in society that has changed a lot of things over the last twenty years. When you look closely, you see that too many people are doing things not for the sake of the things themselves, but just to put themselves in the limelight and maybe get a funny selfie out of it.'

That in turn makes him concerned for the future of Union. On the face of it, there is still a huge desire to stand up for fan power and community engagement. The Union ultras – the organised hardcore fans who largely belong to the generation below Mühle – often speak out on issues of fan rights. They are also community-minded, organising and assisting in various campaigns to collect clothes donations for homeless shelters in Berlin and refugee camps in Greece. In the initial few weeks of the pandemic, they organised a 'community donations fence' near the stadium for people struggling to get hold of key goods in lockdown.

The issue is how many in the Union community are willing and able to uphold that spirit in the long term. 'You have to have stamina,' says Mühle. 'Otherwise, we could end up with a great football club with billions of euros in the bank and lots of success on the pitch, but we'll have messed up the social side of it. The community, the social fabric which makes a club what it is, will be gone.' But the closer Union get to the elite in the Bundesliga, the harder it is becoming to strike that balance: 'The big challenge of the coming years will be how we keep bringing in the money without losing our identity as we do so,' he says.

That identity is partly built on Union's history, its roots in the GDR and its natural self-image as the underdog. But most of all, it is built on the active supporters. Union's road to the top of German football was laid – in some cases almost literally – by fans. Where and how it ends, however, is still an open question.

CHAPTER 5
BLEEDING IRON

CHRISTMAS – 23 DECEMBER 2003

It is a bitterly cold night in Köpenick and Torsten is beginning to wish he had found himself a warmer Santa hat. The one he is wearing barely covers his ears, and it's a bit thin for minus six degrees Celsius. At least the colours are right – red and white to match his Union scarf. You can say what you like about Father Christmas, but you can't fault his taste.

It's only fifty metres or so to the Alte Försterei anyway, and a bit of mulled wine should warm him up later. He has stuffed a few flasks in his bag along with the hymn sheets, which were TeeCee's idea: 'Torsten, I'm not sure I know all the carols off by heart, what do you reckon? I reckon we should do some printouts.' TeeCee had always answered his own questions, ever since they were kids. Still, he was right. If they were going to sing, they may as well do it properly.

As they wander towards the ground, a few stragglers begin to tag along. With every curious passer-by, they seem to have the same conversation.

'Where are you off to?'

'Carol-singing.'

'Carol-singing? Where?'

'In the stadium.'

'You what?'

The idea had come to Torsten a week earlier, after another miserable Saturday at the Alte Försterei. At 1–1 with fifteen minutes to go, and

Wacker Burghausen down to ten men, it had looked like Union might end the year with a win after all. But even with a man extra, they somehow still managed to lose. That made it three defeats on the bounce, and left the club second from bottom, three points adrift of safety in the second division. As he trudged home glumly that evening, Torsten realised he hadn't even wished anyone a Merry Christmas.

The guys from the Alt-Unioner fan club should get together, he thought. They could go to the pub or a Christmas market, but then again why not the stadium? That was where they usually met, and it would be nice to be there without the football – drink some Glühwein, sing some carols, and mark Christmas properly. You can't lose a singsong, after all.

Getting inside would be no problem; there was a gate near the Abseitsfalle pub, on the northern edge of the stadium premises, which Torsten knew was never locked. The question was whether the club would mind. Oskar Kosche, the head of the youth academy, didn't seem to think anyone would care. The groundsman was a bit baffled, but in the end he also shrugged: 'I'll stick two bins out for you, just make sure you clean up after yourselves.'

So here they are: Torsten, TeeCee, most of the other Alt-Unioners and a few dozen others who saw the invite posted on the online forum. Not everyone has heard about the unlocked gate, so there are muffled shouts in the dark as some scale the fences. There are no lights on in the stadium, and with the woods all around them, it is effectively pitch black. But somehow, no one is hurt as they grope their way up the stairs and onto the terraces.

There are eighty-nine of them in total, and they meet on the Gegengerade stand, in the famous old block on the halfway line. There was a time when this was the loudest section of the stadium, when Torsten would scream himself hoarse leading the chants. Now 39, his vocal chords are still strong enough to lead the carols.

'O Tannenbaum, O Tannenbaum! How green your leaves are—'

'Leaves?', a jovial voice interrupts. 'What are you on about? Christmas trees have needles, not leaves!'

'It says leaves here on the sheet!'

It is over a month since Union last won at home, and the Alte Försterei has not seen this many smiles in several weeks. The carollers push on for about an hour before calling it a night. This time, they say goodbye to each other properly: hugs, 'Merry Christmases', the works.

When he gets home, Torsten has a quick look at the online forum. Already, word has got around that it went ahead – that the carol-singing wasn't a joke, and that Unioners really did sing away the Christmas blues on the Gegengerade. 'You nutters! I thought you were having a laugh,' writes one fan. 'Count me in next year,' writes another.

Torsten hadn't thought about next year, but why not? The unofficial Union Christmas Carol Service has been a roaring success. Why not make a tradition out of it?

On that cold night in 2003, Torsten Eisenbeiser could never have imagined what would become of his mad idea. Almost two decades on, Union's annual carol service has come a long way from its first edition, when a few dozen fans snuck into the stadium in the dark with a bagful of Glühwein.

By the late 2010s, the so-called *Weihnachtssingen* had become a world-famous tradition, attracting hundreds of reporters and tourists from around the globe to the Alte Försterei every 23 December. With nearly 30,000 attendees every year, it is now one of the biggest Christmas events in the city – a curious hybrid of rock concert, church service and football match. From a stage in the middle of the pitch, a priest and a choir lead the proceedings, and a Father Christmas delivers a review of the year gone by in rhyming verse. Stadium announcer Christian Arbeit plays trumpet in the band, which switches seamlessly between terrace chants and traditional German hymns as the fans around them get gently roasted on mulled wine, beer and bratwurst. It is a bizarre, joyous occasion, and perhaps the greatest single showcase of the sense of community at Union.

'The *Weihnachtssingen* is the biggest church service in Germany which is not held in a church,' says its creator. Eisenbeiser is a stocky man with a warm smile and a slightly busy air to him. Like Sven Mühle, he is a trained chef, who spent his early career working in the parliament building of the GDR, cooking meals for the likes of Erich Honecker. Like Mühle, you get the impression that he is more of a doer than a talker. He tends to explain things in anecdotes, which he acts out in sparse, quickfire dialogue:

'One day I got a call: "This is Müller."

'"Hello Herr Müller, what can I do for you?"

'"I'm told you need a vicar."

'"A vicar? A vicar! Yes, I need a vicar!"'

The way Eisenbeiser tells it, the story of how the carol-singing grew so big is one of endless logistical challenges: finding a vicar, creating professionally bound hymn sheets, and arranging buses for Union fans who lived outside of the city. Much like Mühle's work, it is all about networking and problem-solving. Perhaps it is the nature of a cook to learn by doing, to improvise and create something which is more than the sum of its parts. Eisenbeiser seems in any case to have a talent for coming up with barmy schemes and somehow making them work.

It is a common trait at Union, and one which underpins the culture of bottom-up supporter engagement. There are plenty of other clubs in Germany and Europe with active fan scenes, where supporters have representation on the board or occupy high-ranking positions. If Union are unique, it is because their fans don't just organise politically, but in almost every aspect of life. Eisenbeiser's carol service is the most famous example, but it is by no means the only one: his friend Tino 'TeeCee'

Czerwinski was the inventor and long-time host of the 'fan meet' – a monthly, semi-private event where players and supporters can meet face to face; Mühle and the *V.I.R.U.S* run their annual dragon boat race, which began in the same year as the *Weihnachtssingen*; since 2006, professional actor and director Jörg Steinberg has staged an annual production of the Union play. A theatrical love letter to the club and its supporters, the play is a gentle comedy about several generations of Union fans, from the miraculous escape from relegation in 1988 up to the notorious ferry trip to Finland. The ensemble cast are all also dedicated Union fans.

It is no coincidence that most of these things were conceived by the same generation of Union fans. If the supporters wanted something in the 1990s and 2000s, they often had to organise it and finance it themselves. Everything had to be improvised, pulled together from what networks and resources already existed, and often at little or no cost. At the time of the first carol-singing, mid-way through the 2003/04 season, Union were coming down off their early-decade high and hurtling towards relegation. They were short of cash and fighting to get through each business week. Eisenbeiser remembers buying stacks of A4 paper out of his own pocket and bringing them to the Alte Försterei so the club secretary had something to print on. 'You can't imagine now what those times were like for Union,' he says.

To this day, Eisenbeiser is not employed by the club. For seventeen years, he organised the carol-singing entirely voluntarily. It takes a certain type of person to do something like that over such a sustained period, and Union seem to have a higher-than-average amount of them. Perhaps it is something in the water. More probably, it is something in the name.

For as long as anyone can remember, Union have been associated with the phrase 'Eisern Union': Iron Union. Nowadays, it is a nickname, a battle cry and a club slogan all rolled into one. It is scrawled across red-and-white merchandise in the club shop, and it is the inspiration behind the club mascot, Ritter Keule, an iron-clad medieval knight with a spiked mace and a nose like a sausage. Iron grey is also an unofficial secondary colour, adorning the team bus, the VIP boxes and, in some seasons, the away kit. Official communications from the club are always signed 'with iron greetings', and Unioners often greet each other with a simple 'Eisern!'

'We're iron because we are a tight-knit community – we help one another,' says Eisenbeiser. 'Other communities do that too, but we have the advantage that it's right there in our nickname. Maybe we are only like that because of the name; maybe the word iron itself is partly what made us what we are today.' If any Union fan knows something about nominative determinism, it is him. His own surname, literally translated, means 'Ironbiter'. 'Growing up around the corner with a name like that, I couldn't really have supported anyone else,' he laughs.

* * *

Anyone who has been to a matchday at the Alte Försterei will have heard the story of how Union became the iron club. Before every single Union home game, a low, melodramatic voice rings out through the stadium over a steady, ominous bassline. 'It was in the golden twenties,' it says, 'when a battle cry like thunder echoed from the terraces...'

The lines, originally written for Jörg Steinberg's play and since repurposed as an introduction to Nina Hagen's anthem, tell the legend of how the battle cry 'Eisern Union' transpired. Union, the story goes, were on the brink of defeat when a lone voice from the crowd screamed the phrase in a desperate attempt to rally the troops. 'Nobody then could have known that they were witnessing a historic moment. A legend was born, which would never, ever be forgotten,' the prologue gasps in conclusion.

According to club historian Gerald Karpa, this version should be taken with a barrel of salt. In the 1920s, he says, the Alte Försterei was far too small for anything to echo around it like thunder. Based on his own research, Karpa thinks the chant originated during a game against Hertha in the late 1930s. It was probably the local baker who first screamed 'Eisern Union', demanding that the team show a little bit more mettle. But the phrase stuck, sliding neatly into Union's enduring identity as the club of the local metalworkers.

It remains, first and foremost, a rallying cry; but iron is also a metaphor for an idealised set of characteristics. As Eisenbeiser puts it: 'Iron is strong, you can't break it, and unless it's very thin, you can't bend it'. Both on and off the pitch, Union fans tend to prize commitment, perseverance and solidarity over style and showmanship. They don't mind if their team plays a dull, efficient brand of football, and they don't generally mind if they lose, provided they show some fight and don't wilt at the first sign of pressure.

To the outsider, the veneration of iron can sometimes seem a little uncomfortable. As Ritter Keule's armour and mace attest, it is above all a military and industrial metal, and it is hardly squeaky clean in the German context. To some, iron evokes Prussian militarism, and a kind of patriotism which few in modern Germany wish to associate with. It has shades of Bismarck and his talk of a nation forged in 'blood and iron', a phrase which the Nazis later bastardised into the racist ideology of 'blood and soil'. When Union commissioned a branded charter plane for away games in 2019, the German airline they contracted declined to decorate it with the Eisern Union slogan, citing possible far-right connotations.

The club were understandably irked. Football, after all, is full of military-industrial nicknames. Arsenal fans are not all firearms enthusiasts, and Sheffield United's Bramall Lane – home of 'The Blades' – is not a knife crime hotspot. Likewise, shouting 'Eisern Union' at an old metalworkers' club does not make you a Prussian revivalist.

Iron, in any case, has a much broader significance in German culture, one which has been used by left-wing and democratic movements as well as the far right. It was first politicised in the Napoleonic Wars, when Prussians traded their expensive jewellery for iron replacements to fund the fight against the French. The iron cross, still a hotly contested symbol of the German armed forces, was also introduced in 1813 as the first military honour to be awarded irrespective of rank and class. Beyond simple military might, iron was a rallying symbol for an embattled community to come together at a time of crisis. It stood for frugality, modesty and solidarity across political and class lines. Even in a society which has long since renounced militarism, those are virtues which still appeal to voters and football fans alike.

Union fans had always put their ideas of iron solidarity into practice, and they did so again in 2004. Just months after Eisenbeiser and his friends broke into the stadium to hold their first ever carol service, he and other fans pulled off what was perhaps the maddest of all their mad ideas. A lot of football supporters would claim to be the lifeblood of their club. At Union, they actually bled to keep their club alive.

Two years after promotion to the second tier, the club had hit the rocks again. Results were bad before Christmas and they did not improve much in the new year, with Union winning just four games in the second half of the season. A change of coach in March couldn't save them from relegation, and the growing financial trouble promised an even harsher fate. By the spring, it became clear that Union were so short of cash that they could well be banished back into the wilderness of non-league football. To get their licence for the third tier, the club needed to present a liquidity reserve of around 1.5 million euros. This was money they simply didn't have, and with the deadline in early June, they had less than a month to raise it.

There followed a mammoth fundraising effort, with fans, celebrities and politicians all chipping in to save Union from potential oblivion. At the centre of it was the Bleed for Union initiative, which allowed fans to donate blood in Union's name at one of four clinics across Berlin. The ten euros compensation fee which was ordinarily paid to the blood donor themselves would then be wired directly to the football club. For those who could not give blood (anyone who spent time in Britain from 1980 to 1996, for example, is still not accepted as donors in Germany because of concerns over 'mad cow disease'), there were countless other ways to donate. Bleed for Union t-shirts were sold at fifteen euros a pop; a 'blood-brothers' friendly' match was organised against Hamburg club FC St. Pauli; and East German rock band City hosted a benefit concert at the Alte Försterei. 'Some people we knew ran a tenpin bowling place, so they did a "Bowling for Union" event,' says Eisenbeiser. 'We were just trying to get as much money as we could from anywhere we could.'

As well as donating blood himself, Eisenbeiser also helped stage an impromptu demo to raise awareness of Union's plight. 'We didn't have any business lobby in Berlin back then, and we needed to get people's attention,' he says. With a few dozen others, he staged a demonstration at the East Side Gallery, an outdoor street art exhibition on the longest remaining section of the Berlin Wall. They hung banners and Union flags from the lampposts, and Eisenbeiser put up two speed limit signs so that the commuters on the main road would slow down and take notice. When the police came to check the protest out, the officers turned a blind eye to the illegal road signs. 'Maybe they were Unioners as well,' he laughs.

In the end, the demonstrations and the media interest probably did more to save Union than the blood donations themselves. It was sponsors' money which made up the bulk of the 1.5 million euros. Just days before the deadline, however, the club were still short of a few hundred thousand euros and soon-to-be president Dirk Zingler and long-term investor Michael Kölmel were forced to make up the difference. Even then, salvation proved to be a somewhat pyrrhic victory. Having bled themselves dry just to secure the licence, Union were forced to sell most of their squad in the summer of 2004 and subsequently plunged straight into another relegation battle in the third division. A year later, they had gone down for the second season in a row.

But while it may not have solved all of Union's financial and footballing woes, the campaign had once again shown to what extent the club were able to fall back on the loyalty and the creativity of their supporters. The huge organisational efforts during the fundraising campaign also brought the fanbase closer together says Eisenbeiser. 'The biggest thing to come of it was not really the money; it was that people started talking to each other more on the terraces,' he says. 'You started getting to know people better, where they came from and what they did.'

Union had always imagined itself as a unique community, but it was in the 2000s that the community came to outshine even the football. Partly because the club itself was in such dire straits, the people around it became even more tightly bound together. That is a legacy which Eisenbeiser says has endured. 'There are still people now who barely go to any games at all. They go to the carol-singing, or the dragon boat race and things like that, because they say, "Yes, I identify with this club, with these colours and with these people, even if I don't really care about football."

'That's the point: we don't go to football. We go to Union.'

*   *   *

Eisenbeiser's anecdotes are full of asides – verbal footnotes to qualify who he is talking about and their relationship to Union: 'She was the one who did this job.' 'He was the one who had this idea.' And all too frequently: 'They are no longer with us.'

Almost two decades have passed since the first carol service and the Bleed for Union campaign. Many of the fans who were behind those efforts, who supported the club through its lowest ebb in the modern era, have now passed away. It is a club tradition that fans who have recently died are given a send-off at the next home game, and in recent years, stadium announcer Christian Arbeit has had to read several obituaries for people whose engagement had made them almost universally popular throughout the fanbase. Eisenbeiser's friend Tino 'TeeCee' Czerwinski, who died in 2018 at the age of 58, was one of them. 'Tino's death really hit me hard,' he says.

As promotion to the Bundesliga began to loom in 2019, Eisenbeiser found himself thinking about the fans who had passed away. The thought that they would never see their club reach the top flight seemed to him an injustice, and it prompted another mad idea. With the help of Sven Mühle and a few others, he devised a scheme whereby fans could provide pictures of their departed friends and relatives which would then be mounted onto enormous banners. If and when Union were promoted, the banners would be raised so that those who had gone would be able to witness the historic moment, even if only in spirit.

The idea proved too complicated to put into practice before the end of the season, so it was instead postponed until Union's top-flight debut later that summer. As the players walked out for the club's first ever Bundesliga match and Nina Hagen's 'Eisern Union' anthem echoed around the stadium, around 450 Union fans raised the huge black-and-white photos of those they had lost. Eisenbeiser wept as he held up an image of TeeCee, and he was not the only one. 'Some of the other faces we held up that day were older guys, who had no living relatives when they died. Union was the only family they had,' says Eisenbeiser. Moments like that and events like the carol-singing, he argues, reveal something about Union which is otherwise hard to put into words. 'We are a family, and that stadium is our front room. They say you can't choose your family, but this one we do choose. These are the people we want to be with.'

The family has changed and grown over the years, and not just because some of its patriarchs and matriarchs have passed away. As well as newer Union fans, the *Weihnachtssingen* also draws supporters from other clubs who happen to be in Berlin over Christmas. Eisenbeiser claims he has seen St. Pauli, Hansa Rostock and even Hertha shirts there in previous years. While some grumble that the visitors water down the event, he thinks it is a sign of strength. 'It's about people coming together. We may not have the same views or follow the same team, but at an event like that, nobody loses. It's peaceful. And maybe that is what has been missing from our society in the last twenty years or so as well.'

He is not the only one who thinks so. In December 2016, a *New York Times* report from the *Weihnachtssingen* raved about its 'old-school romanticism and local-club familiarity' and cast the event as an act of defiant solidarity in the wake of the deadly terror attack on a Berlin Christmas market just weeks earlier. In an increasingly fragmented and fearful society, an event which brings so many different people together in such an intimate setting has a certain romantic appeal.

Like Mühle, Eisenbeiser fears that in general, people are becoming less community-oriented and less likely to throw their lot in for a collective cause. 'The sharp elbows people have today... it's not like they didn't have them in the GDR... but it was different,' he says. As teenagers his generation had sought to provoke the powers that be in socialist East Germany with their rowdy behaviour on the terraces. In middle age, they developed an almost inverse kind of contrariness, remaining defiantly community-minded in an age of individualism. Both are easily romanticised, and in the absence of any significant success on the field, Union's iron-willed insistence on doing things differently was what drew many new people to the club. The more things like Bleed for Union hit the headlines, the more outsiders began to come to Köpenick in search of that community spirit.

Often, the carol-singing was their way in. 'I remember the vicar saying to me in the early years that, sooner or later, we were going to fill the stadium with this event,' says Eisenbeiser. 'I told him he was mad.' But the vicar was right. The runaway success of the Christmas event was the first real sign that Union had a potential fanbase far larger than anybody had previously expected, and its unstoppable rise was a taste of things to come.

* * *

The content of the *Weihnachtssingen* has not really changed over the years. It is still essentially a few hours of carols and mulled wine, with a bit of religion thrown in for good measure. But in terms of size, it has grown beyond recognition.

At some point in the late 2000s, Eisenbeiser remembers busloads of tourists from southern Germany arriving after tour companies started including Union in a Christmas tour of the capital. Demand for the event eventually became so high that the club had to lay plastic matting on the pitch and expand the capacity to 28,500 – around twenty-five per cent higher than it would be on matchday. In 2013, the stadium was so full that people had to be turned away, and the sheer size of the event was turning it into a lucrative occasion for the club coffers. It became ticketed, and from 2013 onwards it sold out every year. 'Even when it's minus ten degrees, they sell more beer on that night than they ever do on a matchday. And that's before you include the mulled wine,' says Eisenbeiser.

The larger the event got, the more it demanded of its organiser. When local TV became interested in showing live images on the evening news, the entire programme suddenly had to be timed down to the last minute to fit with the broadcasting schedule. Media interest at home and abroad became so great that Union's press officers had to ferry Eisenbeiser from inter-view to interview throughout the evening. 'I've spoken to the BBC, *New York Times*, Reuters, ZDF; there is nobody I haven't spoken to,' he says.

By 2019, he had had enough, and decided to pass on full responsibility for the event to the club. He remains tight-lipped about the precise reasons for his departure, and insists there were no hard feelings, but the impression is that the working relation-ship had run its course. He was also, presumably, exhausted: 'At the beginning I would just liaise with one guy, Oskar Kosche. By the end there were fifty different people working on it, from lighting technicians to security teams.' Union had changed and grown more professional, and the event itself had perhaps outgrown its creator. At the seventeenth *Weihnachtssingen* in 2019, the last which he organised, he decided not to do any interviews and simply enjoy the evening. 'It was amazing. It was the first one for ages I really enjoyed, and the first time I became aware of what we had done in all those years.'

Perhaps the surest sign of the event's success is that others have started to imitate it. Huge German clubs like Borussia Dortmund and Schalke now also run their own stadium carol services, though most admit they lack the charm of the original. Union's *Weihnachtssingen* is special because of its history. The founding story of the carollers who broke into their own stadium is part of what draws new people to the service every single Christmas. It may now be a mass event, but it is one which has grown organically out of a genuine sense of community, not out of a marketing idea. That gives it a warmth which other similar events don't have.

But the growth of the carol-singing is also a symptom of Union's quandary. If the club's soul was forged in times of hardship, does that mean that they lose something of themselves in the good times? The Alte Försterei had been a crumbling relic of a bygone era when Eisenbeiser and his friends broke in there in 2003. A decade later, it was a freshly renovated modern stadium, able to host all manner of major events. Union's footballing fortunes had also changed dramatically. Far from being an excuse to forget the miserable results, the 2019 carol-singing was a chance to celebrate Union's meteoric rise, promotion and a recent derby win over Hertha. On the face of it, the carol-singing remains an intimate and warm event, but is the iron still strong underneath the gloss? Everyone sings when they are winning, after all. 'In good times, it is always harder to gauge how real that sense of unity is,' says Eisenbeiser. 'In a crisis, you learn who your real friends are.'

By the end of the 2000s, Union had spent two decades almost constantly in crisis, frequently relying on the people who were willing to muck in simply out of a sense of loyalty and

belonging. In the decade that was to come, the good times were
set to roll for the longest period in Union's history. But before
that, they had one more mountain to climb.

The "Union Madonna", a work created by Andora to mark the 40th anniversary of 1. FC Union and the 100th anniversary of their ancestor Union Oberschöneweide. The writing above the two heads reads: "Semel Unionus, Semper Unionus". Once an Unioner, always an Unioner. © Andora.

▲ Andora's most famous work: The Little Bite. The image
flies from all four corner flags at the Alte Försterei. © Andora.

A fan volunteer gets to work dismantling the old fences between the away block and
the home block during the renovation in 2008. Behind him are the old, uncovered
terraces, a layer of grass and weeds growing on each step. © Matthias Koch. ▼

▲ The terraces at the Alte Försterei as they are today, after the fans volunteered in their hundreds to renovate them in 2008/9. As well as the new roof and fencing, the concrete was also newly laid and the railings painted in Union red. © 1. FC Union Berlin.

Union president Dirk Zingler unveils the monument to the volunteer stadium builders after the project was completed in 2009. © 1. FC Union Berlin. ▼

Union mascot Ritter Keule, whose iron armour is inspired by the battle cry "Eisern Union!". "Ritter" means "knight", while "Keule" can mean both "mace" in standard German and "brother" in Berlin dialect. © 1. FC Union Berlin.

▲ The old brick scoreboard in the Alte Försterei. One of the few parts of the stadium which has remained completely unchanged in the last 30 years. © Stefanie Fiebrig.

Fans watch Germany beat Argentina in the 2014 World Cup Final from the comfort of their sofas at Union's "World Cup Living Room". © 1. FC Union Berlin. ▼

▲ The Old Forester's House which gives the stadium its name. The building was still used by the local forestry authority until the late 2000s. Since 2007, it has hosted Union's head office. © 1. FC Union Berlin.

Veteran defender Michael Parensen celebrates with fans on the pitch after the promotion play-off triumph against Stuttgart. © 1. FC Union Berlin. ▼

▲ A fan raises a chunk of turf ripped from the pitch during the post-match celebrations when Union were promoted to the Bundesliga in 2019. © 1. FC Union Berlin.

The Union ultras raise an enormous tifo of coach Urs Fischer in the club's second ever Bundesliga home game in 2019. A few hours later, they were celebrating a sensational 3-1 win over Borussia Dortmund. © 1. FC Union Berlin. ▼

A photo taken by the author as Michael Parensen crowdsurfed across the sea of fans during the promotion celebrations.

CHAPTER 6
IF YOU BUILD IT

UNION BERLIN 3–5 HERTHA BERLIN – 8 JULY 2009

Twelve hours before kick-off, Sylvia takes a deep breath. Almost every single morning for the past thirteen months, she has stood in the same spot with the same clipboard and addressed the motley crew of volunteers assembled in front of her on the main stand. She has welcomed them all to the building site, given them their paperwork and allocated the day's tasks to the various groups. In more than a year, the routine hasn't changed, but now she is here for the very last time. There are no more steps to pave, no more potholes to fill, no more health and safety forms to hand out. At three o'clock in the afternoon, the building site will officially close, and the most remarkable project of her career will be over. 'It has been one of the most educational and emotional years of my life,' she says, her voice beginning to crack.

Despite the tears, this is a day for celebration. It is a bright July morning, and before the sun goes down this evening, the woods of the Wuhlheide will once again be filled with red and white. Around 19,000 fans will stream through the freshly polished gates and for the first time in 403 days, Union Berlin will play a football match at the Stadion an der Alten Försterei.

It has been a long year. The renovation of the almost 90-year-old stadium was supposed to take only a few months, but it has now stretched over an entire season. As if exile from the Alte Försterei wasn't bad enough,

Union have also been forced to play home games at Friedrich-Ludwig-Jahn-Sportpark, the one-time home of their sworn enemies BFC Dynamo. With a peg on their nose, they have somehow made it to the end of the season as third division champions, promoted without having played a single game in their own stadium. And now, finally, they have their reward. They are back at the Alte Försterei, inaugurating their newly renovated stadium with a friendly against Hertha.

'Köpenick, we're home!' bellows stadium announcer Christian Arbeit from the centre circle as he greets the returning fans before kick-off. After such a long time away, they have returned to a very different Alte Försterei. The dandelions and weeds which used to sprout from terraces are now gone and the once crumbling grey steps are now smooth and pristine. They should remain that way for a while, because unlike their predecessors, they are no longer exposed to the elements. Looming over them, for the very first time, is a roof. It is a roof which has caused Sylvia all manner of headaches and stubbornly delayed this opening day party. But now it is on, firmly attached to the shiny red uprights and grassy slopes below.

The roof is not the only new feature. Above the away end hangs a big screen. It may be second-hand – salvaged from a stadium in Austria after last summer's UEFA Euro 2008 tournament – but for the Alte Försterei it is state of the art. 'Iron thanks to everyone', reads the on-screen message as the fans stream up the slopes and into the new stadium. At the gate, they are handing out red construction helmets with the words 'stadium builder' and 'Eisern' on the side. There is one for every single person who volunteered, whether they gave up their entire summer holidays to shift concrete or just spent a spare afternoon painting toilets.

Union lose to Hertha, but this is one of those nights when nobody cares about the result. As the full-time fireworks display suggests, this is a celebration of a new era. Just a couple of years ago, both Union and their stadium had been written off by most of Berlin. Now the club looks like a worthy second fiddle to their bigger western neighbours. Mayor Klaus Wowereit, whose administration had initially been reluctant to save the Alte Försterei, is now soaking up the party atmosphere from the main stand. His fellow social democrat Gabriele Schöttler, the mayor of Köpenick, beams and chatters to everyone around her. Sylvia nods politely and smiles.

She is exhausted, emotionally as well as physically. Every five minutes or so, another person comes up to her with a card, a gift or just a big, heartfelt hug. Left, right and centre, they are thanking her for what she has done, for the emotional rollercoaster of the last year, and for the shining new stadium in front of them.

But it wasn't just me, she keeps telling them. It was all of us.

In some cities, they say you are never more than six feet away from a rat. In Berlin, the rats are never more than six feet from a construction worker. The German capital, its taxi drivers like to say, is one big building site. From the street battles and bombing raids of the Second World War to the division and isolation of the Cold War, the twentieth century inflicted lasting physical damage on the city. After reunification, that damage made it both a developer's dream and a politician's nightmare. In 2013, tabloid *B.Z.* estimated that there was a worksite every 53 metres in Berlin. It is a safe bet that, no more than six feet from any of them, there was somebody complaining.

Potsdamer Platz is not the only major building site to have caused heated debate since reunification. Since the federal government returned there in the late 1990s, the rebuilding of Berlin has become a fiercely contested battleground in the fight over Germany's national identity and political self-image. The Holocaust Memorial in the very centre of the city is a powerful reminder of the country's historical crimes, and a symbol of its self-critical remembrance culture. At the new Humboldt Forum down the road, the memory politics are a little messier. The demolition of the former East German parliament building in

2006 and its replacement with a faithful reconstruction of the former Prussian royal palace sparked a furious and multi-layered debate over religion, reunification, colonialism and militarism which is likely to drag on for years. At the official opening of the new building in 2021, a street protest outside was already calling for its demolition.

Other building sites are simply embarrassing. The never-ending woes of the infamous Berlin Brandenburg Airport (BER), which opened a full eight years behind schedule in 2020, made a mockery of German efficiency and a national laughing stock of the capital. For years, you could buy postcards in Berlin souvenir shops which quipped that the city could do anything except airports and football. Whether for profound historical reasons or simply because of local pride, architecture and construction matter in Berlin. They fill newspapers, define election campaigns, and bring people onto the streets.

In a city littered with construction cockups, the Alte Försterei is a rare success story. Like all Berlin building sites, it was the result of years of political wrangling, fierce ideological debate and protests. Unlike many others, it was almost exclusively hailed as a good thing. Union's football may have been little to write home about in the 2000s, but their stadium renovation was. From June 2008 to the following summer, the Alte Försterei was transformed into what Unioners called 'the world's most beautiful building site'. The story of the fans who were volunteering to build their own stadium made headlines across the world.

If there was a single key turning point in Union's rise from the backwaters to the Bundesliga, this was it. During the 2008/09 season, 2,333 men and women – most of them volunteers – worked more than 140,000 hours to transform the Alte Försterei from a crumbling wreck into one of modern football's most distinctive stadiums. In doing so, they made Union famous across the globe and changed the way the club was viewed in the rest of

Berlin. They also laid the foundations for a new era of success, giving Union a home which allowed them to break what had long been a vicious circle of financial disasters.

Their efforts are now immortalised in a beer garden on the southern side of the stadium. In the shadow of the terraces stands a tall, stout column made of iron girders, which is decorated with metal plaques bearing the name of every single person who signed up to help. On top of the monument is an enormous red construction helmet, identical in everything but size to the ones which were handed out to volunteers when the stadium finally reopened.

'I still have my helmet in the display case at home,' says Sylvia Weisheit. Her name is buried somewhere low down on the back of the monument along with the other 'Ws', but in truth, she is one of the heroines of the story. As project manager, Weisheit worked night and day to organise and rally the volunteers and keep the building site running smoothly. She allocated tasks, managed the professional contracts, raised funds from sponsors and kept the site logs up to date. Without her, the stadium would not have been built. When I meet her ahead of a friendly match against Swiss side St. Gallen in the summer of 2021, however, she is waiting at the back of a long line with all the other fans. She no longer works here, and she is not one to jump the queue.

Standing with her on the forecourt, though, it's obvious that she's still no ordinary fan. Every five minutes or so, our conversation is interrupted by somebody who wants to say hello. A groundsman with a limp hurries up to give her a bear hug. 'He was one of our stadium builders,' she says. A well-fed man with slicked-back hair and a pink fleece under his jacket changes direction to greet her on his way into the VIP boxes. 'He was one of our sponsors.' A passing journalist exchanges pleasantries and an update on his family. He too once put in a shift or two on the building site.

'This really is a family,' smiles Weisheit. If events like the *Weihnachtssingen* and Bleed for Union had indicated as much, then the stadium renovation put it beyond any doubt. In this case, it wasn't just a case of symbolic grassroots engagement while sponsors' money did the real work. Without the volunteers, the stadium would not have been renovated, and without the renovation, it may have been torn down altogether. Many had already written it off long before construction began, and economically the entire project was a gamble. 'We started building almost exactly at the time the banks started going bust and the financial crisis started,' says Weisheit with a grimace.

In 2008, Union had very little money and only a handful of employees who were able to set up and run a fully functioning construction site. The whole world was about to be hit by economic meltdown, and political will to save the Alte Försterei was in short supply. It should have been impossible. But Weisheit and her 2,000-plus volunteers pulled it off.

'If you have a common goal, and you work towards it, then you can achieve things which seem impossible,' she says. She had been an Union fan since 1977, and for her and the others, it was about more than rebuilding a stadium. It was about keeping the club alive. She quotes the last line of Nina Hagen's anthem. '"We will live forever." That was the aim.'

* * *

For Union to live forever, they had to stay in the Alte Försterei. That was the consensus which drove most of the volunteers to the building site in 2008. For years, there had been murmurs about moving Union to a new location; for years, Union fans had fought tooth and nail to stay put. 'We need the Alte Försterei like the air we breathe,' read one of their protest banners at the turn of the millennium.

The stadium was the oldest, most enduring element of the club's identity. It was older than the colours, the badge and the oldest supporters. It had been their home ever since Union Oberschöneweide first moved to what was then the Sportpark Sadowa in 1920, and it had been the single constant in the club's chequered history ever since. Only in the Second World War, when it reportedly hosted a Nazi flak emplacement to defend against Allied air raids, had football stopped there for any longer than a few weeks.

It also had a long history of fan involvement .In the late 1960s, Union fans mucked in to expand the terraces as part of the East German government's National Reconstruction Programme. A further expansion followed in the late 1970s, but aside from the addition of extra rows and an elevated cabin for the TV commentators and stadium announcers, the ground remained largely unchanged for much of the second half of the twentieth century. That, in fact, was its big problem. By the 1990s, the Alte Försterei was effectively unfit for purpose. Every spring, it would be tinged green and yellow from the dandelions and buttercups sprouting from the cracked grey terraces. Both in terms of facilities and health and safety requirements, it no longer complied with German Football League regulations. From the early 2000s, Union had to repeatedly apply for special exemptions to keep playing there.

That in turn meant a fierce tug-of-war over the future of the stadium between politicians, football administrators and club directors, with the fans making as much noise as possible from the sidelines. Then president Heiner Bertram had been open to uprooting Union and moving them to the centre of the city, but was persuaded against it, in part due to protest and pressure from supporters. The Union fanbase was firmly set against the idea of a new build in a different location or, even worse, a permanent move to the Jahn-Sportpark, which had once been home to BFC Dynamo. Plans for a complete rebuild of the Alte Försterei on the same site also met with similar scepticism. None of the proposals which the club put forward in 2003 pleased the fans, who were particularly alarmed about the prospect of a largely seated stadium. Unioners prefer to watch football standing up. Sitting, they will tell you, is for arses.

Once the new, fan-led administration took over in 2004, there was no more talk of leaving the Alte Försterei. In new president Dirk Zingler and his fellow board member Dirk Thieme, the club now had two people on the board who, as lifelong fans, had the same vision for the stadium as most of the fanbase. They also had the professional know-how to put that vision into practice: Zingler ran a business delivering construction materials, and Thieme was a trained architect. Together, they drew up plans to revamp the Alte Försterei into a modern stadium which would comply with the regulations, but also retain the spirit of the old ground.

But even with the fans onside, there was now an external battle to be fought. The stadium still belonged to the local government, and the club would have to persuade city administrators that a renovation was the best option. However, having squandered public funds in the high-profile *Sportpark* construction scandal just a decade earlier, Union had little political leverage. The Berlin Senate was unwilling to spend taxpayers' money on a stadium which, outside of Köpenick, few people felt particularly strongly about. After nearly a decade of back and forth, many city politicians were urging Union to simply move to the Jahn-Sportpark. That enraged the fans, who took their protests up a notch. City deputies were bombarded with emails, and one pro-stadium initiative staged a demonstration inside the Berlin parliament building. Even the club's official account admits that the tone of the protesters was not always measured, and the spring of 2008 was marked by anger and resentment towards elected representatives.

'The politicians didn't understand why we could never accept the Jahn-Sportpark,' says Weisheit. For the lawmakers, it was a question of practicality and public money. For Union fans, it was an existential question of identity. It was not just that they associated Jahn-Sportpark with BFC; it was also in a completely different part of the city. Berlin is a place where hyperlocal identities run deep, and the club identified strongly with its industrial history in the south-east. Köpenick was one of the last boroughs to become part of Greater Berlin in the early twentieth century, and it still feels more like a satellite town than a district of a major city. To leave would have been to give up the green trees of the forest for the grey concrete of the inner city, and Weisheit insists that it would have broken Union's spirit. 'I'm convinced of it. Our identity is tied to that specific piece of the earth,' she says.

In the end, Zingler persuaded the city to let Union try to save the Alte Försterei themselves. A deal to buy the property for a symbolic fee of one euro fell foul of EU competition rules, but eventually the club and the Senate hashed out an agreement on a 65-year lease. That handed Union control of their stadium and allowed them to start building. They did so at their own risk, beginning work months before the deal was finally signed and sealed in the autumn. Berlin bureaucracy is notoriously slow, and they were neither the first nor the last to try and leap before looking. A decade later, US electric car giant Tesla successfully applied to start building their new factory on the outskirts of the city before they had final planning permission.

Where Elon Musk could afford the risk, however, Union were playing with fire. For the still heavily indebted club, the stadium renovation was make or break. Though the city had loaned them some of the costs, they would be funding most of the renovation themselves. To retain full control of the design, meanwhile, they had eschewed any major commercial investment from outside. If it went wrong, they would be back at square one with less cash than they started with. That meant doing everything on a shoestring where possible. 'Two weeks before we started, the board gave me a budget breakdown,' says Weisheit. When she flicked through it, her heart sank. 'Personnel costs: zero. Equipment costs: zero. I said: "Dirk, how am I supposed to build this thing?"'

'He said: "Sylvia, that's exactly why I got you on board."'

*   *   *

Weisheit was initially reluctant to take on such a formidable task. After training in business education, she had overseen several construction projects during her professional career. But garden centres and hotels were one thing – a stadium was quite another. She and Zingler had long been talking about the club's potential, however, and he insisted that if anyone could pull it off, she could. 'It was quite brave of him really. The project was in two completely male-dominated fields, and he put a blonde woman in charge. I have a lot of respect for that, even today,' she says.

If anyone had doubted her suitability to the role, they were soon proved wrong. Faced with the impossible budget, Weisheit moved quickly to increase Union's wiggle room. She rang every sponsor on the club's books to raise funds and put out a call for fans to volunteer. By the time construction started in early June, 200 people had already signed up, and by seven-thirty a.m. on the first morning, she had thirty-six of them already hard at work.

Within weeks, the project had settled into a routine. Every morning at seven, Weisheit would greet the day's volunteers from her office in the old press box. After signing a basic health and safety tutorial, the helpers would be allocated to one of six professional team leaders and immediately set to work. The days were long. Without shelter from Berlin's freezing winters and baking summers, the conditions could be brutal. Yet the steady stream of volunteers never seemed to slow. Weisheit, herself surviving on just a few hours' sleep a night, was astonished by the level of commitment and the relentless good spirits. 'You always had the feeling that everyone was so grateful,' she says.

For many Unioners, it became a matter of principle and a badge of honour to take part in the collective effort. One fan who had left Berlin in 1991 travelled all the way back from Brazil to work unpaid for almost a whole year. Others used up their entire annual leave doing shifts, often to the chagrin of family members who would have rather been at the beach. For those who couldn't do manual labour, there were other jobs. Andora, who was recovering from an operation at the time, did shifts as a nightwatchman alongside his one-time hero Potti Matthies. On other nights, it was pensioners and families with young children who sat and kept watch in the dark. With the catering budget non-existent, volunteers also provided, prepared and dished out the food and drink. 'This,' as one wisecracking builder quipped at one point, 'is plain communism.'

If the lack of money had seemed a problem at the beginning, it soon became clear that the bigger challenge would be the sheer volume of volunteers. 'I'll always remember the 29th of December,' says Weisheit. 'A lot of people had come home to see their families over Christmas, and we had fifty people signed up to do the shift. But when I arrived in the morning, there were ninety of them waiting in minus fifteen degrees Celsius. I had to find them all useful things to do!'

On that day, they laid the formwork for the last few steps at the top of the terraces. In the first six months, the stands had been transformed from their crumbling brown into a beautiful, smooth, light grey which shone in the winter sun. Repaving the terraces was not the only task, however. Over the course of the thirteen months, the volunteers were responsible for everything except the installation of the roof. They painted the toilets and the handrails, put up new fences, retiled the roofs of the ticket booths and rebuilt the crumbling steps.

Some were stonemasons and professional builders; others were people who had never set foot on a building site in their lives. 'We had people from all walks of life: doctors, professors, successful business people,' says Weisheit. Some were not even Union fans. In the summer of 2008, the team was joined by a student from Leipzig called Otto, who knew nobody at the club but had heard about the project from afar. Weisheit had to find him somewhere to stay, and, as with everyone else, a job he could do. By the time he left, he had become one of the most famous volunteers on the site. 'Maybe that is a female quality: the ability to get people onside and empathise with them,' she says. 'I knew I could lead people because I had led plenty of projects before. It didn't really matter who did what, the point was to make sure everybody could participate.' Years later, she was on the phone with a sales manager at a leading technology company, who reminded her that she had once assigned him to go around the site collecting waste paper.

For many of those who worked on the site, it was a life-changing experience. Weisheit remembers a PhD student learning how to use a core drill, and a painter who was a recovering alcoholic at the start of the project. 'He had just finished withdrawal treatment, and we made him our main painter, because that had been his profession before. Now he has his life back. He's driving again, and even though he still has health problems, he's alive, and he has a different quality of life,' she says.

She too looks back on the renovation as a seminal moment in her life. On the final morning, one year and thirty-six days after she had addressed the first group of volunteers, she struggled to hold back the tears. 'I have done three degrees in my life, but I never learned as much as I did in those thirteen months,' she says.

* * *

Had they known at the beginning just how enormous the project would be, they might never have started it in the first place. 'If you had asked me beforehand, I'm not sure I would have thought it was possible – at least on the scale that we did it,' says Weisheit. 'But then again, we didn't plan to do it on that scale.'

In the initial call for volunteers published on the club website in May 2008, Weisheit noted they would need as many people as possible because the project could last 'up to twelve weeks'. The original idea was to renovate the stadium in a matter of months, allowing Union to return to action there by the autumn. The prospect of a whole year away from the Alte Försterei seemed unthinkable, not least because the only other viable venue for home games was the Jahn-Sportpark. Having done everything they could to avoid moving there permanently, Union were hoping to keep their temporary refuge at BFC's ground as short as possible. As with many things which are supposed to be all over by Christmas, however, the renovation dragged on, and was dogged by constant delays.

The biggest problem of all was the roof. Volunteers could learn to lay concrete or use a core drill but installing a stadium roof required specialists. 'We hired a Slovakian firm, and they had their difficulties,' says Weisheit with a grimace. Initially slated for early 2009, the roof installation became a running soap opera throughout the spring.

It was the Berlin winter which scuppered them first, with sub-zero temperatures and icy roads delaying the delivery of materials and workers in January. The Slovakian company finally arrived and began work in March, with the promise that they would complete the installation within four weeks. By early June, it was still progressing at a snail's pace, and the inaugural friendly against Hertha was now on the brink of cancellation.

The club decided to cut their losses. The Slovakian firm was sacked, and Weisheit replaced it with one she had previously worked with in Austria. It was this new company, as much as the volunteers, who became the true heroes of the piece, installing the roof in record time to complete the stadium and save the long-awaited launch.

Meanwhile, the lost time led to a creeping expansion of the rest of the renovation. While the club waited for the roof to be finished, the number of volunteers didn't abate, and so they began to take on more and more tasks. The initial plan to spruce up the terraces and install the undersoil heating morphed into a full-scale makeover of the entire stadium plot. The slopes behind the stands were re-landscaped, the catering trucks were given a lick of paint, and the potholed ground outside the stadium was levelled out. 'None of that was planned, but we had to kill the time somehow during the delays, so we just started doing things around the edges,' says Weisheit.

On the pitch, too, Union were exceeding initial expectations. In 2008/09 the third tier had been reorganised into a national league, and Union were not among the favourites for promotion. They had finished only fourth in the Regional League North the year before and the new third division was uncharted territory. Not only that, but they had also been uprooted from their usual fortress in the forest. Playing in the Jahn-Sportpark wasn't just unfamiliar, it also meant smaller crowds, with many Union fans refusing to set foot in a stadium they associated with a Stasi club.

Those who did hold their nose and turn up greeted every victory with ironic chants of 'away win!' The more the season progressed, the more they found themselves chanting it, and by November, Union were top of the league and could legitimately dream of promotion. 'We are not building this stadium for the third division, we're building it for the second division,' declared a bullish Dirk Zingler to cheering fans at the club's autumn AGM. The team lost their next game, before charging to an eighteen-game unbeaten run to become third division champions. They sealed promotion with three games to spare on 9 May 2009, as cult hero Karim Benyamina chipped the decisive goal over the Regensburg goalkeeper in the afternoon sun. When the fans streamed onto the Jahn-Sportpark pitch at full time, they sang the name of the Alte Försterei.

Promotion not only meant the end of a long season away from home but it also meant that their construction gamble had paid off. Union were returning to professional level, second-tier football, and they were doing so in a brand-new Alte Försterei. 'That was the most moving moment for me,' says Weisheit. 'What we achieved with that building site was incredible,' she says.

* * *

What they achieved with the building site also changed the club forever. In late April, as the roof drama continued to unfold, Zingler attempted to calm the jitters which were spreading through the Union community. 'In a few weeks, the stadium will be done, and that will be of fundamental importance for Union's development in the next twenty to thirty years,' he said in an interview with the club website. 'The scale of what we have achieved here is something we can't even begin to measure at this point.'

History proved him right. A few days later, Union beat Tennis Borussia 2–1 at Jahn-Sportpark to win the Berlin State Cup final for the third time in their history. It was the last time they would ever play in that tournament. Promotion to the second division meant they were back in the professional league structure and could begin to dream of bigger things than the state cup. Unlike their previous, ill-fated stay in the second tier between 2001–04, they now had a stadium worthy of the league they were in. For the first time, the delicate balance between football and finances appeared to have slipped into a virtuous, rather than a vicious circle. Union went on to spend the next ten years in the same division: the longest period of stability in their history.

As well as steadying the ship economically, the renovation also had a profound effect on the club's image. From the very beginning, the building site had welcomed a steady stream of reporters and TV cameras. Some of the more familiar reporters put in shifts on the site themselves, but it was not just the local papers who wanted a piece of the action. For the first time in their history, Union were attracting international attention, with Italian newspapers, Ukrainian TV crews and French magazines all knocking on Weisheit's door in the course of the year. The sheer volume of requests was exhausting, she says, and at some point, stadium announcer Christian Arbeit had to take on extra duties as a press officer to relieve the pressure. 'We were overwhelmed by it. These days you would have six or seven different communications strategies for something like that, but we only had a few people,' says Weisheit.

The story didn't just provide a good headline; it also spoke to wider anxieties about the way football was changing across the continent. From Arsenal's Highbury to Schalke's Parkstadion, many of Europe's most beloved grounds had fallen victim to football's commercial explosion in the 1990s and 2000s. Fans at many clubs had been forced to bid farewell to their club's traditional home and move to more comfortable, less charming modern arenas, often in different parts of town. Though there were often good commercial and security reasons to ditch the old stadiums, the process also uprooted many clubs, pulling them further away from the communities and traditions on which they had built their names.

Union, by contrast, appeared to have had their cake and eaten it. The new stadium had shored them up economically, strengthened their relationship to the fans and even sharpened their brand. Across Europe, they now had a reputation as a club which went against the grain of modern football. A club that did extraordinary things and tended to prioritise people over profit. 'That's the philosophy of this club,' says Weisheit. 'We tread a line between tradition and commercialism, but we have clear ideas about which lines we do not cross.'

Maintaining that tightrope act would prove to be the defining challenge of the next decade, and not just for the football club. Union, after all, were flourishing in a city which was itself on the rise. A surprise drop in Berlin's population around 2010 proved to be an outlier, and the number of people moving to the capital continued to climb throughout the next decade, pushing its population above three and a half million for the first time since before the war. Berlin was growing more affluent, and rents and living costs were also about to soar in a way they hadn't for decades. Increasingly, the city too was having to toe a line between culture and commerce.

As the population continued to rise, so did the number of building sites. Space in Berlin was becoming more valuable, and that meant many beloved cultural spaces began to feel the heat. In the late 2000s, the Union fans were not the only group in Berlin desperately trying to hold onto their beloved cultural home. Squats, nightclubs and concert venues across the city also found themselves scrapping for their patch of earth as prices soared. Union provided a rare blueprint for success in what was usually a futile fight. Rather than contest a lost cause or accept an unsatisfactory compromise, the club had found a way of reinventing their space in a way which both preserved it and made it future-proof.

Changing the Alte Försterei also meant changing Union's future. After twenty years of struggling to keep their head above water, the stadium opened the door to a new era in the 2010s. The Alte Försterei, once a crumbling wreck in an unfashionable suburb, was about to become the footballing heart of a booming Berlin.

PART THREE
COOL

CHAPTER 7
POOR BUT SEXY

UNION BERLIN 2–0 INGOLSTADT – 8 MARCH 2019

As Christian Arbeit strides out from the touchline towards the centre circle, the volume inside the stadium drops from a chatter to a focused hum. Like a church congregation when the organ stops tinkling before the service, the crowd knows instinctively what is going to happen next. A few more steps – the long-haired master of ceremonies raises the microphone to his lips and says the same word with which he begins every matchday.

'Unioners...'

The greeting is returned with a roar, and Arbeit turns towards the few thousand Bavarians in the away block. '...and Ingolstädters.' A gentle, good-natured boo from the crowd, and the service is underway.

For all the freedom and the fag smoke, there is also a liturgical quality to a matchday at Union. Emerging from the tunnel around half an hour before kick-off, Arbeit greets the faithful and begins a well-rehearsed ritual of call and response. He mentions the stadium, and the whole congregation begins chanting its name: 'Alte Försterei, Alte Försterei, Alte, Alte, Alte Försterei!' He reads out the opposition team sheet, and the crowd responds to each name with a dismissive 'so what?' Later, after a couple of Union-themed rock songs, he returns to announce the home side's starting eleven, and every name is greeted with a cry of 'football god!' When he leaves the pitch for a second time, 20,000 fans raise their scarves as a series of steady, menacing bass notes mark the start of Nina Hagen's anthem. In Köpenick they just call it 'the hymn'.

There are other rituals. At half-time, Arbeit reads out birthday notices, passed directly to him by other fans. When there is a substitution, the players in question are hailed once again as 'football gods'. When Union score, there is no tinny goal music as in other stadiums in Germany, but simply Arbeit's voice, rolling the same words up from his belly into the microphone. He lists the scorer, the new scoreline, and signs off every time with the same back and forth.

'And never forget...' bellows Arbeit.

'Eisern Union! Eisern Union! Eisern Union!' screams the crowd.

Sometimes, circumstance or season will mean there is the slightest variation. If an opposing player has previously played for Union, he is greeted not with a sneering 'so what?', but with an equally devoted 'Fußballgott!' If a player or staff member is about to leave, they will be given an on-pitch send-off. If a popular fan or employee has died, Arbeit will deliver a heartfelt obituary alongside the birthday messages at half-time. And occasionally – very occasionally – he will have something else to say as well.

Today is one of those days. As he steps out onto the pitch in the cool March sunshine, the club's spokesman is wearing not his usual red hoodie, but a white t-shirt with the words 'iron and proud' emblazoned in rainbow colours across the front of it. 'Today is International Women's Day,' he begins. 'And as of this year, a public holiday in Berlin.'

This is not in the order of service, and there are a few surprised grunts among the cheers. Public holidays are one of the many things the capital has less of than other, wealthier German states. In Catholic-dominated, conservative Bavaria, there are up to fourteen a year, covering all manner of minor dates in the Christian calendar. Godless Berlin has just ten, with International Women's Day the most recent addition. For the embattled left-green coalition government, naming it as a new holiday was a cheap political win. It bolstered the feminist credentials of both the city and its administration and gave everyone an extra day off.

Arbeit, by contrast, can hardly be accused of populism as he delivers his Women's Day speech to a football crowd which is at least eighty per cent male. He argues that the fight for gender equality should go beyond mere gesture politics. Respect for women, he says, should be about more than buying a bunch of flowers and a bottle of champagne on one day a year, before returning to business as usual for the remaining 364. Up until this point, the crowd are largely with him, but the mood changes towards the end of his speech. When he quotes German feminist Clara Zetkin there are audible boos.

Zetkin was one of the pioneers of women's liberation in Germany. Like her contemporary Rosa Luxemburg, however, she was also a committed socialist and a national heroine in the GDR. Streets were named after her and her face adorned the ten-mark notes in people's wallets. For some Union fans of a certain age, quoting such a figure in the Alte Försterei is clearly akin to blasphemy. They greet her name with a volley of whistles.

But not everybody is upset. Thirty years after the fall of the Wall, those who grew up under socialism are no longer in the majority at Union. Plenty of fans were born after the GDR ceased to exist, and many more come from somewhere else entirely. In the decade since 2009, Union's membership has quadrupled, boosted by fans from outside the club's usual constituency – from West Berlin, Worcestershire or Wyoming. For these newcomers, the name Clara Zetkin carries no political baggage. Many have never heard of her at all and look around baffled as an apparently innocuous quote on women's rights is shouted down so fiercely by those around them.

This is the new reality at the Alte Försterei. The stadium is no longer just a refuge in the woods for a small, homogenous community. It is becoming an ever-broader church, which increasingly offers a cross-section of Berlin society. The believers now come not only from working-class eastern districts like Köpenick, Lichtenberg and Schöneweide, but also from more hip areas such as Friedrichshain, Prenzlauer Berg, Kreuzberg and Neukölln, which are popular with internationals. Unioners are now older West Berliners searching for a lost football romanticism, and younger immigrants who have come to the German capital on the promise of freedom, excitement and affordable living. Union, like Berlin itself, has become cool. And as the city is already finding out, that is both a blessing and a curse.

It takes about half an hour on the S-Bahn to get from the centre of Berlin to Köpenick, and the journey is a game of two halves. The second half is a gentle rumble through the industrial, the residential and the woodland landscapes of Union country. The first half, from Friedrichstraße to Ostkreuz, is a sight-seeing tour of Berlin's world-famous nightlife.

After Alexanderplatz, the train pulls into Jannowitzbrücke, where a huge power station towers over the side of the river. The back end of the building is home to Tresor, one of the elder statesmen of the city's techno scene. To the right, just opposite the Chinese embassy, is the equally iconic KitKatClub, famed for its fetish parties and strictly kinky dress code. Further on towards Ostbahnhof, a brightly coloured building complex is visible on the nearest riverbank. Holzmarkt – a beach bar, artists' studios, and nightclub – is a direct descendent of the famous Bar25, which closed in 2010. As the train approaches Warschauer Straße, the tracks and river part ways and an imposing grey building looms in the open sky over a low-build retail park. This is Berghain, the most famous of all Berlin clubs and a byword the world over for the city's taboo-free, twenty-four-hour party culture. Its notoriously scrupulous door policy is an attraction in itself. For the less committed, an abandoned East German train depot nearby offers an entire complex of other clubs which are easier to get into.

All these venues are close to where the Wall once stood and all of them were founded in the decade or so after reunification. They are places which grew out of that unique period in

Berlin's history, when historical trauma and a sluggish economy meant the city was still full of unfilled spaces. Increasingly, though, the space around them has been filled, and now they are surrounded by building sites, shiny new office blocks and retail and commercial centres. Berlin has changed radically in the last thirty years, but few areas have been transformed quite as much as the central districts of the former East. More than any other, they have been subject to that familiar cycle of gentrification: a depressed area becomes a cultural hotspot, the culture brings cash and development, and slowly but surely, people begin to be pushed out.

'Berlin is poor, but sexy,' said mayor Klaus Wowereit in a newspaper interview in 2003. It was a phrase which would define the capital and the debate over its future for more than a decade, becoming both an advertising slogan and a curse. As a largely deindustrialised and heavily indebted city, Berlin's main assets in the immediate post-Wall period were cheap living costs and a flourishing alternative cultural scene. Wowereit sought to use those assets to attract investment, and Berlin's economy did indeed grow significantly in the following fifteen years. But as prices rose and space became scarcer, its sexiness also came under threat.

Union, in many ways, is a world apart from all of that. By the time the S-Bahn train reaches Köpenick, it is in a very different part of the city from Berghain, Tresor and the rest. But the football club does not exist in a vacuum, and in many ways, it faces the same problems as the city's other major subcultures. 'If you have too many people who are only here as spectators, then eventually it won't be that great anymore,' says Christian Arbeit when I meet him in September 2021. He is talking about Union, but he could just as well be talking about Berghain.

As stadium announcer since 2006 and club spokesman since 2009, Arbeit has been the face of Union for much of the last two decades and has seen both his club and his city boom in popularity during that time. He meets me in one of the stadium's beer gardens, and for the middle part of the interview, we have to shout at each other. It is the day before a matchday, and behind us, someone is testing the loudspeakers in the stadium. At one point, they play a well-known advert for a brand of Berlin beer that also happens to sponsor Union. A quickfire series of clips showing ravers, mechanics, dominatrixes and DJs is overlaid with the 2003 song *'Berlin, Du Bist So Wunderbar'*. With its slickly synthesised organ notes, hip-hop beat and scratchy vocals, the song – and the advert – are a classic example of the poor-but-sexy product. Come to Berlin, it says, we have party boats, sex clubs and 1920s-themed nights.

When Arbeit first took the microphone, Union were not all that sexy. They were just one of many struggling lower-league clubs in the city, still in the fourth division and reeling from the financial and footballing woes of the early 2000s. After the stadium renovation and promotion to the second division, however, they established themselves as the undisputed second force in Berlin. They too became more prosperous, and footballing success quickly began to dovetail with the city's cultural cool. In the beer advert, one of the DJs is wearing a t-shirt with the Union badge on it.

By the time they were promoted to the Bundesliga, Union's reputation as the 'cool club' in Berlin was an established media narrative. 'It is cooler than ever before to be an Union fan,' Berlin lifestyle magazine *Tip* declared in the summer of 2019. A few weeks later, public broadcaster ARD ran a video feature headlined 'Five Reasons Why Union Berlin Are So Cool', which included Eisenbeiser's carol-singing and the stadium renovation. 'You could argue that those things weren't actually that unique, and that they could have happened anywhere else,' says Arbeit. But the point is that they didn't. They happened in Berlin, and as such, they could slip seamlessly into a wider cultural romanticisation of the city, encompassing everything from Berghain to David Bowie. 'Union,' one of Germany's most famous DJs, WestBam, declared in an interview with the *FAZ* newspaper in 2016, 'are more techno than Hertha.'

As the techno scene knows all too well, however, being cool is a double-edged sword. As the spaces have filled in the urban landscape around the nightclubs, so too have they filled around the lifelong fans on the terraces at the Alte Försterei. Between 2005 and 2010, the number of members at Union rose steadily from around 4,000 to around 6,500. In the decade since, it has grown exponentially to reach almost 40,000. In many respects, the club is now unrecognisable from the one which was promoted to the second tier in 2009.

So, at what point is it no longer the same club; no longer the same city? At what point does 'poor but sexy' cease to be a description of reality, and start becoming a nostalgia trip, or even a plain lie? Does Union, like Berlin, risk losing its soul the more successful it becomes? When I ask Arbeit, the club's face and mouthpiece, he narrows his eyes and chooses his words carefully. 'The club will never stop changing,' he says. 'But hopefully it does so slowly enough that it can still recognise itself.'

* * *

If anyone can tell whether Union is still Union, then it is Christian Arbeit. First as a fan and later as the public face of the club, he has had a closer view than anyone of the dramatic changes of the last three decades. Since his father first took him to the Alte Försterei as a 12-year-old in 1986, he has rarely left the club's side. When his daughter was born, he took her to home games and pushed the pram around the bottom rung of the terraces to send her to sleep. When he lived in London for a year as a student in the early 1990s, he would trek from the Fulham Road to Victoria Station every Monday to buy the German papers and check Union's results. At the end of the 1992/93 season, he took an expensive flight back to Berlin to watch a decisive promotion game against Bischofswerda. Union won, and he returned to London with a case of Berlin beer in his hand luggage.

At that point he could never have imagined that the club would become his career. When he became stadium announcer in 2006, it happened almost by accident. Having been roped into moderating an event for his then employer, a cinema chain, he was asked by Union if he could do the same thing at the stadium. 'I remember being quite surprised to find that my knees were shaking a bit the first time I did it,' he says. 'It was almost as if I was standing outside of myself and watching my own performance.'

He has obviously overcome the nerves since then. In 2006, Union were drawing crowds of around 6,000 at best. Nowadays, Arbeit regularly marches into the centre circle in front of 22,000 fans, many of whom have only ever known his voice on the stadium PA. 'There are those fans who I grew into the role alongside, and those for whom I have just always been there,' he says. Many of the rituals which now seem such an integral part of a matchday at Union are in fact Arbeitisms, and relatively recent ones at that. The cry of 'football god!' after each name on the team sheet, for example, emerged out of necessity in the late 2000s. At most grounds in Germany, the stadium announcer reads out the player's first name, and the fans bellow back the surname. 'But back then, about half of our players were either called Christian or Daniel, and often nobody knew which one I was talking about,' laughs Arbeit. 'So, one day, I just told the crowd that I would say the full name and they could just say "Fußballgott."'

The team sheet is more diverse these days, and so are the terraces. Ever more people are coming to savour the Alte Försterei atmosphere, many of them drawn by rumours of a cooler type of football in the depths of East Berlin. To some extent, Arbeit and his rituals are part of that image. When he is not working, he plays guitar in a band. Until recently, he wore his hair at shoulder length, with a beard to match. As Bundesliga stadium announcers go, he is pretty rock'n'roll, and he knows it. 'What I do out there is also a kind of entertainment,' he says.

But the look has changed in recent years. Arbeit's hair was shaved off in the wild promotion celebrations of 2019, and he decided not to grow it back. He has a neat short-back-and-sides now, and he wears shirts more often than he used to. He seems wary of making it all too much about himself and cautious about over-romanticising Union. The media may portray them as a rebel club, but Union remain surprisingly coy about the idea. As head of communications, Arbeit takes care to downplay certain narratives, including the legend of the East German dissident club. 'It would be pretty easy for us to live off that story and to keep fuelling that myth, but we don't do that,' he says.

Union's steady rise from the lower leagues back into the big time came at a time when East German history was becoming a pop culture phenomenon. In the 2000s, two films about life in communist East Berlin had been released to international acclaim – the sentimental comedy *Good Bye Lenin!* and the more solemn, Oscar-winning tragedy *The Lives of Others*. Despite their success, both were accused of simplifying the East German experience. *Good Bye Lenin!* was criticised for its cutesy *Ostalgie* – or nostalgia for the East – while *The Lives of Others* was slammed for applying Hollywood tropes of good, evil and redemption to an altogether more complex society.

For good or ill, the two films helped to establish two very different and equally powerful images of the GDR, both of which were reflected in Berlin's burgeoning tourist industry. The nostalgic kitsch of *Good Bye Lenin!* chimed with the steady development of a kind of Cold War amusement park, complete with Trabant Safaris, keyrings containing chunks of the Wall and a museum dedicated to daily life in the GDR. *The Lives of Others* brought home to western audiences the darker side of repression and dictatorship, which was also the focus of museums at the former Stasi prison in Hohenschönhausen and the Wall Memorial at Bernauer Straße. Spanning both genres was the East Side Gallery, an open-air exhibition just down the road from Berghain with a series of murals on the longest remaining section of the Wall. It was originally painted in 1990, and renovated and restored in 2008 – at almost the same time as the Alte Försterei.

While the city was happily peddling these two visions of its past, Union also offered a bit of both. Nina Hagen's anthem delivered the requisite *Ostalgie*, and the legend of the anti-Stasi football club dignified it with an altogether more heroic back-story. These too were simplified versions of history, and Union may have been careful about how much they indulged them. But they did draw people in and provided a sexy backdrop to the club's improving fortunes on the pitch. By the mid-2010s, Union were not only the most successful former GDR-Oberliga club in Berlin, but also in the whole country. As former giants like Dynamo Dresden and Hansa Rostock yo-yoed between the second and third divisions, the Berlin club's stability and location made them the natural destination for any East-curious football hipster.

The rebel myth was quietly fuelled by the idea of a club which still kicked against the system, even in the modern day. Union's fan-first approach has often been characterised as 'anti-commercial', a direct rebuke to the financial excesses of the modern game. Under president Dirk Zingler, they have repeatedly taken the side of supporters in major debates. In 2018, they put forward a ten-point plan to reform professional football, which included salary caps, a fairer distribution of marketing revenues, and a clear commitment to the 50+1 rule.

In the ongoing debate about whether to keep 50+1, both the club and their fans see themselves as partisans on the side of the virtuous. Detractors of the rule argue that it discourages investors and weakens the Bundesliga in comparison to other European leagues. But as it has lost ground financially on its richer neighbours, the Bundesliga has also begun to consciously market itself as an alternative to the financial excess of Spain or England. 'Football as it's meant to be' ran the slogan in a recent campaign emphasising the atmosphere in German stadiums. Union have one of the best atmospheres in the league, and they too sell an idea of a football which still has rough edges, where authenticity and community are more important even than winning. That has proven a remarkably attractive narrative for fans disillusioned with big money in football.

'You can try to get success through investors, but then you may as well give up on the idea of football as something which has anything to do with ordinary people and their lives,' says Arbeit, adding with some pride that Union have got to the top flight and into European competition without a wealthy benefactor. 'We are showing that there is another way. I'm not sure I could even enjoy it if the Emir of Qatar bought us the league title. Because at the end of the day, what would that have to do with this club, with this social space?'

But the anti-commercial image is also one that Union tend to wear lightly, preferring instead to style themselves as advocates for a purer and fairer kind of football. For Arbeit, it is less about money or the 50+1 rule itself and more about a more generally inclusive approach. 'Plenty of people both inside and outside the club have tried to pin us down with a single slogan over the years, and we've never really felt comfortable with any of them,' he says, adding that the only guiding principle is the sanctity of a matchday at the Alte Försterei. 'It's about the people who come to the stadium. The people who are physically here.'

First and foremost, that means attempting to provide a purer football experience than in other stadiums. Aside from the LED boards around the pitch, there is astonishingly little advertising at the Alte Försterei. There is no official payment partner, no 'substitutions sponsored by' and very few adverts at all on the big screen. There is, in fact, only one big screen – the other scoreboard is an old-fashioned brick hut where someone has to lean out of the window to change the numbers. 'There is no blimp in the sky, no quiz, no half-time show,' says Arbeit. 'And if I don't have much to say, I shut up and there's just some music.' Coupled with the fact that tickets are cheap and there is only a negligible mark-up on beer and food, and you have a much less commercialised stadium experience at the Alte Försterei than at other grounds.

This is not to say that Union are above making money from their fans. A replica shirt still costs ninety euros, and the club shop is as full of branded toasters, rubber ducks and cheaply produced t-shirts as any other. The key difference, says Arbeit, is that it is not shoved down fans' throats. 'We give people the option to buy all sorts of things if they want to, but I don't go on about it during the game.' Fans can ignore an advertising poster or a social media post, he argues. 'But anything we do in the stadium on matchday they can't get away from, so we keep it to as little as possible.' Union fans, the logic goes, should be football supporters first and consumers second.

While there is undoubtedly a kind of idealism behind that, it is also a pragmatic line to take. If the club were to actively play up too much to the resistance myth, they would open themselves up to accusations of historical dishonesty. If they were to bang the anti-commercialism drum too hard, they would potentially curtail their own business opportunities. But no football fan actively wants to be treated as a consumer, so prioritising the stadium-going fan is something everyone can get behind. It marks Union out from other clubs, which in turn makes them more attractive to potential sponsors. At the same time, it gives the fans the sense that they are part of something more authentic, and that they are more involved. Arbeit feels that it is that, more than anything else, which makes Union recognisably Union.

'The reason the experience at the Alte Försterei is great is because people feel a part of it – they feel like they belong,' he says. 'They know that this is their club, and if they have an idea, they know they have somewhere to take it, and we should never allow ourselves to lose that.'

*　　*　　*

'The story of this club is the story of crazy ideas and the courage to turn them into reality,' says Arbeit. But beyond Bleed for Union and the *Weihnachtssingen*, not all those ideas have been universally well-received.

In 2014, Union's reputation for doing things differently was given another boost when they transformed the Alte Försterei into a 'World Cup Living Room', where fans could watch Germany games on the big screen. The stands were decorated with retro East German-style wallpaper, and the pitch was adorned with around 800 sofas which the spectators had brought from their own homes. The bizarre sight of hundreds of fans lounging on their own settees inside a 20,000-capacity stadium made headlines across the world. 'I still meet people who say, "Oh, that was you guys? I saw pictures of that!"' says Arbeit.

Among the fanbase, there was a more mixed reaction. Many Union fans avoided the event, and the ultras staged a handful of protests. On one occasion, three sofas were even stolen from the pitch and dumped ceremoniously into the nearby river. Some accused the club of selling its soul by endorsing a tournament organised by FIFA, which was then mired in corruption scandals. Others were sceptical of an event which they felt had little or no relevance to Union. The fact that it received international attention only heightened the sense that this was a stunt for the outside world, not the community itself.

Their scepticism betrayed a fear familiar to many sub-cultures who suddenly find themselves subject to attention from outside. Like many of Berlin's most famous cultural establishments, Union is a space where people can express their identity in a way which is impossible – or at least much more difficult – elsewhere. 'It's a place where you can break out of social norms,' says Arbeit. '*I belong here, I can scream and swear here, I can be what I am here,*' runs a line in one of the rock songs which plays during his pre-match rituals. Union, in that sense, is not so different from the fetish parties in the KitKatClub.

A cultural space is just as susceptible to gentrification as a neighbourhood, and as Arbeit says: the more people who are just there to gawp, the more that space begins to disappear. In a 2015 interview with *GQ*, Berghain bouncer Sven Marquardt explained the nightclub's famously arbitrary door policy in similar terms:

I feel like I have a responsibility to preserve Berghain as a place where people can forget about space and time for a little while and enjoy themselves. The club evolved from the gay scene in Berlin in the nineties. It's impor-tant to me that we preserve some of that heritage, that it still feels like a welcoming place for the original sort of club-goers. If we were just a club full of models, pretty people all dressed in black, it would be nice to look at for a half an hour, but god, that would be boring. It would feel less tolerant, too.*

That is a constant balancing act in Berlin. The city's openness offers safe spaces for minority subcultures of all kinds, but that in turn creates hype. The storm in a teacup over the 'World Cup Living Room' was perhaps the first occasion on which the hype around Union began to rub some people up the wrong way and cause internal friction.

Arbeit insists that the club did not go out of their way to court the cool image. 'We don't do anything specifically to please other people, and we don't do anything specifically not to please them. We can't help it if people like us,' he says, though he admits that it was not always comfortable when Union's outside popularity hit new heights in the mid-2010s. 'There were plenty of people in the fan scene who saw that with a lot of scepticism,' he says.

Perhaps they were aware of how quickly coolness can dissipate. In 2009, *Time* magazine ran a feature describing Berlin as 'capital of cool', a phrase which would become as irritatingly ubiquitous in media coverage of the city as Wowereit's 'poor but sexy' line. By 2016, *Vice* had already declared Berlin clinically dead. 'Berlin has happened. It's past cool,' the magazine honked, before ironically interviewing hipsters in Peckham to find out why.

Beyond the superficial media coverage, though, lies a more substantial question about how places can become victims of their own popularity. How do you maintain a balance between those for whom the stadium or the nightclub is simply an experience, and those for whom it is a way of life? At Berghain,

---

* quoted with permission (TBC)

they employ the world's most famous bouncer to filter out the voyeurs and maintain the social equilibrium inside. Union may not have quite as strict a door policy, but Arbeit explains that they also do not actively court new fans. Even the enormous boom in membership in the last few years is organic growth, he says. 'We show people where and how they can become members, but we don't do membership campaigns in a classical sense.' Unlike other clubs from Europe's top leagues, he adds, they have not sought to widen their fanbase in the Far East or the USA. 'If we focus our energies on things like that, then we will lose our core purpose.'

He is perhaps exaggerating a little bit. Union do work with foreign influencers, and at least on their own website, they very actively encourage people to become members. In some ways, the idea that they would eschew big marketing campaigns is itself on brand. In a video campaign with adidas in the summer of 2021, Union gently mocked the very notion that they or their provincial surroundings could be considered cool. 'If you want to be a proper football club like us, then you had best base yourself in one of the coolest cities in Europe,' said the voiceover, before cutting to a clip of women's team player Josy Ahlswede looking bored in front of a deserted kebab shop in Köpenick. But then Berlin cool is often just that – understated, self-deprecating, dressed down.

Whether for Union or for the club scene, the understatement is also an exercise in self-preservation. The more visible you are in Berlin, the more likely you are to be overrun by tourists and thrill seekers. Ideally, you only want the kind of newcomers who will actively participate. 'It's a bit like Sleeping Beauty,' says Arbeit. 'To get to her, the prince first has to know where she is, and then he has to cut his way through the thickets. With us, people know where we are, but you still have to walk through the forest before you can kiss us awake.'

* * *

On the Warschauer Bridge, the once expansive view over East Berlin is now as crowded as the pavement itself. Between Ostbahnhof and Warschauer Straße, the S-Bahn tracks used to look over an old rail depot on the banks of the Spree which was once home to Ostgut, the original incarnation of Berghain. In the mid-2000s, Ostgut was turfed out to make way for a new indoor arena and, slowly but surely, an entire new commercial estate popped up around it. Now, in front of the East Side Gallery, dull neon lights illuminate the offices of a major internet clothing retailer, a multi-storey car park and a mall. The last trace of the old rail depot is the Postbahnhof, a station-turned-event-space now dwarfed by the enormous high-rise office buildings which shot up in the late 2010s.

On the other side of the tracks, at least, the high grey walls of Berghain are still visible. When I travel through on my way to meet Christian Arbeit in Köpenick, I can clearly read the huge banner which hangs from the club's roof. Part of an art exhibition the club hosted when the parties stopped during the pandemic, its message is a reproachful jibe towards the rest of the city: 'Tomorrow is the question'.

It is a twist of irony that Berlin's nightclubs, themselves shrines to *carpe diem* hedonism, are so consumed by the question of tomorrow. For almost as long as they have existed, Berghain, Holzmarkt and co. have been in a losing battle for space with MediaSpree, the sprawling property investment project behind both the commercial estate at East Side Gallery and much of the urban development along the East Berlin riverfront. Protesters have occasionally managed to slow progress, but they have not managed to 'Sink MediaSpree', as the name of one citizens' initiative has it. The urban spaces which were a playground for creatives in the early 1990s have slowly been filled, closed off and monetised.

That, in the end, is the problem with 'poor but sexy'. As the *Taz* newspaper remarked fifteen years later, Mayor Wowereit's phrase was powerful because it so clearly contained the seeds of its own destruction. When Berlin sold its reputation as a creative paradise, the target market was not more struggling artists, but people who had money to spend. The city's economic growth has been driven in part by nightlife tourism, but also by tech start-ups, media companies, property developers and research institutions. The new money has slowly eroded the affordability of the city and put the cultural scene on the back foot. It has also affected ordinary people, many of whom had benefited little from either the old sexiness or the new wealth. In the hippest districts in Berlin, the unsexy poor are the first to be priced out.

Fears of a similar process also simmer under the surface at Union. After all, many of the new fans at Union are neither poor, nor have they experienced much misery even in football terms. 'The main difference between the old fans and the ones who have come in the last ten years is that the new fans have only ever really known success,' says Arbeit. Since he became stadium announcer in 2006, the club have been promoted three times and never once been relegated. With that in mind, it is little wonder that the old guard might worry about glory-hunters and hipsters; that a fan from Munich, Amsterdam or London may come only to consume and not participate at Union; that their presence alone might increase competition for tickets and dilute the atmosphere which makes the Alte Försterei so special.

But Arbeit still doesn't see a fundamental conflict between the newcomers and the people who were there before Union was cool. 'I don't have the feeling that we are losing something essential,' he says. 'Partly, that's because space is limited anyway. It wasn't as if 15,000 more people could suddenly come to Union when we got promoted, because there were still only 22,000 spaces in the stadium.' The club also has more tools to control gentrification than the city does – at least within its own space. 'We shouldn't overestimate ourselves – it's not like we can stop somebody from losing their job or being priced out of their apartment, but we do keep an eye on what we can control. How expensive is a ticket at Union, for example?'

The prices have indeed barely changed at Union in the last decade. A season ticket still costs around 200 euros, and the price of a matchday ticket can be as low as twelve. That is not exceptionally cheap by Bundesliga standards, but it is certainly a good deal cheaper than elsewhere in Europe. In that sense, Union still delivers on the promise of 'poor but sexy', in that it offers an experience which anyone can afford. 'It's not that we are a club for poor people, but it is definitely our responsibility to make sure that even people on low incomes have the opportunity to come here,' says Arbeit.

Remaining accessible to the poorest in society, of course, becomes harder and harder the higher you get in professional football. 'Nowadays, we have the players' Lamborghinis in one car park, and in the next car park along, which also belongs to us, there is a soup kitchen,' notes Arbeit. But he insists that the club are keen to show they appreciate that social gap and ensure that nobody should be turned away from football purely for financial reasons. 'Otherwise you end up with the same situation you have in England. If a ticket costs £60, then people can't afford it and you get an entirely different crowd. Then it's no wonder that the famous atmospheres of English football just don't exist anymore.'

By keeping prices low as their popularity grows, Union are trying to thread the needle between gentrification and stagnation. So far, it has just about worked. Far from killing the atmosphere, the membership boom since 2010 has kept the stadium full for the most sustained period in Union's history. At the same time, the fanbase is more economically and ethnically diverse than it has ever been: the club now has around 13,000 members from outside of Berlin, including some in places as far flung as Israel, Chile, Taiwan and South Africa. In an era of social fragmentation, argues Arbeit, that is important. 'There is a social mix in this stadium which you rarely see elsewhere, and that is partly because we are still affordable for everyone,' he says.

But affordability is not the only thing people are concerned about, and Union still have a significant challenge on their hands when it comes to the balance between success and authenticity. As their fanbase grows, the expectations of the club will begin to change, and that will cause more friction. For now, more than eighty per cent of Union's Berlin-based members still hail from their traditional catchment area in neighbourhoods which were once part of East Berlin. Yet the longer Union's success lasts, the more the rest of the city will start knocking on the door. Nobody can remain Sleeping Beauty forever.

CHAPTER 8
SOUL SEARCHING

UNION BERLIN 2–1 ST. PAULI – 17 APRIL 2010

Imran is here on business. All around him, the forest is filled with red: red scarves, red shirts, and red noses from a sunny spring morning of drinking. But he has no scarf, no shirt, no beer. This is not his team; this is not his stadium. This is not even his Berlin.

If anything, he is supporting the away team. He likes St. Pauli. Who doesn't like St. Pauli? Who could fail to like a proudly anti-fascist club from Hamburg's red-light district with the Jolly Roger as their unofficial emblem? It has been fun working with them this year, and he is pleased with the campaign they have put together for the club centenary. 'Non-established since 1910' – that's a football club you can get on board with. Rebels with a cause; pirates, not prawn sandwiches. Union? Much less fun. Köpenick is hardly the beating heart of Berlin counterculture. In a decade of living in the capital, Imran has never once felt the urge to come out here to watch a game.

But he's here now, and as he and his girlfriend wind their way through the car park towards the main stand, he is rather taken with the place. It may say 'VIP' on their tickets, but he feels reassuringly unimportant as he trudges through the door. The lounge itself is little more than a line of prefab huts which have spilled from the car park onto the nearby training pitch. The main stand is the smallest of the lot, dwarfed on all sides by the stone terraces. The stadium is fit to burst, and everyone in it seems to be within spitting distance of the pitch. Some of them could even reach out and touch the corner flags.

And then there is the noise. The singing begins long before kick-off, and crashes around the newly built roofs on the stands. Some of the songs are even genuinely melodic, something Imran knows more from southern European and Turkish stadiums than German ones. A player who is returning from injury is greeted with a roar so fierce you would think he had come back from the dead. In the away block, the St. Pauli fans are also putting on a good show, with a storm of brown and white flags. 'St. Pauli is the only option' reads the banner they have put up behind the goal. An hour ago, he might have agreed, but looking at this stadium, Imran is no longer so sure.

Just before kick-off, the hairs on the back of his neck stand up as a deep, theatrical voice fills the stadium. 'It was in the golden twenties, in the middle of a desperate fight, when a battle cry sounded. A battle cry that echoed like thunder...' When the first guitar riff sounds, Nina Hagen's voice shrieks out of the speakers and the whole stadium begins to sing, Imran keeps his poker face. He is here on business – for the away team. But his girlfriend nudges him in the ribs and leans over to whisper something in his ear.

'This is your club.'

🐻

In the autumn of 2011, an advert started popping up in Berlin cinemas. In a meeting room overlooking the Alte Försterei, a group of marketing executives are presenting their ideas to a bored-looking club president. A smug man with thick-rimmed glasses and a V-neck jumper wants to rename the stadium after an anti-diarrhoea medication. A woman with a clipped voice and a pristine business suit suggests appealing to both women and hardcore fans with the 'Always-Ultra-Arena'. An eager thirty-something with a striped tie proposes a cooperation with a brand of toilet roll. There is a cheap pun on the word 'arse', and then the president has had enough. He dismisses them, and the Union badge flashes onto the screen above a tagline:

'We are selling our soul... but not to just anyone'.

Even a decade later, there are few slogans that more succinctly sum up Union's delicate tightrope act between commerce and community. The club are constantly adjusting certain elements of their football-first approach – replica shirts get more expensive, and new sponsors prove more or less controversial. Some red lines remain constant, though, and the name of the stadium is the thickest red line of all. Other clubs sell their home to the highest bidder, but Union's ground is called Stadion an der Alten Försterei. Full stop.

Ideology comes at a price, however. Selling the rights to the stadium name is a significant money-spinner for other clubs, and not selling them means having to make up the lost revenue. That is where the cinema advert came in. 'The idea was that they were selling shares of the Alte Försterei, which is understood to be the soul of the club,' says Imran Ayata, the real-life communications executive who led the agency team behind the campaign. 'And they weren't selling it to anyone because you had to be a member to buy a share. It was a way of getting the money to build a new main stand, while also involving the fans at the same time.'

Just a few years after Union fans renovated the Alte Försterei in 2008–09, the club were gearing up for their next big building project. The main stand, which had been given little more than a lick of paint in the initial renovation, was now to be torn down and replaced with a shiny new build, complete with VIP boxes, office space and, for the first time, an in-built players' tunnel. To help finance the project, the club created a holding company and sold off shares to the fans. At 500 euros a pop, the stocks were not cheap, nor did they come with the promise of enormous returns in years to come. Nonetheless, the scheme was a roaring success. Over the course of December 2011, more than 4,000 club members bought more than 5,000 shares and raised almost three million euros for the new stand. For many fans, the chance to own a share in the Alte Försterei was an opportunity not to be missed. As Ayata says, the stadium is the soul of the club.

'Whenever people ask what is special about Union, I tell them to go to the stadium. The Alte Försterei is a place which electrifies people as soon as they set foot in it,' says Ayata. When he first went, he was working for a major Berlin PR company on a campaign for St. Pauli's centenary. A few months later, Union invited him to work with them on their 'soul-selling' advert, and slowly but surely, he fell in love with the club. Now a member, a season-ticket holder and himself the proud owner of a stadium share, his eyes light up when he talks about the soul he helped to sell: 'Regardless of whether we have won or lost, I always come back a little happier from that place. Other people need psychoanalysis, I just need the Alte Försterei. As banal as it sounds, I love getting on the train out there, and getting out of my normal life.'

Ayata is one of thousands of new fans who have adopted Union in the last decade or so. Like many others, he was drawn there because it was different to his day-to-day life. He talks about the thrill of being completely involved in a shared experience, and a sense of belonging in an environment which was otherwise quite alien to him. Slowly but surely, he has come to consider himself an Unioner, but the ride has not always been easy. It has also meant confronting the conflicts and contradictions in his relationship with the club. As a German of Turkish descent, he has both experienced racism on the terraces, and found himself defending the club against the snobbery of outsiders. At the same time, he has watched Unioners struggle with their own identity as the club's popularity has exploded.

Union is now Ayata's club, but he was by no means the last one in the door. As more new fans arrive, the fanbase is becoming more diverse in every way. That presents new challenges for the Union community that are quite different to the material ones they faced in the 1990s and 2000s. The changing milieu opens up new questions about belonging, about how gentrification is transforming Berlin, and about how the Alte Försterei itself is changing. Union are too attached to their stadium to sell its name or move to another part of Berlin, but what if the rest of Berlin comes to them? What happens then to the soul of the club?

*　*　*

Berlin, like London or New York, is a metropolis of small villages. Unlike London or New York, it has no central financial district, and it had a tense international border running through its centre for much of the last century. That gives it a different sense of gravity to other cities. While there is still a busier inner area and a quieter outer rim, there is no stream of commuters flooding in and out of the same square mile at rush hour, no single commercial centre per se. People tend to live, work and play almost exclusively in their own neighbourhood, or *Kiez*, as the Berliners call it.

Ayata's *Kiez* is nowhere near Köpenick. He lives in Mitte, goes out in the adjacent district of Kreuzberg, and works on a street which is a stone's throw from both of those districts. I meet him there in a high-ceilinged conference room at his 'campaign agency' on Potsdamer Straße, just inside former West Berlin. The house, an ornate, listed early twentieth century building with French windows and a broad staircase, used to hold the offices of the city's biggest broadsheet newspaper. Now, in Ayata's offices on the top floor, well-dressed advertising professionals lounge on sofas and perch at breakfast bars with their Macs. Everything is airy, fashionable, and well-lit. There are not many Union stickers on the lampposts around here.

But then why would there be? This is not just on the other side of the old division, it is also in a very different Berlin to Köpenick, with its brick-gothic town hall, cobblestone old town and gruff pubs with net curtains in the windows. For Ayata, that is part of Union's appeal to newcomers: the forests of the Alte Försterei are an escape from ordinary life. They offer a sense of belonging in a setting which is, by definition, very far from home. That, he says, is not a feeling which is unique to Union. 'I think a lot of football fans have the same thing. It is one of the few communities in life that you choose to be a part of – completely voluntarily. Nobody forces me to go there; nobody is forcing me to like it. That's part of the appeal. It's not just about experiencing something together. It's about interaction.'

For Ayata, who grew up in Germany supporting Galatasaray and Liverpool, interaction is the major draw. Having previously followed his teams only on the television, he has always found it exhilarating to be in the stadium, sharing the emotion with complete strangers. And the Alte Försterei is particularly exhilarating because of the way it is designed, he argues. 'You don't just sit there eating your chips, you *stand*. That makes a huge difference, because it demands a different kind of involvement than if you are just sitting there. Seated stadiums turn football into a kind of bourgeois theatre.'

Standing for three or four hours is harder work than sitting. The Alte Försterei is often a place from which you return with beer-stained clothes, aching heels and a sore throat from shout-ing. But it is also a place which has the power to make you feel alive, he says. 'I love the roughness, the coarseness. Both the good sides and the ugly sides of it.'

He is not alone. Standing is one of the fiercely defended sacraments of football fan culture across Germany. In England, old-fashioned standing terraces were abolished in 1989 following the Hillsborough disaster and are only now beginning to be cautiously reintroduced. In Germany, they have endured, providing both affordability and a livelier atmosphere. The difference between having an allocated seat and being able to stand in an open block may seem small on an individual level, but when multiplied across an entire crowd, it is significant. A standing crowd packs more people into the available space. You smell your neighbour's sweat, inhale their smoke, and are often drenched in their beer when your team score. But it is also a more fluid experience. Rather than being a static pixel in a fixed jigsaw puzzle, each fan becomes part of a living, breathing organism.

The difference is particularly noticeable at the Alte Försterei, where so much of the stadium is standing room only. Where other German grounds limit their standing areas to a few blocks in specific locations, Union's is surrounded on three of four sides by a standing crowd, with the only seats on the main tribune. Though the different blocks do have their different characters, the stadium experience is largely the same everywhere in the ground. It is naturally egalitarian, and the sense of a collective makes it easy for new fans to pick up the unwritten rules of stadium etiquette. Although, at Union, the unwritten rules have in fact been written down. There are four of them, and they are called the *Laws of Boone*, because they were codified in the early 1990s by a fan of the same name:

1. Never boo your own team.
2. Never leave before the final whistle.
3. Never make a scapegoat of an individual player.
4. A hoarse voice is the Union fan's equivalent of aching muscles.

Rules one and three both follow the same logic: that the fan is there to support the team, not petulantly demand success. Rule two is designed to wheedle out the fans who are there to gawp and consume rather than take part. Rule four sounds a lot snappier in the original German ('Heiserkeit ist der Muskelkater der Unioner'), and it is the basis for the electric atmosphere. In other stadiums, the standing and seating areas also divide the louder fans from the more passive ones. At Union, where the whole stadium is standing, everyone should be loud, and everyone should be hoarse the next day.

The rules are self-enforced. 'I've seen new fans try to have a go at our players, and people tell them to stop,' says Ayata. On the one occasion in recent years that a significant number of fans did leave the stadium before full time – at a 3–0 cup defeat to Kaiserslautern in 2013 – they were aggressively booed by others around them. Even as more and more new people arrive at the club, there is a concerted effort to protect the atmosphere, and not let the Alte Försterei become like any other stadium. At the same time, the rules also provide a foothold for new arrivals in the community. If you follow the *Laws of Boone*, you can't go far wrong at Union. And more often than not, you will quickly get hooked on the atmosphere.

Nonetheless, there is still a noticeable difference between older and newer fans in the Alte Försterei. Ayata admits that, even after a decade following the club, his experience of the stadium is not the same as that of the more traditional Union fans who come from Köpenick. The latter tend to come in larger groups for a start. Family members, old school friends and neighbours will stick together on the terraces. The game is a chance to catch up and socialise – an extension of the pub at the end of the street. For the new fans, especially those who come from another district, it is different. Ayata tends to go with one or two friends, or even alone. Beyond the odd chat about the game itself, he rarely finds himself chatting to the strangers around him. When he does, there are often phrases, jokes or cultural references which make little sense to him as a German from the former West. 'They are bound by a shared history – both through the GDR and the club. That is a sense of community which comes from social practice, it's not something ideological or imaginary,' he says. 'Someone like me can never marry into that. I can never say that I went through that time, that I was there.'

That doesn't mean he can't identify with it in a different way or get involved with the pageantry. When the whole stadium launches into Nina Hagen's hymn with the words 'We from the East', Ayata sings it with as much gusto as anyone. He may not literally be from the East, but this is still his club. 'There's a lovely Turkish saying which says that if you sleep with the blind, you wake up cross-eyed,' he says. 'The Union fans have all these crazy quirks and I like that I have picked some of them up.'

*   *   *

Ayata has often been faced with the question of how compatible he and Union really are. The fact that he chooses to go to the Alte Försterei still surprises many of his friends. '"*You* go to Union?" they say to me. "You're left-wing, and you go there? *You?*"'

Depending on who you ask, there are different assumptions about Union, and the type of people who go there. Among younger people, particularly those new to the city, there is an idea that they are a proudly left-wing club, an East Berlin equivalent of St. Pauli. Others are convinced the opposite is true, associating Köpenick with a lack of diversity, and even with right-wing extremism. These are the people who are surprised that Ayata goes to Union. After all, he is not some naive hipster, fresh off the Ryanair flight with a half-baked idea of football rebellion. He is a respected communications professional who works with the Social Democratic Party and the major trade unions. He is a serious author who has written two novels about the experience of first- and second-generation immigrants in Berlin. The fact that he would choose Union, rather than a more left-leaning club like St. Pauli, Babelsberg or Tennis Borussia, seems peculiar.

It is true that there is less ethnic and cultural diversity in Köpenick than there is in Kreuzberg. The Turkish-German community, which is the largest minority group in the country, has traditionally been more present in the central areas of former West Berlin. When the first generation of Turkish immigrants arrived in West Germany as so-called 'guest workers' in the 1960s, it was in those areas that many of them settled. East Germany had an entirely different history of immigration, which is still reflected in its demography today. Official statistics show the states of the former East have not only fewer Turkish-Germans, but by far the lowest proportion of Germans with what officials call an 'immigration background'. In Berlin, no borough has fewer foreigners and Germans of foreign descent than Treptow-Köpenick.

The former East Germany, meanwhile, has a complex reputation politically. A rise in patriotic sentiment after reunification, high-profile acts of far-right violence, and recent electoral successes for the far-right AfD party have all given it a bad name in recent decades. Köpenick itself is considered a relatively safe seat for the radical left Linke party, but it is also a place where the neo-Nazi NPD have their national head-quarters. Both the far left and the far right consistently poll higher there than in central and western districts. Given all this, many people in the more international areas of Berlin tend towards a more unflattering view of Union. 'I would often hear my friends saying that Union are just *Ossis*, just Nazis, blah, blah, blah,' says Ayata. 'To begin with, I thought they were right, because I didn't know the club. Then I started going and I thought, "Wow, the people I know talk about this place, but they know nothing about it."'

Nowadays, he says, the question of why he goes to Union almost seems like a personal affront. 'I feel a little bit attacked myself, and I go straight into defensive mode. I start defending the social environment and the people. I find myself saying there is no racism at Union. Even though I know there is.'

Very few football stadiums in Europe are free of racism, and the Alte Försterei is not one of them. Some Union fans still sing a song which uses a racial slur, and just as in other stadiums, individual acts of racist abuse are not unheard of. 'I have been racially insulted at Union several times,' says Ayata. 'There have also been plenty of occasions where I have felt uncomfortable. The question is: how do you deal with that?'

The most common answer to that question is that other fans should actively discourage such behaviour, and report incidents when they see them. In theory, that should work well at Union, where supporters are used to upholding the *Laws of Boone* amongst themselves. And sometimes, racism is indeed met with laudable interventionism. When Union hosted Israeli side Maccabi Haifa in the Europa Conference League in 2021 a small group of home supporters reportedly hurled anti-Semitic abuse at nearby Jewish fans and attempted to set fire to their Israeli flag. The club responded quickly and decisively, identifying the perpetrator and opening proceedings to revoke their membership. The group who reported the abuse also said that other Union fans had intervened on their behalf.

But cases like that are the exception rather than the rule. There are also countless other incidents that go unchecked and unchallenged at Union games. Even Ayata admits that he tends not to get involved if he sees or hears racist behaviour in the stands. 'I am normally quite brave in those situations, and I tend to step in, but when it has happened in the stadium, I have generally kept my mouth shut. You never know when there's alcohol involved,' he says. As much as many fans would like to think they always speak up, the reality is that many do not feel able to.

It is not that there is no anti-racism at all at Union. Plenty of fans wear anti-racist slogans on badges or t-shirts, and in 2021, a new fan club called *Grenzenlos Eisern* ('Iron without borders') was founded to combat discrimination and intolerance in the stadium. But Union is not St. Pauli. The fanbase is not unanimously left-wing. It includes plenty of people from both extremes of the political spectrum, and the peace between them can be fragile. The club itself tends to wear its political convictions lightly. Union's club statutes declare that it is 'religiously and politically neutral', albeit with an 'obligation to democratic and humanist values'. But they actively avoid political statements and have also been criticised in the past for their lacklustre response to accusations of racism.

'The club have done some good work to combat racism in the past, but they're not anti-racist or cosmopolitan per se. They are a *Kartoffel* club from Köpenick,' says Ayata with a wry grin. *Kartoffel*, meaning potato, is pejorative slang for white German, and he uses it with the same levity that he uses the word *Kanake*, a highly offensive racial slur, to describe himself. It's a provocative word, and he is teasing a little, both of us fully aware that he can use it and I cannot.

'I know what it's like to be constantly confronted with clichés and prejudices,' he says, acknowledging that any discussion of racism is more loaded when it comes to the former East Germany. 'Yes, there are racists at Union, but there are also racists at western clubs like Hertha or Werder Bremen. It's football. Football isn't a nice, comfortable champagne reception where everybody gets on with each other. Everything we have in our society we also have in football. There are arseholes, and if you're unlucky, you find yourself standing next to one. If twelve or twenty per cent of people in the stadium vote for the AfD, then that's a reflection of society, and I can live with that. Nobody is forcing me to go there, and nobody is forcing me to like it. The interaction with other people is part of the appeal, and sometimes that is friendly, and sometimes it isn't.'

But Ayata is also adamant that he does not want to romanticise the club, nor to whitewash away the uglier sides of the crowd. Racism undoubtedly exists in the Alte Försterei, and too often, the famous Union spirit has not delivered a robust response to it. At a club so proud of their sense of solidarity and community, it still leaves a bad taste when racism is ignored, rather than challenged. 'There is no developed culture of anti-racism at Union. And because there is no culture of intervention, you are alone in those moments,' he says.

Perhaps that culture still needs time to develop. As a small, lower division club in a largely white part of town, Union's fanbase was for a long time much more homogenous. There was little pressure on the Union community to address issues of racism and discrimination. As more people start coming and the fanbase becomes more diverse, these questions are likely to become only more frequent. In the past, the Union community has responded well to the needs of minority fans when they have been raised. In recent years, they have mobilised campaigns to organise more accessible transport to away games for fans with disabilities and clumped together to pay for the season tickets of fans on lower incomes. The onus is now on them to show that solidarity also applies when it comes to issues like racism, sexism and homophobia.

Because the bottom line is, it shouldn't be a surprise that Ayata chooses to go to Union. 'I've been going for so long now that it doesn't seem odd to me anymore,' he says, a little wearily. 'It's more interesting to other people. For me, I am just an Unioner'.

* * *

Ayata is not sure at what point he began to think of himself as an Unioner. 'With Union, it's a bit like Berlin,' he says. 'You have the real Berliners, and then you have the people who have chosen to move here, and after a while start referring to themselves as Berliners.'

In Berlin, too, Ayata is the latter. He was born in Ulm, in south-western Germany, studied in Frankfurt and moved to the capital in the early 2000s. He has lived most of his adult life in Berlin, and yet he is still identifiably from elsewhere. He is far too friendly for a start, with none of the gruff directness for which Berliners are famous, and his accent and intonation are softer and more southern. As a Swabian, he is from a region which is synonymous with the gentrification of the capital. As the city has grown more expensive in recent years, many long-term Berliners have been pushed out of areas which had previously been affordable to them. According to a popular cliché, wealthy, middle-class Swabians have now become the majority in former districts of East Berlin like Prenzlauer Berg and Mitte. Go to a dinner party in Berlin, and you will undoubtedly hear the tired old platitude that nobody in Berlin is really from Berlin. Meet another immigrant to the city, and they will suspiciously ask you how long you have been there.

That is also true at the Alte Försterei. As Union's fanbase has grown, the phrase 'I have been an Unioner since...' has become an increasingly common refrain. For some, the defining quality is not how long you have supported Union, but how fervently you do so in the present day. If you uphold the *Laws of Boone*, it doesn't matter whether you have been there six months or six decades. For many others, longevity is a claim to authenticity, and a way of establishing a higher spot in the hierarchy of fans.

Ayata admits that he is as guilty of this as anyone. He too finds himself occasionally rolling his eyes at fans who don't know the words to every terrace chant, and he freely admits that it is a reflex borne of insecurity. 'We know from the sociology of migration that the newest arrivals are often seen as a kind of threat,' he says.

But both in Berlin and at Union, there is a reason why longevity matters to people. As Ayata points out, his experience of Union now is different to that of the older fans because it is not based on the same experiences of the past. He did not live through the GDR, and he did not give his own blood or work on the building site. The club's identity is built on the stories of hardship from years gone by, but fewer and fewer fans can now tell those stories from first-hand experience. As a communications man, Ayata worries that the stories will soon become clichés which can be packaged and commodified. Union are already selling items in their fan shop which hark back to things like Bleed for Union and the fan campaigns to save the Alte Försterei. 'Marketing, after all, is an exercise in story-telling,' he says. 'The lovely thing now is that everyone tells the story of Union in their own way. There is no official version which the club try to impose. It's good that they don't. But I'll be interested to see if that is still the case in five years' time.'

Because regardless of how they perform on the pitch, it is reasonable to think that Union's rise will continue for some time yet. A similar-sized club in Stuttgart or Dresden would have a natural limit to how much it could grow. 'But Berlin is such a huge place, and it has so much potential. There will always be more money flooding into this city,' says Ayata.

Even in the ten years since he started going, the eastern half of Berlin has changed radically. The changes in the coming decade are set to be even more drastic. As eastern areas like Lichtenberg and Rummelsburg also become more gentrified, Köpenick is getting closer and closer to the centre of the city. With the opening of the new international BER airport in 2020 and the closure of Tegel Airport in the West, the weight of the city has already shifted towards the south-east. The Alte Försterei also lies directly between the centre of the city and the small town of Grünheide, where electric car giant Tesla is building its first European Gigafactory, promising thousands of new jobs. This part of the city is going to get wealthier, its population is going to grow, and its demographic is going to change.

'The gentrification itself is not necessarily the problem for Union, but it might be one of the causes,' says Ayata. 'The real pressure is coming from the fact that, presently, the demand for tickets is too high.' When they were a mid-table second division club, a 22,000-capacity stadium was about the right size for Union. The closer they got to the Bundesliga the more games started selling out. By the time they were promoted the competition for tickets was so fierce that even lifelong members began to miss out. The idea of a hierarchy within the fanbase suddenly took on much more importance.

In 2021, the number of members reached 40,000, double the number of spaces in the home areas of the stadium. The longer Union stay in the top flight and the more people move to Köpenick for other reasons, the bigger that discrepancy is going to get. 'But what can you do? You can't build a wall around Köpenick,' says Ayata. 'That's always the biggest misconception about migration – that you can tell people where they have to go. If they want to go somewhere, they will find a way.'

The only answer is to find a way of letting them all in. And that is exactly what the club planned to do.

* * *

Just four years after the new main stand was officially opened, Union announced yet another major construction project. In 2017, plans were announced to expand the Alte Försterei from a capacity of 22,012 to 37,000. The main stand would stay as it was, and the three terraced stands would each be extended by another level. The new, expanded site would also include a new fan shop, an on-site pub and office spaces. Originally set for completion in 2020 to coincide with the stadium's 100-year anniversary, the project had still not begun at the time of publication in August 2022. Promotion, the coronavirus pandemic, and bureaucratic wrangling over the transport infrastructure all helped to delay construction.

Sooner or later, though, the expansion will go ahead, and in general it has been well-received among the fanbase. The plans retain the essence of the stadium as it is now. It will remain around eighty per cent standing, with only one or two new seated sections. The current terraces will stay exactly as they were before, just with another half a stadium on top of them. For most Union fans, whether new or old, it seems like a good compromise. But the change will still be dramatic. When the new stadium opens, 15,000 more people will suddenly be able to go to the Alte Försterei every single weekend. That will be the biggest expansion in the history of the stadium – the biggest makeover yet for the soul of the club.

To not expand, though, would simply be to ignore the problem. It is not just the competition for tickets which means Union are now too big for a 22,000-capacity stadium. To keep financial pace with the rest of the league, they need to make more of their home. In its current form, the Alte Försterei doesn't conform with UEFA and Bundesliga regulations, which require a certain number of seated tickets. For the time being, the club have negotiated an exception for domestic football, but UEFA have not been so flexible. When they qualified for the Conference League in the 2021/22 season, Union had to play their home games in Hertha's Olympiastadion. Just as in the 2009 season, when they were forced to play at BFC's ground, they did their best to swallow an unwanted situation. When Union were playing, the stadium was lit up in red, and the blue athletics track around the pitch was covered with a red carpet. But as Ayata points out, that was just the politics of symbolism. 'It was a vain attempt to maintain something which could not be maintained,' he says, and quotes Adorno: 'Wrong life cannot be lived rightly.'

He doesn't just mean that Union can never be at home in the Olympiastadion. The very fact that they had to move exposed the fundamental tension between wanting to succeed and grow and wanting to preserve a less sanitised football experience. You can't have the Alte Försterei as it is at the top level of modern football. 'When you are a professional club in the Bundesliga, there are so many regulations and necessities – eventually you reach a point where your hands are tied,' says Ayata. As they get closer to the elite of modern football, Union will have to make compromises; they will have to choose which bits of their soul to sell – this time for real.

Once the cogs of growth start moving, it is hard to slow them down. 'You can't win that fight because people are already in motion,' says Ayata. Even if he himself would sometimes like to freeze time and turn back the clock, he knows it is useless. He has been at Union long enough to consider it his club, but in that time, he has also seen the club he fell in love with transform into something new. In the coming years, even more people will flood into the Alte Försterei – people with different ideas about what the soul of Union is, and what it should be. Ayata has long made his peace with that.

'I don't know if I think it's good, but ultimately I do think it is right that new people should come to Union and question what has gone before,' he says. 'Because that's just how this city is.'

CHAPTER 9
HOW LONG IS NOW

UNION BERLIN 0–1 FORTUNA DUESSELDORF – 28 JULY 2007

Jacob's head is pounding as the S-Bahn trundles past Alexanderplatz and out towards Warschauer Straße. That last beer in Zapata was probably a mistake, but it felt like a good idea at the time. It was one of those nights when the air is so thick that you just have to keep smoking. One of those conversations where even the most banal point is a hill to die on. He remembers having something profound to say about Tony Blair's resignation. That was a month ago now – it seems longer than that.

He's only been in Berlin a few weeks, but it may as well have been a lifetime. He is in love with the city, and especially with the artists' collective Tacheles. He loves the artists, he loves the graffiti, he loves mounting the prints and flogging them to the tourists downstairs. He loves the long nights in the in-house bar, Zapata, and he loves the building itself, half-demolished, open to the street – a crumbling wreck to the untrained eye, but a blaze of life and colour inside. He loves the stench of piss in the staircase and the relentless carousel of people. He has never felt freer than he does in that building, in this city.

It is intense though. Sometimes you need a bit of Radio 4 just to come down from it all. Last Sunday he listened to Kevin Pietersen reach his ton in the cricket against India with a cup of tea. It made him think he should go to the football on his next day off, get away from the arthouse for a bit.

SCHEISSE! WE'RE GOING UP!

The Kurier *said Hertha weren't playing this weekend, so here he is, on his way out to the arse end of nowhere in East Berlin to watch a game in the Regional League North.*

The train starts to fill up a bit after Ostkreuz, every station bringing a few more red shirts. There's a decent crowd by the time it gets to Köpenick, and he follows the crowd as it streams across the platform towards the exit. But at the bottom of the station steps, half of them go left and the rest go right. Jacob hesitates just long enough for a guy by the döner stall to catch his eye. He barks something in Berliner which sounds like a 'Can I help you?' Jacob tries his German. 'Fußball?' The guy nods and grins. 'Follow me, I show you.'

'Will there be any tickets left?' Jacob asks as they join the trickle of other fans up the cycle lane towards the woods. The guy looks at him to see if he's joking and bursts out laughing. 'There are always tickets,' he says. 'We haven't sold out for years.' So Jacob pays at the little window, buys himself a beer, and climbs up the steps to the stands. The stadium is about a third full, and the roofless terraces are exposed to the sun. The concrete is well-worn, with weeds and moss and buttercups poking from the cracks.

The football is equally shabby. Union are toothless, and Düsseldorf deserve their lead in the 75th minute. The home side throw the kitchen sink at them in the last quarter of an hour, though, and the stadium erupts when the referee gives a penalty five minutes from time. A stocky bloke with a belly steps up to take it – Torsten Mattuschka, number 17. He looks confident, but the keeper goes the right way: a penalty miss to end an underwhelming start to the season.

To Jacob's surprise, the crowd seem entirely unfazed by defeat. They give the team a rousing send-off before meandering happily back to the beer stands. As he wanders back along the woodland path towards the station, Jacob is grinning too. His hangover is gone, and his head is now filled with the drum beat from that last terrace chant. He takes the programme out of his back pocket and flicks through to see if he can find the fixture list. He'll be coming back here. This place is nothing like Tacheles. But it might just be another home from home.

🐻

It is now more than a decade since Jacob Sweetman first went to Union, but he still remembers the baffled looks he got on that July afternoon. 'At the beginning, I was definitely seen as some sort of curio. There just weren't any English people going then,' he says. People did not come to Berlin for the football in any case and Union were still a footballing backwater, even by the low standards of their own city. 'To suggest then that it could have become some kind of hip football club... it would have seemed impossible,' he says.

We are sitting in a typical candle-lit bar on the canal in Kreuzberg, the multicultural residential district which used to run alongside the western side of the Wall. This is an area which has a higher-than-average density of hipsters. It is where David Bowie recorded *Heroes* in 1977, where squatters chased the police out of town during the 1 May riots of 1987, and where the KitKatClub first opened its doors to latex-clad partygoers in 1994. These days, it has lost some of its edge, but its gentle freedom still attracts the world. At the table next to us, a group of relatively new Berliners talk in English about the trials and tribulations of German grammar. Across the street, the Turkish market-sellers pack up their stalls. Just one block down the canal is the Admiralbrücke, where tourists and junkies swig cheap beer on the pavement and listen to the street musicians.

The bar's toilet, like all Kreuzberg toilets, is covered in stickers. Antifa stickers, rock band stickers, stickers for food trucks. On the back of the cubicle door, there is one that reads *'Yalla FC Union'*. This is about as far west as you are likely to see an Union sticker, and almost as far east as you will see a sticker in Arabic. The East Berlin backwater is creeping west – and slowly tapping into a milieu which few Berlin football clubs have ever managed or bothered to break: hipsters, internationals, English-speakers.

Perhaps it was inevitable. During the 2010s, Union's steady rise began to draw more international attention. The new myth of the cool club sticking it to the football establishment began to pop up more and more in English-speaking media. In 2016, the *New York Times* raved about the Christmas carol service. A few years later, the *Guardian* wrote of Union's 'anti-establishment bearings and intensely involved fan culture'. Whereas Sweetman arrived with little to no knowledge of the club, football lovers moving to Berlin today will at least know the headlines: the rebels who bled for their team; the carol-singers who built their own stadium.

Sweetman has played more than a bit-part role in that myth-building. He began to write about Union almost immediately after his first visit, both for the city's English-language magazine *Exberliner*, and later for *No Dice*, a quarterly on Berlin football which he co-produced between 2011 and 2016. He has now written more extensively in English about Union than anyone, and he continues to shape the romanticism which surrounds foreign coverage of the club. When the BBC came to Berlin to profile Union in 2019, they spoke to him outside the stadium. 'They are a rebellious football club in a rebellious city,' he told *Football Focus* viewers.

But by then, neither the club nor the city were really the same ones which Sweetman had found in 2007. Union didn't just have international media attention; they had a spanking new stadium and were now two divisions higher up the league pyramid. Berlin too had changed. The artists' collective Tacheles, where Sweetman worked upon his arrival in the city, was long gone, its demise a sign of the changing times. In the 1990s, the crumbling former department store had been one of many buildings occupied by artists and alternatives in an under-populated former East Berlin. As the city grew richer and other squats were cleared, Tacheles held on, becoming a romantic relic of a bygone era. But eventually, it too became unsustainable. When it was finally closed in 2012, many commentators mourned what they said was the death of the city itself. 'But that's the thing about Berlin,' says Sweetman. 'Everybody always tells you that everything was better ten years ago.'

Things change fast in Berlin, which is partly why reports of its death are so common, and so often greatly exaggerated. In hindsight, the great cultural movements of the city always claim they were on the cutting edge, but most of them were chasing the past. David Bowie came to Berlin in the 1970s, looking for something Christopher Isherwood had found there in the 1920s. A decade later, half of the great and good of rock'n'roll had turned up looking for what Bowie had discovered. In the 2000s, people pined for the 1990s and the early years of techno. In the 2010s, they pined for the squats and the space of the 2000s. There is always something new happening in Berlin, and everyone is always saying that the latest generation has ruined everything. 'Fuck, Mark Twain was writing about this in the 1890s,' Sweetman laughs. 'You know, people complaining about all these foreign artists coming in.'

There was a similar paranoid nostalgia behind Union's fear of going up. The club too had been on a helter-skelter of transformation since the fall of the Wall, and like the city, they had slipped into a more comfortable, stable status quo in the 2010s. Berlin's anxieties about losing its golden age began to play out on a smaller scale at Union. The hipsters who had colonised Kreuzberg began to turn up at the Alte Försterei, bringing with them questions of gentrification and cultural appropriation. Sweetman, who had been a novelty when he first went to Union, found himself increasingly torn. He had fallen in love with the club and wanted to evangelise about it to his fellow non-Germans, but he also didn't want Union to change.

'There used to be a busker at Weinmeisterstraße who would always play "Wish You Were Here" by Pink Floyd,' he says. 'I always thought it was deeply ironic, because if there's one place they don't wish you were here, it's Berlin. They like it as it is, with a population of three and a half million. They're rude to tourists because they don't want them to move here and ruin it for everyone else. And at the same time, they keep getting drunk and telling tourists how brilliant it is.

'I've got to stop doing that,' he chuckles.

* * *

Sweetman was by no means the first British immigrant to be smitten with Union. Ten years before his time, the club even had an English stadium announcer. In his short stint in charge of the PA system, Des Squire would play The Beatles and The Lightning Seeds before kick-off at every home game and baffle the fans by making up silly nicknames for the players. But Squire, who now does a similar job at Berlin's ice hockey stadium, was long gone by 2007, and Union had hit rock bottom again in the meantime. By the time Sweetman arrived, English fans were practically unheard of. He remembers taking some friends to an away game in Erfurt on the *V.I.R.U.S* party train, and having people goggle at them between the Schlager hits and the shots of Kümmerling, a cheap herbal liqueur. 'They were like: "Who are these English weirdos and what the fuck are they doing with us, this crappy little third division side?"'

Union fans tend to give each other nicknames, and Sweetman was initially labelled 'the Ipswich fan', after the club he supported back home. Far from making him feel more foreign, it endeared him to even more people. German fans may be scornful of the English game in its modern form, but they also still have a romantic fondness for the motherland of football. England is seen as the birthplace of the traditional fan culture which German fans fight tooth and nail to protect. Stadiums like the Alte Försterei, where the four straight stands bring the fans as close to the action as possible, are hailed for their 'Englishness'. When Union played Queen's Park Rangers in a pre-season friendly in 2018, 2,000 ultras travelled to London to cheer them on.

In general, though, the traffic now flows in the opposite direction. It is the Bundesliga which is widely considered to have the healthiest fan culture in Europe these days, and many British fans now regularly travel to Germany in search of a stadium experience which is less sanitised and less expensive than the modern arenas of the Premier League. Before the pandemic hit, German stadiums were enjoying a mini boom in British tourism, driven in part by low ticket prices and budget airlines. The so-called 'Easyjetset' generation – the first for whom weekend trips to Europe were both practical and cheap – has long been a driving force behind Berlin's nightlife. The same flights which fill the bars and clubs with tourists every weekend work just as well for football fans. For the same price as a ticket at Arsenal or Tottenham Hotspur, it was possible to get a return flight from London to Berlin or Cologne, watch a Bundesliga match and still have some money left over for beer. The fact that more and more European football is now shown live on UK TV means that tourist fans can continue to follow their adopted team from afar, even if they only make it to the stadium once or twice a season.

At Union too, English and non-German-speaking fans have become more and more noticeable over the last ten years. While many also go to Hertha, Union's stadium atmosphere and outlaw reputation has made it a more attractive destination for groundhoppers. On-field success has also helped, even if the football has rarely been exhilarating. Between 2009 and 2019,

Union established themselves as the most stable club in the second division. Genuine relegation scares were rare, and there were a couple of optimistic promotion bids. Having cemented their status as the capital's second footballing power, they were operating in a reputational sweet spot: big enough to draw new fans, but small enough to retain the charm of the rebel club.

Derbies against Hertha, who spent the early 2010s yo-yoing between the first and second tiers, also fuelled the underdog narrative. In 2011, Union played Hertha in the Olympiastadion for the first time in a competitive match. As rank outsiders, they snatched a sensational smash-and-grab win thanks to a late free-kick from Torsten Mattuschka, whom Sweetman had seen miss a penalty just a few years before. This time, the Union block was fit to burst and Sweetman was not the only Englishman in there. Mark Wilson, another British Berliner who was relatively new to the city, was so enchanted by Union's win that he decided to take out membership. Shortly afterwards, he and a handful of others got together in Köpenick's shopping mall and founded a blog called 'Union in Englisch'. The website is still an unofficial hub for the international fanbase, offering everything from advice about how to get tickets to English translations of terrace chants. Its regular podcast, *Mattuschka's Right Peg*, is named in honour of the famous derby win.

'Union in Englisch' remains an excellent resource for the curious international fan and a useful rallying point for the dozens of foreign fans who were unable to engage with the club's official channels in German. At Union, where many of the board members were educated in the GDR and learned Russian at school, English was for a long time rather neglected. Only in the late 2010s did the club introduce an English-language website, social media channels and customer support. Not just a response to growing interest from international media, it is also increasingly a necessary service. Union now have members in more than thirty different countries, and around one in seven live neither in Berlin nor the surrounding area.

For Sweetman, who was once the only one writing about Union in English, that is a bittersweet development. He is too good-natured and too generous to really begrudge any new Union fan the same experience he had a decade earlier. Like Ayata, though, he guiltily admits to the odd flash of possessiveness when faced with casual supporters. 'It does annoy me when people say they love Union, and then say they've only been once,' he says. It is an understandable reflex, one conditioned from living in a city where things you love are frequently swept away by the relentless transformation. 'I just love Union so much, and I don't want it to change,' he says at one point, with a hint of melancholy. Like many Berliners, he knows what it feels like to lose a fundamental part of his own city.

∗   ∗   ∗

'Tacheles, for me, was probably the most exciting building I've ever been inside in my life. It was just wild,' says Sweetman. 'It was joyous, and at the same time, it was totally intense. It was full of all these fucking weirdos and lunatics, and drugs. It was chaotic. It was frustrating. It was romantic. And it was doomed.'

The old department store building on Oranienburger Straße was already half-demolished when it was occupied in 1991. Having saved what remained from also being torn down, the new inhabitants transformed it into a Kunsthaus – an arthouse. The name 'Tacheles', a German loan-word from Yiddish meaning 'straight-talking', alluded to its noble aims to be a space where artists could live and work freely – outside of the constraints of dictatorship or the market. Its existence was precarious from the very beginning, and that was part of the essence of the place. On one side of the building, which could be seen from a hundred metres down the street, there was an enormous mural with the words 'How Long Is Now'.

As it turned out, now was longer in Berlin than it would have been elsewhere. Just a stone's throw from Museum Island and in walking distance of Alexanderplatz, Oranienburger Straße is bang in the middle of town, in what would have been prime real estate in any other city. But Berlin had been divided for more than a generation. It wasn't until 1999 that it was fully re-established as the capital of Germany, and it would take even longer for its economy to bounce back to something like normal. So Tacheles survived, and as Sweetman tells it, became a symbol of the creative optimism of its founding years. 'There was this romance about it, about what had been and about Berlin after the fall of the Wall.'

Tacheles fit a vision of Berlin which diverged from the sombre history and the Cold War kitsch. Accessible at all hours of the day and night, it was a living monument to the sense of freedom and space which has always driven artists and misfits to the city. Sweetman was invited there in 2007 by his friend Tony, who earned his keep selling art by Tim Roeloffs, a Dutch artist who had joined the collective in the early years. 'We would flog prints and t-shirts to the tourists. It was like shooting fish in a barrel, because the images were so good, so Berlin, so Tacheles,' he says. By this point, the building and its artists had become an attraction, complete with bars, a cinema, and a concert hall. 'Every tourist in town came to Oranienburger Straße,' says Sweetman. 'It was a fucking party. It was the whole world.'

Why then, if he was working at the best party in the world, did he feel the need to go to Union? Why did he regularly take time out from the experience of a lifetime to go and watch low quality third-tier football on the other side of the city? 'I was looking for something,' he says. 'I think I needed Union because I had Tacheles.'

The arthouse was, by definition, international. Sweetman learned little to no German there and turned instead to print to pick up the language. He began to read the *Berliner Kurier*, a no-nonsense red-top tabloid from the old East. It was there that he read that Union were playing on his day off, and it was at Union that he found a way of integrating beyond the nightlife, the artists and the myths of Berlin. 'In Tacheles, I didn't need to speak German. It wasn't like being in Germany. It was international and cosmopolitan in a way that Union was not back then,' he says.

Tacheles and Union were both theoretically in former East Berlin. Yet both geographically and culturally, they could hardly have been further away from each other. Years after arriving, Sweetman interviewed Union player and local boy Steven Skrzybski just around the corner from Oranienburger Straße. 'He had never heard of Tacheles,' he says, almost daring me to believe it. 'But then why would he have heard of it? He grew up in Kaulsdorf, right on the edge of East Berlin. They didn't listen to techno growing up there. They were totally removed from it all.' Sweetman's world was equally far removed from the trees of Köpenick. But like Ayata, that was partly what drew him to Union. 'I found myself going to all these games, often on my own, and I don't really know why I did. I had nothing in common with any of these people, not even a language. But there was just something inherently likeable about them,' he says.

The irony is not lost on him. The original artists, most of them East Berliners, had fled the mundanity of ordinary life to occupy and set up Tacheles. Sweetman, a foreigner for whom the Kunsthaus was thrilling and new, sought occasional refuge in the ordinariness of the Unioners. 'It felt honest in a way Tacheles never was,' he says. 'Tacheles was about being cool and showing off. Union was never about that.'

If there was one thing both had in common, it was openness. At Union and Tacheles, Sweetman found the sort of freedom which people talk about less and less as the city has become more built-up and more affluent in recent years. In his second season, when Union were playing at Jahn-Sportpark during the stadium renovation, he remembers sitting on the grass behind the tribune and smoking a joint before kick-off. 'You could go along and get pissed, stoned – you could do what you like,' he says. Even as a writer, he was afforded freedoms which would be unthinkable now Union are in the Bundesliga. The club, still overlooked by large parts of the Berlin media, were only too happy to give wide-reaching access to a small, English-language magazine.

It was the same at Tacheles, a project which could only have been conceived in a period when Berlin was full of space. 'It was totally open, every weirdo in the world could come in. It was very rare for someone to get banned – only violence would get you kicked out,' says Sweetman. He admits, however, that the openness belied the tensions which had long simmered between the arthouse's residents. By 2007, Tacheles was already struggling to survive the rapid pace of change in Berlin. After seeing out a ten-year lease which had been given to them by the building's owners in 1998, the artists suddenly became squatters again at the end of the 2000s. The developer had gone bust in the meantime and ownership of the building had effectively passed to a bank. To sell the asset, now worth considerably more than it had been a decade previously, the bank needed to turf the occupants out. So began a long and at times messy stand-off over the future of the building, which the arthouse eventually lost.

The end was further complicated by a bitter split between the artists who worked upstairs and those closer to the bars and businesses on the ground floor. 'I learned later that this was originally seen as an East-West divide. The guys from Café Zapata had come from West Germany in the early days and tried to make money out of the bar, while the artists, who were largely from the East, saw it as something more noble. You start to see that this stuff underpins everything,' says Sweetman.

While the factionalism may have hastened Tacheles' demise, the cracks ran far deeper than the acrimonious last few years. Sweetman says there was always a fundamental difference in the way the locals and the internationals saw the arthouse and its future. 'The ones who were forward-looking were always the South American artists, the Japanese, the Australians. They were the ones who could see a future for it. I think the Germans in there, and especially the East Germans, already thought it was over. They saw it becoming sold out. They saw it becoming touristy. It is such a parallel to Union.'

*　*　*

Tourists remain a tiny minority at the Alte Försterei, but as that minority has grown, attitudes towards them have begun to change. English-speakers are now no longer exotic, and not all of them receive the same warm welcome Sweetman remembers getting in 2007. 'About five years ago, I stopped speaking English on the tram on the way there,' he says. 'I definitely feel a lot more self-conscious about it now. The English are not as welcome now as they were when I first went.'

He is not the only one who has noticed the shift. Shortly after promotion, the *Tagesspiegel* newspaper spoke to two foreign Union fans who said they had begun to experience more aggression from other supporters, some of whom insulted them as hipsters and 'event fans'. It is not that the English-speakers are unwelcome per se, and aggression towards foreigners remains rare at the Alte Försterei. But as more newcomers arrive at Union every week and English becomes more common, its significance has changed.

English is the language of globalisation, with all the advantages and disadvantages that come with it. English means tourists, who are more likely to gawp, and it often means more lasting economic change. In the 2000s, more and more start-ups and academic institutions emerged in Berlin operating primarily – if not exclusively – in English. They were just one element of a wider influx of western money into central Berlin, which has completely changed its eastern districts.

Sweetman, whose regular spot is near the ultras on the Waldseite, the hardcore block behind the goal at the forest end, sees the flashes of hostility as symptomatic of a broader divide between older fans and newcomers. 'There is definitely a sense of us and them,' he says. 'Them being the sort of leftie, Prenzlauer Berg-types.' A residential East Berlin district whose grand pre-war buildings had become dilapidated by the end of the Cold War, Prenzlauer Berg is the area which has gone through the most dramatic process of gentrification in the last twenty years. Cleaner, safer and more prosperous than it was thirty years ago, it has also become unaffordable for the overwhelming majority of Berliners. Most people blame the Swabians, of course, but the Anglo-Saxons have also played their part. Along with Mitte and Friedrichshain-Kreuzberg, it is also the area of Berlin with the highest number of Brits and Americans. English, therefore, is also seen as a symptom of gentrification.

For Brits in Berlin like Sweetman, that is often a source of guilt. 'I've worked as a tour guide for eight years, and I recently stopped doing tours through Kreuzberg,' he says. 'I felt like I wasn't a small part of the problem, I was a fundamental part of the problem. I felt like I was making money out of people's lives being ruined.' He has a similarly guilty conscience about Union, and the myths and narratives he has helped to create over the last decade. 'It was OK when I was just on my own or with a few people, but then it starts to feel like you're undermining the whole thing. Maybe I give myself too much credit, but I worry about my own influence. I worry that I sell it as something it's not, and that I attract outsiders based on these stereotypes.'

He probably is giving himself too much credit. There are still only around a hundred native English-speakers among Union's membership, and the English-speaking community has neither single-handedly gentrified Berlin nor significantly changed Union. But his sheepishness is a common trait in an immigrant community which knows that it can afford to assimilate less than others. 'The big debates about integration are always aimed at the Turkish and Arabic communities, but who is it who really has cafés and bars where they only speak their own language?' asks Sweetman. Conservative politician Jens Spahn made a similar point in 2017. 'I find it increasingly annoying that, in some Berlin restaurants, the waiters only speak English,' he huffed in an interview with *NOZ* newspaper. It was a typically crude bit of populism, but there was little outrage from the city's anglophone community. Many of them felt he had a point.

Because so many people can speak it across the world, English is a natural lingua franca in areas where people from different cultures and countries come together. That is especially the case in Berlin, where the local language is notoriously difficult to learn, and many Germans are more than happy to speak English. If you work in the right industry, it is possible – even easy – to set up and live a new life in the German capital without learning much more than a few phrases of German. In certain areas, even among those who do speak German, there is a tacit understanding that English will do.

Guilt about the language is then easily conflated with guilt about gentrification. When people move to Berlin from other, more expensive cities, they bring different price expectations, push up rents and put pressure on existing communities. The fact that many only stay two to three years only exacerbates the problem. It is a process which has taken place across the world, from Brooklyn and Bristol to Amsterdam and Athens. In places where English is a widely spoken second tongue, language is just another very tangible barrier between the gentrifiers and the gentrified. Listening to Sweetman, it feels like the people who say Berlin was better ten years ago are the ones who feel most guilty about having changed it.

So, how long *is* now? When and how does change happen? Is there a critical mass of new wealth or popularity that will always spark irrevocable transformation? In Berlin, where recent decades have seen an incremental growth in population and a steep rise in the price of living, these questions are pervasive. Tacheles grappled with them, the entire English-speaking community grapples with them, and increasingly, Union are having to grapple with them.

At the heart of it all is a simpler question: who is the city for? Still traumatised by the Wall and for years very keen to attract new industries, Berlin has long styled itself as an open city, where people from anywhere in the world can live in any way they want. The difficulty is making sure that they can do that while also preserving the people and the spaces which make the city what it is in the first place. 'Union's problem will always be keeping that balance,' says Sweetman.

* * *

The Tacheles building is covered in scaffolding on the day I meet Sweetman. The 'How Long Is Now' mural, still visible for years after the arthouse closed, has now been erased, the gap it once faced filled in by the polished facade of the new development. The architects have kept the old name, but their vision of a slick, saleable space for apartments, offices and shops is nothing like its predecessor. 'Tacheles failed in the end,' says Sweetman. 'And as soon as it went, that was the end of Oranienburger Straße. I went there recently and there's nothing there anymore. Not even the women working in the street.'

Prostitution, which is legal in Germany and was once synonymous with Oranienburger Straße, has indeed deserted the area. Along with much of the edginess which once defined the street, the sex workers have moved on as the area has become richer. What was once one of Berlin's edgiest corners is now one of its smartest, full of brightly lit restaurants and artisan coffee shops. There are still a few establishments which have survived, even thrived in the change: a popular falafel joint has expanded into the next-door building. An ivy-covered bar still holds weekly trad-jazz gigs in a smoke-filled cellar. Another old place down the road advertises itself as 'the last unstylish pub on Oranienburger'.

You could say it was dead. You could say it was just different. From the open-air theatre on the corner of Monbijou Park to the 150-year-old synagogue, to the Georgian bistro run by a top-hatted chocolatier, there is still life around Oranienburger Straße – it has not yet been completely sanitised into office blocks and chain cafés. It is just another kind of life, one which is more sober, more well-fed, and less affordable than the one which made it famous; one which is at the same time in tune with a city which, after long years of trauma, is beginning to heal and settle. Berlin is only dead if you think Berlin is a time as well as a place.

Tacheles was the product of a sweet spot in the city's history, a brief period when artists were more interested in the centre of the city than developers were. 'The fact that it lasted as long as it did was a miracle. It was a unique situation that you could have an explosion like that in the middle of a city,' says Sweetman. Union, he notes, are in the opposite situation. Their position on the edge of Berlin meant that they were easily forgotten in the fallow years, but now they are thriving, they have space to grow.

The question is how much they want to grow. Even after a decade in the second tier and several close shaves, Union fans remained decidedly schizophrenic about the prospect of promotion to the Bundesliga. 'Union weren't supposed to be this successful,' says Sweetman. 'They shouldn't be a Bundesliga club. All we ever wanted was to be in the Bundesliga, and when you get there, you step back and think: is this what we want? I quite liked it when we were playing against Wolfsburg's reserves.' Like many, he worries that a prolonged stint in the top flight could make the club more commercialised and soften their rebellious streak. It is the same unease that was expressed in the 'Shit, we're going up!' chant. For a long time, promotion to the Bundesliga was little more than a pipe dream, a lyric in a song which would never become reality. When it did become real, Unioners were confronted not only with what they stood to gain, but also with everything they stood to lose.

The day after promotion, the tabloid *B.Z.* ran a light-heart-ed headline comparing Union's victory over Stuttgart to Berlin finally sticking it to the wealthy south-westerners who had taken over its central districts. 'Berlin throws out the Swabians!' chirped the front page. In reality, promotion would only mean more Swabians, more new fans, more hipsters and yuppies on the terraces. The new money and the new popularity cannot be reversed any more than the real estate developments in the centre of Berlin.

That is not only a bad thing. In the end, nobody wants to preserve everything in aspic. Tacheles may have been a liberating space for many people, but it was also a troubled place haunted by addiction, in-fighting and, as Sweetman says, the knowledge that it couldn't last forever. The centre of Berlin may now have less space, less freedom in it, but it is also a cleaner, safer and healthier city than it was twenty or thirty years ago. At Union, the Alte Försterei has rarely had a more electric atmosphere than it has had in the last ten years, when the team has been winning and the stadium has been full to the rafters almost every single weekend. Nostalgia tends to remember the good things and forget the bad. And ultimately, even Sweetman tries not to indulge in Berlin's chronic homesickness for the past.

'I've heard Union fans say that the penalty shootout defeat to Osnabrück in 2000 was the best day of their lives,' he laughs. That legendary defeat in the third-tier play-offs, the last dramatic failure of the 'Unpromotables' era, was a defining experience for many fans of a certain age, and is now a memory from a simpler time, when Union were reliably useless in big games. But that time is gone now, and Sweetman prefers to enjoy the present. 'Maybe it was great for those guys. But personally, I fail to see how anything was better than promotion in 2019. Because that was so, so special.'

PART FOUR
SCHEISSE!

CHAPTER 10
WE'RE GOING UP!

UNION BERLIN 0–0 VFB STUTTGART – 27 MAY 2019

The night begins in smoke and flame. As the team bus turns off the main road and into the stadium car park, the fans are waiting. In the descending dusk, they line the route with flares and rockets until the bus is engulfed in an enormous cloud of red fire. For a few moments, the players on board can see nothing but smoke and hear nothing but singing as driver Sven Weinel guides the bus carefully down the tunnel of fire. Inside the stadium, as the rest of the fans file in, the big screen shows pictures of the inferno. The flames seem to leap out of the screen. The spring air is cool, but the atmosphere still feels hot and humid.

In theory, Union are not the ones feeling the heat. They are the underdogs, battling for an unlikely promotion while Stuttgart attempt to avoid catastrophic relegation. Unlike the five-time German champions from the south, the Berliners have everything to win and nothing to lose. A few weeks earlier, the fans had made it clear that there would be no retribution, wailing, and gnashing of teeth if Union came up short. 'Head off, heart on, everything possible, nothing expected,' read the banner they hung up on the training ground fence. Yet now they are here, there is no shaking the tension. Both head and heart say that this chance is not to be missed.

For weeks now, promotion has been tantalisingly close. On the final day of the league season, 5,000 Unioners travelled to Bochum, while a further 5,000 crammed into the stadium car park to watch the game on the big screen. In the pouring rain, they stood and sweated as Union fought back from two goals behind to salvage a draw. But it wasn't enough. A point meant third place, and third place meant the play-off against Stuttgart. They drew the first leg 2–2 and are now back on home soil for the return match, two away goals to the good. In the Alte Försterei, a 0–0 draw will suffice.

'We won't do it,' says a quiet, greying Berliner standing on the Gegengerade before kick-off. Stralsund in 1974. Chemie Leipzig in 1984. Osnabrück in 2000. He knows from bitter experience that Union don't win these kinds of games. The guy in front of him, an Australian, is brimming with the optimism of the newcomer. 'I dunno man, I think it'll be fine!' Neither of them sound completely convinced.

Sitting on his little plastic chair on the touchline, Union coach Urs Fischer looks the calmest man in the stadium. In just one season at Union, he has already won Köpenick hearts and minds with his straightforward manner, tracksuit, and baseball cap in the dugout. Were it not for his thick Swiss accent, he could easily pass for a local. Yet unlike the locals, he has no need to be nervous. The 53-year-old has led Union this far not with rousing speeches or furious emotion, but with pragmatic, well-organised football and careful planning. As the players walk out before kick-off, the fans on the Waldseite raise a huge artwork showing two hands clasping a beating human heart. Fischer, composed and concentrated as ever, doesn't even seem to notice as the gruesome spectacle rises slowly from behind the goal to loom over the pitch. They are the heart; he is the head.

The motor is the team: a diligent, cheerful bunch whom Fischer has made more than the sum of their parts. Like their coach, the players have no roots in Köpenick. Left-back Ken Reichel is the only Berliner in the starting line-up, and he was born on the other side of the Wall. But there are adopted heroes. Captain Christopher Trimmel, a goofy-grinned Austrian who galumphs tirelessly up and down the right wing; Michael Parensen, a now part-time veteran who joined from Cologne a decade ago when Union were still in the third division; and Rafał Gikiewicz, a Polish goalkeeper with a mad streak as wide as his piercing stare.

WE'RE GOING UP!

As the first half snarls into gear, the stadium seems to sweat with nerves. First touches are heavy. Blood soaks into bandages after Stuttgart defenders Holger Badstuber and Ozan Kabak clash heads. The only release of tension comes when the visitors have an early goal ruled out for offside. The Union fans, who otherwise make a point of booing the video assistant referee, cheer him like one of their own this time around.

But 0–0 is no party scoreline. In the second half, the sense of an oncoming collective migraine sets in. Union's Nigerian striker Suleiman Abdullahi hits the same post twice in a matter of minutes. Stuttgart have a penalty appeal waved away by the referee. A few minutes from time, hot blood runs cold in the crowd as the ball falls to Stuttgart's Benjamin Pavard on the edge of the Union penalty area. The French right-back has form with this kind of chance. A year earlier, he scored the goal of the tournament at the 2018 World Cup with a blistering half-volley against Argentina. Now, from almost the same position, he slams the ball towards Gikiewicz. The Polish keeper dives full length to palm it away and leaps to his feet, his eyes burning their icy blue.

A few minutes later, it is over. Beer falls like rain from the sky, and on the pitch, the exhausted red shirts fall to their knees as one. On the touchline, assistant coach Sebastian Bönig drops to the ground and buries his face in the grass. 'Böni' is another adopted son, who made 122 appearances for the club in the mid-2000s before returning to the coaching staff in 2014. If there is one man in the dugout who feels like the fans do, it is him. As the fans stream onto the pitch, he hammers his fist against the turf, as if to be absolutely sure that the world is real.

Soon, the whole stadium is alight. From the forest end, rockets fly high into the night sky, clearing the clouds which have loomed heavy all evening. Across the pitch, smoke billows from the flares and sweat pours off the screaming faces. Bönig is not alone in his desire to touch something, to make the moment physical. Some clamber onto the crossbar and snip souvenirs from the goal net. Others go downwards, ripping out ever larger chunks from the hallowed turf. By the time the crowd clears a few hours later, the grass looks like a moonscape, the green pocked with brown craters.

For a while, the line between supporter and professional blurs. Fischer embraces a beaming stranger on the touchline. Captain Trimmel, who has been forced to watch from the stands with a suspension, pulls on a shirt and dances arm in arm with the fans. Parensen, the silver-haired veteran defender, crowd surfs across the jubilant masses from the touchline to the centre circle. And Christian Arbeit grins in joy and terror as a shirtless ultra ceremonially shaves off his shoulder-length locks. As the players gather on an impromptu pitchside stage to lead the celebrations, striker Sebastian Polter grasps a beer in one hand, a burning flare in the other. 'I remember the final whistle and the half hour afterwards, but nothing more,' he tells RBB TV a few days later. 'I celebrated in the pub with the fans, and I got home about six in the morning with some mates and some other people I didn't know.'

Two days later, the smoke still hasn't cleared and the drink is still flowing. An estimated 60,000 litres of beer are consumed at Union's victory parade along the river Spree. The drunken flotilla of fans and players begins at the East Side Gallery and sails off towards the Alte Försterei. On the banks and bridges between Kreuzberg and Köpenick, thousands of fans line up once again to hail their heroes with flares and fireworks.

They have been preparing for this party for a long time, but none of them in Köpenick on this bright Wednesday afternoon can possibly imagine what lies ahead. For five decades, Union have been denied a sporting triumph on this scale. For fifty-three years, they have been underdogs. The world has changed, and so have they, but their place in the footballing hierarchy has remained more or less the same. Now Union are in the Bundesliga, and nothing will ever be the same again.

Stefanie Fiebrig's eyes light up when she talks about the party in May 2019. 'I'd seen Union get promoted twice before, but when we went up to the Bundesliga, it was different,' she says. 'It was a party marathon. By the end of the week I could barely even see straight.'

Her husband, Sebastian Fiebrig, describes promotion as a noise. Until then, his and Stefanie's blog *Textilvergehen* had occupied a relatively quiet niche in the German-speaking corner of the football internet. After the images of the pitch invasion were beamed around the globe, they became part of a national – and international – conversation. 'Union were suddenly being talked about in all these different languages. It was incredible,' he says. 'We realised that we were part of this global noise, and it was like: woah! After a while, like all background noises, you start to blend it out and hear the important things again. But we had to gather ourselves first.'

Union going up was always going to capture the imagination. In the weeks before and after the play-off against Stuttgart, media interest in the club exploded like never before. Typically for Berlin, the infrastructure struggled to contain the hype. At training sessions, there would usually be just a few print reporters and one or two cameramen watching from the press enclosure on the touchline. In the spring of 2019, it was overflowing with TV crews, feature writers and foreign correspondents. In the little press conference room in the bowels of the Alte Försterei, the journalists jostled for space among the thin wooden tables. 'You could barely breathe in there; it was bursting at the seams. Everybody had the feeling that something was happening here, and they had to keep their finger on the pulse,' says Stefanie.

At *Textilvergehen* they were happy to stay on the fringes of the scrum. The Fiebrigs' blog follows the club as rigorously as any of the local newspapers, and it is essential morning reading for fans and reporters alike. But despite its name, which is a poetic word for pulling back an opponent by their shirt, it has never really been about scoops and sharp elbows. Sebastian describes it as a kind of aggregator, a platform for debates and issues within the fanbase which are otherwise overlooked.

'There are so many things which are not so relevant for the traditional media but are important for Union fans. People want to discuss them, and they need to discuss them; that's what we try to do. We aren't neutral, but we are critical,' he says. Both Stefanie and Sebastian have a media background – she as a photographer and graphic designer and he as a print journalist – so the site's output is professional. The Fiebrigs and their co-bloggers produce two regular podcasts, write a daily 'State of the Union' newsletter, and keep tabs on an often lively comments section.

Their readership has boomed since promotion, and not just because Union have become more popular. Being in the top flight also meant fiercer debates within the fanbase, as the club reassessed its identity, its expectations, and its role in football and society. While going up was a reason to party, it also shook many of the certainties which Union had built up over the previous ten years. Many feared that the club would have to change in its new environment, and that the things they valued most highly might get lost. 'People were scared that we would lose our identity in the Bundesliga. That was a very big concern,' says Sebastian.

The slow, manageable changes of the previous decade had been turbo-charged, and inevitably, that led to questions. How would Union deal with the soaring demand for tickets? Would success change the stadium experience? Would it change Union's approach to wider social issues? And as more people kept flooding in, would the club retain its East German identity?

'We are suddenly interesting, and maybe that means it's not quite as cosy as it used to be. But how cosy was it really back then? Should we be open or not? That was the big question, and it was really a social question,' says Sebastian.

Textilvergehen was by no means the only online forum on which these conversations played out. But it was arguably one of the most important, because its audience was so diverse. The blog is read by fans and media, by older locals and the newer international crowd. 'We have a lot of people with very different opinions, and the debates can be fierce, but people know how to behave so it's a healthy discussion culture,' says Stefanie. She and Sebastian are both long-time Union members, and both holders of the club's official 'silver honour' award for extraordinary commitment. They have also argued tirelessly for the club to remain open to newcomers, and their blog is an important foothold in the community for many new fans. As digital natives born behind the Berlin Wall, they are as close as you get to the middle of the Union Venn diagram. They understood both the hopes and the fears surrounding promotion.

Two years after they had first sung '*Scheisse*, we're going up!', the proverbial faeces had finally hit the fan. Union were going up, and amid the wild partying, many fans found themselves asking each other the same question.

Is this really what we want?

* * *

What do football fans want? If the point of fandom were only to see your team win, then nobody would support anyone but Bayern Munich and Real Madrid. But most fans do not support a club because the club is successful, they support it because, for whatever profound or half-baked reason, they have decided they identify with it. Losing a game or a trophy is part of the journey; losing your identity is the end of the road.

As much as the Union fans enjoyed winning, it had never been part of their football identity. It would need a certain amount of time to get used to their team as a top-flight outfit, and the board knew it. Club president Dirk Zingler initially described promotion as a 'holiday', a kind of year abroad in a league in which Union could never feel at home. 'Zingler never really believed that; he was just trying to make sure people weren't overwhelmed,' says Sebastian. 'The club hierarchy were much further along in their thinking than most of the fans, and they had to coax people into it step by step.'

Some needed more coaxing than others. By 2019, Union had been in the second division for ten years – the longest period of stability in the history of the club. While many fans had grown attached to the second division, there had also been plenty of time to consider the prospect of going up. Their first brush with promotion had come as far back as 2013, and when they came even closer four years later, the '*Scheisse*' banner was raised on the terraces. But not everyone feared promotion. In the 2018/19 season, another banner with the initials 'A.J.' on it also became increasingly visible at home and away games. The letters stood for '*Aufstieg jetzt*' ('promotion now'). One of the banner's creators told *B.Z.* newspaper that the idea was to 'pull people out of their lethargic thinking'.

Most fans fell somewhere between the two stools. After a decade in the second tier, they recognised that the club was ready for a new challenge. But there were also huge reservations about how the Bundesliga would change Union. The club had been promoted before, but they had seldom made a jump between two such different leagues. Being in the top flight didn't just mean a more glamorous fixture list; it also meant commercial consequences which would affect every single aspect of the club. 'The debate about going up was all-encompassing: it was about how the stadium should be; what our fan culture should look like; how we should react to certain types of media coverage; it was about an entire picture of what Union should be, and that was something everyone had a strong opinion on,' says Stefanie.

As ever, the stadium experience was a central issue. The Alte Försterei had been a slightly larger than average stadium in the third division, and slightly smaller than average in the second. In the Bundesliga, it was entering an entirely new dimension, in which it was not necessarily a good fit. Both the Fiebrigs wrinkle their noses when they talk of their first impressions of other top-flight stadiums. Where previously they had been taking away trips to charming, old-fashioned grounds like Fürth and St. Pauli, now they were watching Union in huge, modern arenas, complete with flashing lights, cheesy goal music and multiple layers of advertising boards. 'Even proud old clubs like Schalke had all this village disco rubbish,' Stefanie says. 'We looked around at these stadiums and thought OK, this is the league we're in now. And it didn't feel good,' she adds.

For a league which is famous for its atmospheres, the Bundesliga's stadiums are remarkably uniform in architectural terms. Almost all of Germany's biggest grounds were either built or rebuilt in the last twenty years, in part thanks to a wave of investment around the 2006 World Cup. Some clubs like Bayern Munich relocated to completely new, out-of-town venues. Many more, including Schalke, Cologne, Stuttgart, and Eintracht Frankfurt, simply built a brand-new arena on the site of their old ground. As a result, most Bundesliga stadiums look extremely similar, and all of them are designed with modern commercial requirements in mind. As well as the flashing lights and copious advertising space, there are also outrageous mark-ups and internal payment systems to squeeze every penny out of every fan. To Union fans, all of this was the exact opposite of what they cherished about their own ground back home.

It also offered a disturbing vision of a potential future for the Alte Försterei. After all, many of these stadiums were not completely new builds; they were old grounds whose character had been eroded or erased by renovation. And renovation was also looming in Köpenick. Union's ground only held 3,500 seated spectators, less than half the amount required by Bundesliga regulations. In order to use the stadium at all in the top flight, they had had to apply for an exemption to the rules, which had been granted partly because the club already had plans to expand. The expansion would have to go ahead sooner rather than later, and while most fans were happy with the concept, it was still going to change the physical and commercial dynamics of the stadium. At a club where the matchday experience is so crucial to the shared identity, that was a scary thought.

Right from the outset, Union fans set out to prove that being in the Bundesliga wasn't going to change them, and as it happened, the fixture list gave them a perfect chance to do so. Union's first game in the first division was at home to RB Leipzig, a club which, for many fans, epitomised everything they rejected about elite professional football.

To the purists, RB represented both the creeping com-mercialisation of the game, and the undermining of fan democracy. They had been founded in 2009 as the German outpost of Red Bull's football empire and had risen from the lower divisions to the Champions League in the space of a decade. Their business model not only gave them a competi-tive advantage, but it also disenfranchised fans. RB were technically a club with voting members like any other. Yet, they were one which had effectively limited its membership to just seventeen people. That meant they followed the letter of 50+1 but rode roughshod over the spirit of it. For fan groups across the country, that was a red flag to a bull.

Union supporters had protested against Leipzig before, and they planned to do so again in the top flight. In a statement ahead of the game, the ultras urged all ticket holders to remain silent for the first fifteen minutes, a so-called 'atmosphere boycott' to remind both Red Bull and the watching world that fans were at the heart of football.

This was a controversial call. Union had dreamed for decades of reaching the Bundesliga, and now they were going to mark their arrival with fifteen minutes of mournful silence. There were fans, and even some players, who publicly criticised the silent protest, and called on the ultras to abandon the idea. But the majority were on board, and ahead of kick-off, Christian Arbeit whipped the crowd into a frenzy with a rousing speech on the virtues of fan membership before the home crowd settled dutifully into silence for the first fifteen minutes. Union lost 4–0, but the fans stayed long after the final whistle to serenade the team and went home with smiles on their faces. To paraphrase another defeated ideologue, they felt they had lost the game but won the argument.

The Leipzig game was Union's promotion dilemma in a nutshell: is it better to lose on the moral high ground or succeed and make compromises? On that day, as thousands of people deliriously celebrated a thumping defeat in the summer sun, the answer seemed obvious. 'Are our values and traditions no longer important? Should we celebrate away all our past protests just because we've got to the top and are now part of it all?' asked the ultras in a statement in the matchday programme.

But even the question felt like a tacit admission that, once you are 'part of it all', not all values and traditions can be sacred. Despite their objection to the Red Bull model and committed defence of 50+1, Union could not escape the fact that they too were now in the big leagues. And that meant they too were making moral compromises.

* * *

On 14 June 2019, just a fortnight after promotion, Union announced a new shirt sponsor for the coming season. With its boilerplate sentences and contrived quotes, it was the sort of announcement which would usually be met with a shrug. On this occasion, it sparked outrage.

'Union and Aroundtown have a lot in common,' said the new sponsor's British CEO Andrew Wallis. It is fair to say not everyone agreed with him. Aroundtown was a major real estate company registered in Luxembourg. Its subsidiary, Grand City Properties, was one of the seven biggest players in the Berlin property market. At a time when city politics were gripped by a bitter war over housing and rental prices, it was a highly controversial commercial partner. Short of airport planners and actual organised criminals, there was perhaps no group of people with a worse reputation in Berlin in the late 2010s than property developers.

'Aroundtown stands for the opposite of what Union stand for,' wrote *Textilvergehen* in an angry post the following day. Like many others, they argued that against a backdrop of evictions, rising rents and gentrification across Berlin, this was a deal which sat uneasily with Union's image as a community-oriented underdog. To team up with a major property company was at worst a betrayal of the club's community values, and at best highly insensitive. 'It was a remarkably tactless decision because it happened at a time when rent prices were skyrocketing in Berlin,' explains Sebastian. 'Aroundtown were representative of something which affected everyone in the city.'

Between 2010 and 2020, average rents doubled in Berlin. Longstanding subsidies had been phased out, a property boom had set in, and living costs were climbing quicker in the capital than anywhere else in Germany. Where people had once happily moved regularly from cheap flat to cheap flat, they were now forced to cling onto older contracts like lifeboats as the rental market became ever hotter. 'It used to be that you would ask people "Oh where are you moving this year?" But now nobody is moving because it's become so expensive,' says Sebastian. 'We can never move out of our place now,' adds Stefanie with a slightly hollow laugh. Others have no choice but to move. As well as high-profile evictions of former squats like Tacheles, the boom has also pushed many ordinary people from their long-term homes. Germany has comparatively strong tenant protection laws, but the most ruthless landlords find ways around them, such as carrying out large-scale 'modernisations' to hike up rents. Almost everyone knows someone with a horror story.

Aroundtown itself was more involved in the commercial sector than in private rentals, but it was hardly small fry. According to a 2019 report by the left-wing Rosa Luxemburg Foundation, its subsidiary Grand City owned more than 8,000 units in the capital, around a quarter of its 7.2-billion-euro portfolio. The report also suggested that the company was structured to avoid paying capital gains tax and stamp duty, a claim which Aroundtown CEO Wallis sought to play down in an interview with the *Tagesspiegel* shortly after signing the deal with Union. Speaking to journalists in an England shirt at the company's offices in northern Berlin, he insisted that Aroundtown and its subsidiaries paid their due taxes in Germany and that it did not use underhand methods to force up rents or force out tenants. 'Grand City has never done modernisations in the same way that others have done them,' he insisted.

Yet the optics of the deal were undoubtedly abysmal, especially given the political context. Just a week before the deal was announced, the Berlin Senate officially tabled plans for a city-wide rental cap, which aimed to freeze rent prices for five years. The flagship policy of the city's left-wing coalition government, this was the most radical attempt yet by legislators to curb spiralling Berlin rents and rein in property companies like Aroundtown (when the move was announced, Grand City's share price reportedly dropped by eight per cent). The policy was later thrown out by the constitutional court, but that did not end the bitter war over housing. At a referendum in September 2021, Berliners voted overwhelmingly in favour of a landmark citizens' initiative urging the Senate to forcibly buy back property from any company which owned more than 3,000 apartments in the city. The poll was non-binding, but if nothing else, it was further proof of how dramatic many people considered the situation to be.

Whether or not the Aroundtown deal was a fundamental betrayal of Union's values depended on who you asked. 'There were some people who took a pragmatic view, and said the money has to come from somewhere. And then there were others who said they would never buy a shirt with that sponsor,' says Stefanie. For her part, she thinks it could have been worse. On the wider spectrum of morally questionable sports sponsorship deals, a company which sells office space in an overheated market is perhaps not quite up there with a human-rights-abusing oil state or a gambling website. 'I'm just glad it wasn't a betting company because that would have been just as awful,' says Stefanie, and points out that the Aroundtown deal at least had no bearing on the stadium experience. 'As long as I don't have advertising at every corner kick and every substitution, then I can live with a shirt sponsor which I don't like.'

Sebastian thinks that much of the controversy came from outside and arose from a misconception about Union's self-image. 'We do have a moral idea of how a football match should be staged, but that doesn't mean we are an anti-capitalist club. Do we ourselves have higher morals which we need to adhere to, or is that an idea which is projected onto Union from outside? That's the big debate here, and it's one which is still ongoing.'

It was the timing which made that debate so pertinent. Union, after all, had struck deals with controversial sponsors before. In 2009, an ill-fated partnership with a nebulous, UAE-based sports promotion firm was quickly shelved amid revelations about the Stasi past of one of its executives. Grand City, meanwhile, had already been involved with Union's youth academy for several years before Aroundtown became the main sponsor. But the 2019 deal felt different. It wasn't just that the housing crisis had a direct effect on the lives of many fans; it was also that this had happened in a moment when the world was watching Union, and when the fans were already worrying about their future.

While most fans made their peace with the Aroundtown deal, it still shook people's trust, and fuelled more immediate, football-related concerns. If the board had no qualms about gentrification in the wider city, what about gentrification on the terraces? Now Union were in the top flight, space in the stadium was about to become almost as precious as space in the city. And that would open up yet more questions about what – and more importantly who – the club should be.

* * *

To get an idea of how much the Bundesliga could change Union, you just had to look at the membership numbers. During the failed promotion charge in 2017, 5,000 new people joined the club in the space of a year. At the time, that was the most significant rise in membership in Union's history, but it paled in comparison to what happened two years later. When they did go up in 2019, it took just two weeks for the club to attain 5,000 new members. By the end of 2019, the membership had gone up by seventy-five per cent to around 35,000. For the first time in the club's history, there were now more members than there were spaces in the stadium.

Even though Union kept prices low, tickets became gold dust overnight. With half of them going to season-ticket holders and more still going to fan clubs and sponsors, that left around one ticket per every two remaining members. In the second division, it had still been possible to pick up several tickets on general sale. In the Bundesliga, getting hold of them became a lottery, with members having to enter a random draw just to get one for themselves. Union's notoriously dysfunctional ticketing website did little to alleviate the frustration.

Inevitably, that reopened the question of fan hierarchy. When resources are scarce, it is natural to ask who has the greater claim to them. When long-time stadium-goers suddenly found themselves forced to watch on TV or unable to get tickets for their friends, there was bound to be some grumbling. Had they not been coming here longer than these neatly turned-out hipsters? Did they not identify more with the club? 'In some ways, you could see it in a larger context. When so many people come to Berlin and to Germany then there are different reactions and reflexes, and one of them is a loss of identity,' says Sebastian. Just as it feels like we are skirting the elephant in the room, Stefanie finishes his thought: 'How East German do you have to be to be an Unioner?'

This was the biggest identity question of all. Union have now existed for longer in reunified Germany than they ever existed in the GDR, but most of their fans still have distinctly East German biographies. Sebastian grew up in the city of Jena, and Stefanie speaks with the rounded vowels of Brandenburg, the region which surrounds Berlin. Both are of a generation which was born in the GDR, experienced the fall of the Wall as children and came of age in reunified Germany. As Stefanie points out, even many younger Union fans, born long after 1989, would still identify strongly as East Germans. 'You find a lot of people who have a certain way of thinking, even if they didn't experience the GDR themselves. It's passed on from their parents and it's still part of who they are,' she says.

As a club, Union are happy to play up their East German-ness. Nina Hagen's anthem is a case in point, but there are plenty of other examples. Another club song, 'Stimmung in der Alten Försterei', was sung by the late Achim Mentzel, a pop star and entertainer who remains immensely popular in the former East and utterly baffling to most other Germans. In the club shop, there is a line of products based on Pittiplatsch, a children's cartoon character who originated on East German TV in the 1960s.

Often, this sort of stuff is dismissed as *Ostalgie*, the cultural yearning for a lost past under socialism. In the summer Union were promoted, the *Tagesspiegel* published an article under the headline 'Union's *Ossi* affectations are annoying'. Written by an East-German-born writer for a paper with a largely West-Berlin-based readership, the piece sneered that Union had 'written *Ostalgie* and "outsiderism" into their unofficial statutes'. The Fiebrigs dispute this. 'Calling it *Ostalgie* suggests that we want to go back to the past, and nobody is saying that,' says Sebastian. But to repress any sense of a shared eastern identity is equally problematic, he argues. 'That is something people react to allergically in the former East: being told how you should do things and that your own experience doesn't count. The idea that your own experiences and qualifications are somehow worth less is a very East German trauma.'

The Bundesliga, like many institutions in reunified Germany, was exclusively West German before 1990 and has had a disproportionately low East German representation ever since. As the league's first former GDR club for ten years, Union were caught between two extremes. On the one hand, they were being hailed as representatives of an entire region. In the same breath, the media were criticising them for clinging on to their eastern identity too tightly. They were in a bind familiar to many minority groups: damned if they did, and damned if they didn't. 'Integration is not a one-way street,' says Sebastian. 'People often say this about foreigners, but they don't understand that it also applies within Germany. As an East German, I know all the cultural codes from West Germany. But my West German colleagues don't know any of the East German codes.' Essentially, it is a question of 'othering': West German cultural references are normal and neutral, while East German ones are exotic *Ostalgie*.

When Union's fanbase had been almost exclusively made up of people from the former East, that issue had been less present on the terraces. The cultural imbalance between east and west had been a feature of wider society, rather than of the Union community itself. The wave of new fans and the increased attention from outside, however, threatened to bring it inside the Alte Försterei. What had once been an almost exclusively East German space was now opening up at breakneck speed, putting pressure on a culture which already considered itself on the back foot. That perhaps explains why people like Jacob Sweetman noticed a growing hostility towards English-speakers. Even Sebastian says that a young Union ultra once sneeringly called him a hipster for drinking a particular type of fizzy drink.

It is possible to overstate all this. East German identity is not monolithic, and the frictions emerging at Union were not all to do with the east-west divide. They were also driven by issues of class, wealth and lifestyle choices. But promotion did shine a light on some of the underlying tensions around Union's identity. The Fiebrigs urge a level of mutual understanding. 'Ideally people would engage with the culture, and try to understand it, instead of just looking at it from outside and saying: we don't understand that, and you should do it differently,' says Stefanie.

Sebastian puts it more succinctly: 'You don't have to be an East German to be an Unioner, but you have to understand East German.'

*   *   *

Is it better to stew in your own juices or open yourself up to the world? From the modern stadiums and controversial sponsorship deals to the wider questions of identity and demographic change, promotion reminded Union fans of what it was they thought was worth protecting. But it also gave them a platform to impose their own ideas about football on a much wider audience. The question was: would Union change the Bundesliga, or would the Bundesliga change them?

'Unioners have this missionary zeal – it's partly why some people find us annoying,' says Sebastian. 'When someone is new in the stadium, we always want to explain to them why it is so special, and why we do this and that. The experience at the Alte Försterei is so important to us, and we want to make the world aware of it. And if you accept the idea that it's like a religious service, with its own liturgy, then the idea of a mission fits quite well.'

It was Union's evangelism which stopped them from turning inwards. As they faced up to the pressures of promotion, the club attempted to strike a careful balance between the old fans and the new. Season ticket numbers were capped to give as many people as possible a chance of getting a ticket, and the club continued to make it easy for people to become members. On the terraces, meanwhile, hostility towards newcomers remained the exception, rather than the rule. At the first few Bundesliga home games, foreigners attempting to find a ticket tout at the station on matchday were less likely to be told to get lost, and more likely to be reminded not to pay over the odds. 'If you've created something extraordinary and people want to be part of it, then that's a good thing. It means you are spreading your values,' says Stefanie.

It helped that the matchday liturgy itself remained largely unchanged. The fact that the Alte Försterei was so small may have increased competition, but it also had its upsides. In a larger stadium, the difference between the new, casual fans and the more passionate supporters may have been more noticeable. But at Union, there are no posh seats to suck away the atmosphere. The nature of the stadium is such that everyone mixes with everyone on the terraces, and after promotion, the place remained as raucous as it always had been. In terms of atmosphere, Unioners could still see themselves as an example to the rest of the league.

In other ways, though, the Bundesliga also began to change them. Fan power, that other great sacrament of the Union creed, has also changed with the massive influx of new members. In previous years, the AGM had been a cosy affair held at small or medium-sized venues in Köpenick. In 2019, to allow as many members as possible to attend, it was moved to the new Verti Music Hall, a huge, modern concert venue among the neon lights of the Mercedes-Benz Arena. With a much bigger voter base, the dynamics of supporter democracy have begun to change. A larger electorate can be a strength, providing more checks and balances on the decision-makers, but it can also make democracy more cumbersome, and encourage the use of executive power.

Before those long-term questions, though, came a more immediate problem. In their first season in the top flight, the fans had a few, glorious months as the team took the Bundesliga by storm. Sensational victories over Borussia Dortmund, Borussia Mönchengladbach and city rivals Hertha kept the fire roaring in the Alte Försterei and enchanted more and more viewers around the wider world. The BBC turned up to film a game against Freiburg, and the club itself started producing a documentary which would be screened in German cinemas and on international broadcasters like BT Sport. And then, just as the gospel was being heard by more than ever before, their church was forced to shut its doors.

When the coronavirus hit in March 2020, the debate changed completely. Suddenly, the question was no longer who should be allowed into the Alte Försterei, but whether anyone should be allowed in at all.

CHAPTER 11
WE ARE THE SICK

UNION BERLIN 1–0 PADERBORN – 16 JUNE 2020

It is a warm night in June, and all is quiet in the Alte Försterei. An hour before kick-off, there is no queue at the old ticket gates, no bustle at the bratwurst stands, no sea of red on the terraces. Birdsong floats out of the woods and the stone terraces stare glumly at each other across the empty pitch. It is not normally this warm at the end of the season. The season does not normally end in mid-June. But it is 2020, and nothing is normal anymore.

For the fourth time this summer, Union are preparing for a home game in an empty stadium. Three months after the pandemic first swept into town, Berlin is still only cautiously emerging from its first lockdown. Beer gardens, restaurants and bars have been open for around a month, but most people are still working from home. With large events on hold until the autumn, the football stadiums remain decidedly shut.

As the sun sets behind the woods, the quiet feels all kinds of wrong. Football is not supposed to be played behind closed doors. In German, they call these matches 'ghost games'. In theory, they are meaningful fixtures, elite sporting clashes which can make someone's fortune or define their career. But without the spectators, the circus has been robbed of its claim to legitimacy. It exists only as a shadow, a pale imitation of the life which usually buzzes around it.

Even the sport itself feels a little ersatz. A win against bottom side Paderborn tonight, and Union will clinch survival with three games to go and guarantee themselves a second season in the top flight. It will be one of the greatest achievements in the club's history, but beyond the press, the backroom staff, and a few hangers on, nobody will be here to see it. As the old saying goes, if a tree falls in the forest...

In Köpenick, though, there are always people in the forest even if there are none on the terraces. In the last few weeks, a few dozen Union fans have been congregating outside the stadium during home games. Unable to cheer on their team from inside, they assemble in little groups on the woodland path to watch on their phones and belly-sing their support from a distance. With no other noise but the thud of the ball and the barked instructions of the coaches, the exiled fans are clearly audible from inside the stadium and have begun to raise eyebrows. The German Football League, wary that it has been given special dispensation to finish the season, has urged fans to watch from home to avoid infection. There are police patrolling the path tonight.

Not that it is much of a deterrent. As the game gets underway in the evening sunlight, the first cries of 'Eisern Union!' ring out from the canopies. They may not be allowed on the path, but they can still hide among the trees, even if that means climbing up to the higher branches. As the game grows more and more tense, the muffled cries from outside are joined by louder ones inside the stadium. Union miss a few early chances, and the substitutes jiggle around in their seats from the nerves. Up in the rafters of the main stand, the club directors yelp in agitation at every ball into the box.

On the half-hour mark, the voices settle in anticipation. The home side get a free-kick between the halfway and the eighteen-yard line, and Christopher Trimmel lopes up to take it. Union's captain and set-piece specialist has ten assists already this season, most of them from dead balls. He sends this one floating ominously into the box, where a Paderborn defender flicks it helplessly into his own net. As it nestles in the bottom corner in front of the empty away block, the substitutes spring up in triumph. A few seconds later, when the broadcast catches up with reality, a roar goes up from the forest.

For the remaining hour or so, Union string out the torture. Flooding bodies forward, they waste chance after chance. Midfielder Robert Andrich hits the post, and the Paderborn goalkeeper hurls himself in front of every shot. By the time injury time is up, the midsummer sun has long since set on Köpenick, and even dusk is fading into darkness. Striker Anthony Ujah dribbles the ball towards the corner flag and the referee blows three sharp whistles. Union are safe. They will have a second year in the Bundesliga.

The initial roar booms through the empty stands, but the flurry of celebration quickly flickers out. It is hard to keep the adrenaline pumping in an empty stadium, and as they wander around the pitch in their specially made t-shirts, the players look listless. 'Lads can you celebrate a bit please, you just avoided relegation!' shouts one of the photographers from the edge of the pitch. A handful of them do a half-hearted little dance for the cameras.

Back in the dressing room, however, they soon find their rhythm. The beer begins to flow, and slowly, the party begins to migrate outside. The fans from the forest have made their way around to the front of the stadium to cheer the players as they leave, and as midnight approaches, the players trickle out of the main stand to join them. Coach Urs Fischer takes a bow as he is given a beery guard of honour, midfielder Grischa Prömel leads the chants with a towel around his waist, and the stewards try desperately to maintain the requisite physical distancing.

They are not entirely successful. As the broadcasting truck tries to leave the car park without running over the revellers, Ujah leaps onto the back of it with a beer in hand and is given some hefty slaps on the back as he jumps off and runs back through the cheering crowd. Captain Trimmel goes one step further and celebrates arm in arm with a group of supporters. He is later fined several thousand euros for breaking the German Football League's Covid regulations.

In the cool summer night, there is a sense that this is ultimately a happy ending. Despite the worst fears two months ago, the season has not been cancelled. Union have stayed up, and when president Dirk Zingler joins the car park party shortly after midnight, he urges fans to look positively at the future. 'This season was for you; we have done this for you,' he says, before promising that a return to normal is not far away. 'We will do everything we can to make sure football can take place with fans again.'

His words are met with raucous cheers, but in time, they will prove to be far more controversial than anyone present imagines. Normal will not return for a long while yet. Union's pandemic has only just begun.

While the players were partying in the car park, club historian Gerald Karpa was rooting around in the dark for a lost ball. 'When the final whistle went, I saw that somebody booted the ball over the stand,' he says. 'So, I went down afterwards to see if I could find it. And there it was! One of the stewards had thrown it back over the fence, so I picked it up and kept it to put in the museum one day.'

The ball was his reward for some unexpected extra work. Karpa was one of many Union employees who took a step back as the club scrambled to stay afloat in the early months of the pandemic. He had been put on shorter hours via Germany's furlough scheme and had taken a holiday in June on the assumption that, as a non-essential employee, he would be expected to stay at home on matchdays. When he was asked to come to the Paderborn game, he initially refused. 'I thought it would be odd: all my friends have to be in the pub, and I get to stroll around the stadium? But Christian Arbeit persuaded me that I had to come because it was a game of historical significance,' he says.

He was not the only one who felt a bit underwhelmed by it all. From Andora to Jacob Sweetman, many of the people interviewed in this book claim they watched little of Union's final push for survival on TV in the 2019/20 season. Many, like Karpa, didn't have the right TV subscription, and with the pubs closed for much of the season, had little option but to listen on the radio or read the reports in the papers. But there was also a more fundamental question. 'Being an Unioner – a real Unioner – means going to the Alte Försterei,' says Imran Ayata. Without the stadium, the atmosphere, and the social side of things, Union simply wasn't Union anymore.

When they were worried about promotion, the last thing anyone expected was a global pandemic. But in 2020, the old curse struck again. Just as the Prague Spring and the 9/11 attacks had overshadowed Union's European successes in the past, so Covid-19 loomed over their first season in the Bundesliga. The virus changed Union more radically and more quickly than promotion alone could ever have done. In the blink of an eye, many of the things which had been considered sacred were gone: fans were shut out of the stadium, the Christmas singing was cancelled for the first time ever, and even the AGM was moved online. At a time when Union were doing better than ever on the pitch, the fans had never felt more alienated. It was as if the lifeblood of the club had been drained.

That created a dilemma. On the one hand, Union had to keep their treasured community together. On the other, they were now a club on the biggest stage, and therefore had to position themselves in an increasingly tense national debate about public health. Covid-19 coincided with the back end of Angela Merkel's long reign as Chancellor, when Germany already had a cautious eye on its future. After sixteen years of adept crisis management and consensus politics, there were fears that the country might become more unstable without the widely respected leader at the wheel. The virus fuelled those concerns and emphasised the tensions which had begun to brew in a nervy society.

While there was no mainstream political opposition to restrictions or vaccinations in Germany, that didn't mean the conversation couldn't get heated. In a system where rules differed from state to state, there could be blazing rows over the minutiae of public policy. How many people could sit at a table in a restaurant? Were non-prioritised people jumping the queue for vaccination? What percentage of the capacity of a football stadium was morally justifiable? At times, the temperature of public debate rose to almost un-German levels.

'Having rational discussions became more difficult in the pandemic. You'd try to explain in a calm and matter-of-fact way why you had a different opinion on something, and people would shout at you,' says club spokesman Christian Arbeit. 'We had to follow our own compass.'

Union did what they had always done: they prioritised the stadium-going fans. At a time when stadiums were empty, that meant trying to keep the sense of community alive as much as possible. It meant taking fan-friendly positions in the bigger debates about how football should deal with the crisis. And ultimately, it meant trying to find ways to get supporters back into the stadium.

But at a time when the whole world was adjusting to a new normal, Union's fan-first approach didn't go down well with everybody. On the pitch, things kept getting better for Union. Off it, the club's approach to the pandemic saw them faced with growing media criticism and internal tensions within their own fanbase. As they tried to adjust their identity to top-flight football, Covid-19 turned up the heat even further.

*   *   *

Union's pandemic began with a fan protest. On 1 March 2020, a 2–2 draw at home to Wolfsburg was almost abandoned after a controversial banner was raised on the terraces. It showed red sniper crosshairs imposed on a picture of a face. The face belonged to Dietmar Hopp, a software billionaire who owned mid-table Bundesliga club TSG Hoffenheim. The banner was part of a coordinated demonstration in stadiums across Germany.

Hopp, whose money had turned village club Hoffenheim into a major force, had long been a bogeyman for football traditionalists. In the previous decade, he had been engaged in a long-running feud with Borussia Dortmund fans, who had voiced their disapproval of his methods with insulting chants and the ominous crosshairs banner. The dispute escalated in early 2020, when the DFB ruled that Dortmund fans would be banned from Hoffenheim for two years for displaying the banner, reneging on a previous pledge to abandon collective punishments for supporters. Fan groups across the country began to protest in solidarity with anti-Hopp banners, and when the club hierarchy at Bayern Munich decided to defend Hopp and condemn their own fans, German football descended into full-blown class war. The end of February and the beginning of March were marked by angry arguments between the suits and the supporters over freedom of speech and the right to protest.

At this point, the pandemic seemed to be a sideshow. The word 'lockdown' had not yet entered the German vocabulary, and nobody in the stadium for the game against Wolfsburg realised that this would be their last visit to the Alte Försterei for months. Some fans had brought bottles of hand saniiser with them, but very few had stayed away for fear of infection. It wasn't until later that evening that the headlines announced the first positive coronavirus test recorded in Berlin. The Hopp protests, not the virus, were the biggest crisis facing German football.

But events soon caught up with the Bundesliga. On 11 March, the day the World Health Organisation declared a global pandemic, Hanover's Timo Hübers became the first German footballer to test positive, and Cologne and Borussia

Mönchengladbach played the first ever German top-flight game held behind closed doors. Union, who were due to play three days later in a long-awaited first home clash against champions Bayern Munich, were also ordered to close their stadium. A few days later, the game was called off entirely as the entire league season and life as everyone knew it was put on hold. That weekend, instead of manning the football stadiums, police officers strolled through the streets of Kreuzberg at midnight closing the bars.

The fact that the Hopp protests were so fresh in the mind was important because it informed how football fans reacted to lockdown. Already deep in an ideological squabble with the millionaires at the top of the game, the ultras carried on in the same vein once the virus became the main issue. One might expect football fans to be devastated to see matches cancelled, but in Germany, supporters had actively been campaigning for exactly that. 'No football in Covid times!' ran the headline in a statement by the Union ultras on 13 March. The only reason to keep playing behind closed doors, they argued, would be to keep the TV money flowing into the pockets of those at the top. 'Money seems to be more important than the people,' wrote the ultras, urging the league to suspend the season.

The decision to do so happened that very afternoon, and the fans immediately began pouring their efforts into community action. Union ultras hung banners on railway bridges with messages of support for key workers and set up a donations fence at the Tanke beer garden, for those struggling to get hold of key goods. The club, meanwhile, did its best to maintain a sense of community going while everyone was shut away in their own homes. Under the slogan 'Waiting for Union', they organised an endless series of virtual activities including watch parties of past games, virtual mask-making workshops and 'Union Yoga' videos. As the players took a wage cut and many employees were put on to Germany's reduced hours furlough scheme, the club also turned to the fans for help, encouraging them to buy virtual beer and sausages on the club shop website to make up for lost matchday revenues.

But state aid and fan generosity were not long-term solutions, and slowly, clubs began to sound the alarm and demand that the league be resumed in some form. Once again, the fans protested. To them, games behind closed doors stood for everything they hated about modern football. It was the absurd logic of a system which prioritised TV profits over stadium-going fans. 'The game is already sick and it should stay in quarantine,' wrote the Union ultras in another statement rejecting the proposed restart in April 2020. To allow professional football when pubs and schools remained shut and thousands of people were out of work would be insensitive, they argued. 'Restarting the Bundesliga season would be plain insulting to the rest of society, and particularly to those who are really serving others.'

For once, the public agreed with them. Why should millionaire footballers be allowed to pursue their profession when ordinary people could not? In Germany, when somebody is given special treatment, people talk about them being given 'an extra sausage'. In 2020, most people felt that football already had its fair share of sausages and shouldn't be given any more. A poll in May showed that almost two thirds of Germans thought the Bundesliga season should simply be cancelled.

But Germany is a country where sausages are plentiful and cold economic logic tends to prevail. Whatever the ultras and the public said, the clubs still needed the TV broadcasting income, and that would only be guaranteed if the season was continued. Eventually, the politicians relented. In mid-May, just days after restaurants and bars had been allowed to reopen in Berlin, the Bundesliga became the first major European league to restart.

For Union, that meant a dilemma. Through all the changes of the previous years, the club's guiding principle had always been to put stadium-going fans first. But how did you apply that to an empty stadium? Elsewhere, clubs were putting up cardboard cut-out fans or decorative tarpaulin to cover the empty seats. When matches were shown on TV, broadcasters piped in fake crowd noise to make it feel more normal. These practices were largely welcomed by sports fans around the world, but for German football ultras, they were sacrilegious. They saw them as another sign that professional sport cared only about the TV product, and that the ordinary stadium-going fan had become expendable, even commodified.

Union were broadly sympathetic to this view, and while the club did not object to the restart, they did approach the ghost games with a kind of pious austerity. Rather than decorating their stands, they made a point of leaving the terraces completely untouched. Unlike other clubs, they also decided not to make announcements over the tannoy to an empty stadium. 'We didn't want to simulate normality,' Christian Arbeit later told Swiss newspaper *NZZ*.

As it turned out, they didn't even need to simulate an atmosphere. Right from the beginning of the restart, Union fans began to make regular pilgrimages to the woodland path behind the Alte Försterei. At almost every home game in the last few weeks of the 2019/20 season, there were at least a few dozen fans out in the woods, shouting as loudly as they possibly could to spur the team on to survival.

But this was only a short-term fix, and there was a sense that something had to give. With other parts of the economy opening in the summer of 2020, the club began to explore ways to bring the lifeblood back into the Alte Försterei. And that put them on a collision course with a lot of other people.

WE ARE THE SICK

'We are Unioners. We are the sick ones. We break through all barriers,' goes a line in one of the most popular terrace chants at the Alte Försterei. Sick, in this case, means a bit mad, a bit wild, and until the pandemic, it was generally considered a good thing.

In a crisis where consensus is king, however, the rebel spirit earns you fewer plaudits. When the barriers are supposed to be self-imposed, attempting to knock them down is frowned upon. In a city like Berlin, where rules are often interpreted somewhat liberally, many people had to recalibrate their idea of right and wrong after Covid-19 hit. It is one thing to ignore a smoking ban or travel on public transport without a ticket, but in a pandemic the line between the allowed and the acceptable becomes harder to draw.

Union found that out the hard way. In mid to late 2020, their policy of putting stadium-going fans first often put them at odds with the prevailing consensus, and that in turn led to a notable shift in the media narrative around the club. When they were promoted in 2019, they had been everyone's favourite underdog. By the end of 2020, they were more like the Bundesliga's pantomime villain.

It began in March 2020, in the week before Germany first went into lockdown. The full extent of the crisis was beginning to sink in across the country, and the Bundesliga was already gearing up for games behind closed doors. When Health Minister Jens Spahn suggested that all mass events be called off, Union reacted spikily. 'Herr Spahn hasn't recommended that BMW shut its production line, and he can't recommend that we close down our business,' said president Dirk Zingler. The point he was making, that professional football was as much a part of the economy as anything else, was not unreasonable. But in the fraught atmosphere of that week, it did not go down well. Zingler's comments were seen in some quarters as typical of an incompetent and contrary capital city. 'Does Berlin think it is immune from the virus?' sniffed Hamburg-based news magazine *Der Spiegel*. 'Once again, our capital is a source of shame.'

In terms of media coverage, that early altercation set the tone for the rest of Union's pandemic. On 10 July 2020, after six weeks of empty stadiums, the club formally announced their intention to return to a full stadium from the first day of the 2020/21 season by organising mass testing for their fans. They were once again met with a wave of criticism. Shadow Health Minister Karl Lauterbach said he thought Union's plan was 'untenable', while local conservative politician Tim-Christopher Zeelen called it 'almost grotesque'.

The club were somewhat taken aback. They had not foreseen that even the suggestion of re-opening would be so controversial. 'We were completely convinced of what we were proposing,' says Christian Arbeit, who as club spokesman, shouldered most of the opprobrium. 'At that point, we could never have imagined that the lockdowns would last as long as they did. We thought there would be much more pressure to come up with safe concepts for getting back to school and putting on events again.'

But while football fans were by now desperate to get back into stadiums, the wider public was more conservative. Returning to school was one thing, but beyond a small group of extremists, there was little ideological opposition to lockdown measures. Even in the less dangerous summer months, Germany tended to maintain a more cautious footing than some of its neighbours. There was never a 'freedom day' on which all restrictions were suspended, and even smaller measures like the mask mandate were more stringent. Less than a year into the pandemic, cloth masks were deemed no longer sufficient as face coverings, and medical-grade masks became compulsory.

In hindsight, Union's proposal seems relatively uncontroversial. According to the detailed plan they unveiled to journalists later that summer, the club would pay for every ticket holder to take a PCR test, allowing them to safely forgo masks and physical distancing in a full stadium. As Arbeit points out, it was a model which was considered acceptable just months later. But in August 2020, when vaccines and mass testing were still not widely available to the general public, it seemed radical.

That meant criticism, of both the very substantial and the slightly more hysterical kind. According to one old football joke, Germany is a country with eighty million national team managers. In the pandemic, it became a country of eighty million virologists. Suddenly, football journalists were quizzing club directors about the risk of airborne infection in a packed tube train.

Crucially, Union failed to drum up the political will to implement their plan. 'We had meetings with the politicians and with the Charité university hospital,' says Arbeit. 'There were people even at that point who were saying: this is all workable, but it's too early. Not because it's impractical, or wrong, or would be better in six months' time, but just because the mood isn't right at the moment.'

In a city where events are a significant part of the economy, Union perhaps thought the mood might be different. According to Berlin's Club Commission, nightlife tourists generated an estimated 1.5 billion euros in 2018. That income flow had been almost wiped out by the pandemic, and when they announced their concept Union openly stated that they hoped it could be a game changer for the entire events sector. But while more high-class organisations such as the Berlin Philharmonic were hailed for similar trial projects just a few months later, Union's proposal was met with scepticism: the mayor of Berlin

Michael Müller said there were 'high hurdles'; a director at Borussia Mönchengladbach said Union should show humility; and the editor of a leading football magazine accused them of wantonly putting their own fans' health at risk. A narrative was beginning to emerge that Union had never taken the pandemic seriously.

The tension between the club and their critics reached its crux in the autumn, by which point stadiums had been reopened at reduced capacity. With infections rising in the capital and a second lockdown looming, the city changed the rules in October 2020 to ban singing at mass events. When Union failed to implement this rule at a friendly match, they were once again slammed, with *Der Tagesspiegel* claiming that 'Union only abide by laws they agree with' and accusing the club of 'arrogance'. They pointedly enforced the rule at the next home game, encouraging fans to bring pots and pans from home so they could still support the team without singing. On one of the strangest and most uplifting afternoons ever witnessed at the Alte Försterei, Union battled to a 1–1 draw with Freiburg to a cacophony of clanging, rattling and drumming from the 4,500 fans on the terraces.

Ultimately, this was less an issue of right and wrong, and more one of communication. Having only been promoted the previous year, Union were still getting used to the fact that they were now in the spotlight, and that every tiny comment and inflection was subject to scrutiny. 'The way things are perceived when you say something as a Bundesliga club is totally different to when you are in the second division. That's something we realised,' admits Arbeit. He goes as far as to suggest that, in a football culture which is still heavily focused on big West German clubs, Union's success was always going to rub people up the wrong way. 'It was OK when we were little and cute in the second tier, but in the Bundesliga we are a real threat. If we stick around, we are taking away a spot which would otherwise be for a Werder Bremen or a Schalke. And then we're no fun anymore.'

But as the pandemic dragged on, it was not just Union's media image which came under strain because of their stadium policies. It was also the relationship between the club and their fans.

* * *

Without the Alte Försterei, Unioners were further away from each other than they had ever been. 'The people I stand with on the Waldseite... it always seemed like our lives were so intertwined,' says Jacob Sweetman. 'But when the stadiums were empty, I kept wondering what it was going to be like when we went back. Who would be there? Would we come back more divided?'

This was arguably the biggest concern for Union. From the very start, the club's approach had been to put fans first, and even when they had faced widespread criticism for doing so, they had been happy to stick to their guns and go against the grain. But what if the fans themselves were divided? Union's fanbase was now bigger than it had ever been, and opinions on Covid-19 policies differed as much as they did in society at large. If some fans thought one thing and others thought another, who did you put first then?

By the autumn of 2021, the state of public debate in the whole country had become more fraught, and the spirit of solidarity from the early months had long since given way to low-level suspicion and anxiety. Germany's vaccine rollout, which was initially slow in comparison to the UK, the US and Israel, caused a lot of pearl-clutching in a country which hates disorder and loves to self-deprecate. A few months later, the relatively low uptake in comparison with countries like Italy and Spain prompted a more fundamental divide. Case numbers had been comparatively low for much of the summer, but as they began to rise in the autumn, the conversation over vaccine hesitancy became more emotive. When Bayern Munich and Germany midfielder Joshua Kimmich admitted in October 2021 that he had not yet been vaccinated, football was once again thrust onto the front line of the debate. At Union, the vaccine issue briefly threatened to polarise the fanbase.

At the beginning of the 2021/22 season, Bundesliga stadiums were beginning to move towards a point where they were allowed to hold games at full capacity. But where Union had once been the first club to demand a full stadium, they were now one of the last to make it happen. Rules still differed from state to state, and in Berlin there were two options. If the stadium was full, every ticket holder had to be vaccinated or recovered. If it was at reduced capacity, they could simply show a recent negative test.

To the surprise and anger of many fans, Union consistently plumped for the latter option, keeping their stadium half-empty so that unjabbed fans could continue to come to games. Their argument was that shutting the unvaccinated out of public life would only deepen already dangerous societal divisions. But as reduced capacity made it even harder to get hold of tickets, many fans who had received the jab asked why they should be punished to pander to the unvaccinated.

On one level, this merely reflected the wider discussion in Germany, and was a precursor to the debate over vaccine mandates that would grip the country in early 2022. Essentially, it was a question of ethics, a weighing up of freedoms and rights of the individual against those of the collective. In the case of Union, you could reduce it to a mathematical sum. If the vast majority of Unioners were vaccinated, was it legitimate to reduce their chances of getting a ticket by almost fifty per cent to protect the rights of the very small minority who weren't?

It was a question which caused noticeable friction within the Union fanbase. In October 2021, ahead of a game against Wolfsburg, Dirk Zingler made a surprise appearance at the pre-match press conference. 'I am vaccinated. My family is vaccinated. Ninety per cent of people who work here are vaccinated. Everyone at the club thinks vaccination is an important part of getting out of the pandemic,' he said. The fact that he even had to say it, the fact that he was even there, spoke volumes. The 'Union family', as he so often called it, was divided, and he knew it: 'We recognise that this is an issue which gets people going. The Union community is no different to society in that sense.'

Amid growing impatience among the vaccinated and an increasingly extreme anti-vaxxer movement, this was a difficult tightrope to tread. Zingler made it clear that he felt the state was abdicating responsibility onto event organisers instead of making clear rules one way or the other, and he stuck to his guns. He pointed out that the city government's mobile vaccination bus would park outside the ground on matchday, which he argued was more constructive than simply shutting unvaccinated fans out of the ground. But that argument was not enough to placate his critics, and the debate rumbled on for another few weeks.

Textilvergehen blogger Sebastian Fiebrig, admits that the mood became more fraught as the pandemic wore on. 'The discussions became a lot more emotional because everyone had their own experience of Covid,' he says.

For Fiebrig, part of the reason why many fans felt aggrieved by the club's position was simple lack of communication. 'The fans were generally more out in the cold,' he says. During the pandemic, there were fewer opportunities for contact and direct discussion with people like Zingler. As well as the AGMs being online, the regular fan councils had taken place far more sporadically. 'Internal discussions were much more fragmented, and that meant a lot of people didn't understand why certain decisions were being made,' he says. The culture of community and conversation had always been kept alive first and foremost by the physical act of going to games. In the pandemic, it was shifted into the altogether more toxic sphere of social media, and that meant the Union community also split into its various echo chambers.

Online debate, after all, lives off polarisation. Without regular social contact, differences of opinion seemed sharper than they had before. As everywhere, the worst were full of passionate intensity, and the best simply logged out. On *Textilvergehen* Fiebrig noted both the tone becoming rawer in the comments and the readership figures dropping as the pandemic wore on. 'I assume it's because it was no longer a part of their social day-to-day,' he says. 'That social aspect – experiencing football together – is very important. The sport alone isn't enough for people. Especially at Union, it's not the quality of the football which means 20,000 people make this the focal point of their lives.'

In some ways, the divisions the club were facing only confirmed their broad position that the stadium-going fan is king. Without the social side of things and the physical act of going to the Alte Försterei, Union were at risk of losing something essential. Watching on TV, their fans were merely football fans at a small-to-medium-sized German club. For their famous sense of community and solidarity to endure, they had to be in the stadium.

* * *

If the vaccine debate had been allowed to fester, it may have done more damage to the Union community. Fortunately for the club, it was quickly made irrelevant by the pace of the pandemic. As infection rates began to rise again in late 2021, the Berlin government moved to effectively ban the unvaccinated from mass events. That took the decision about whether to let them in out of the club's hands and paved the way for a return to full capacity.

The Alte Försterei finally returned to its former glory at a derby against Hertha in November 2021, with 22,000 fans cramming onto the terraces for the first time since the beginning of the pandemic twenty months earlier. Once again, there was criticism from outside, but inside the stadium, it felt like something was healing. As they cooked up the usual eardrum-bursting atmosphere, the Unioners could forget for a moment the divisions and strains of the previous two years.

It helped that they had something to cheer about. An early goal from Taiwo Awoniyi and a superb long-range strike from captain Christopher Trimmel put Union on their way to a comfortable victory over their city neighbours, prompting delirious scenes in the packed-out stadium. It was only one result, but as the win pushed Hertha towards the relegation zone and Union towards the top four, it was hard not to see it as a changing of the guard.

Union had always been the underdogs, and they had always been the East Berlin club. In 2021, they had a claim to being the biggest club in Berlin, a city which was moving further away from its historic division. Since promotion in 2019, they had gone from strength to strength, avoiding relegation in their first season in the Bundesliga and qualifying for the newly created Europa Conference League in their second. As crowds trickled back into grounds in the autumn, the fans who did get into the stadium were treated to thrilling European ties and ever more sensational wins over superior opposition. Midway through the 2021/22 season, Union were briefly considered genuine contenders for a Champions League spot. This was dreamland, and a great antidote to the troubles of the pandemic.

'I was stuck in this state of euphoria for a while. I kept thinking that Covid was like a dementor, sucking all the life and the joy out of everything, and Union were my patronus,' says Sebastian Fiebrig, referring to the magical creature summoned by Harry Potter to ward off the soul-sucking baddies. He was not the only one who had developed a taste for winning. Soon, the idea that Union had once feared going up started to fade as the club began to dream of ever more success. The pandemic had raised similar questions to the ones raised by promotion. They were questions about whom Union belonged to, about the club's own values and responsibilities to society, about how the club adapted to success and attention, and what that meant for its relationship to the city.

But Covid-19 also focused minds, reminding Union fans of what it was they held most dear. It turned out that it was not success that they feared, but the loss of community. It was the human interaction and the sheer thrill of the stadium experience which had made Union special over the previous half a century. And it was that which was worth protecting as the club moved into a new era.

The pandemic had shaken Union. But just like every other major upheaval they had endured in the past it had not broken them. The present was bright. The question now was how to shape the future.

CHAPTER 12
FUTURE MUSIC

UNION BERLIN 1–1 SLAVIA PRAGUE – 9 DECEMBER 2021

The Olympiastadion leaks cold. When the Nazis designed it for the notorious 1936 Olympics, they put it at the centre of a bombastic east-to-west axis, flanked by a huge parade ground on one side and a vast expanse of concrete on the other. Aside from a couple of fascist sculptures, there is nothing to break the Siberian winds as they sweep through the limestone columns and down into the stadium bowl. When the stadium is half-empty, which it usually is, it is even harder to stay warm.

On this night, Covid restrictions mean there are only five thousand spectators, less than a tenth of the full capacity. The eastern curve, home to the Hertha ultras and normally the loudest part of the ground, is empty. This time, Union are the home team, and most of their fans are huddled into the northern curve of the arena. They wear hats, ski jackets and several layers of scarves around their necks. The snow, already lying thick on the ground outside, blusters in under the stadium roof.

On the other side of the pitch, people the size of ants cluster around the dugouts and cameras on the home straight of the running track. One of them, Union president Dirk Zingler, is giving a TV interview ahead of kick-off. He too wears a red-and-white woollen scarf to protect himself from the cold. At around three metres long, it seems to swallow his head when he wears it wrapped around his neck. But he would be wearing it even if it was a baking hot day in summer. Zingler's grandmother knitted it for him when he first started going to Union in the 1970s. Nowadays, he only gets it out for special occasions.

Zingler's voice crackles a little as he tries to tell the TV reporter what this game means. When he took over as president seventeen years ago, Union were about to be relegated into the fourth division. Now, they are one win away from the knockout stages of a European competition. They have already won two of their five games in the Conference League this season. If they beat Slavia tonight, they are through.

It would be nice if they had real home advantage, admits Zingler. The Alte Försterei has too few seats to comply with UEFA regulations, so Union have had to rent Hertha's ground from the city and play their home ties in an unfamiliar stadium. Even now, three or four games in, it is still a strange sight to see Union fans swarming over the Olympiastadion and the blue running track covered with red tarpaulin. In many ways though, it is also the perfect metaphor for an upside-down world. This city only has one stadium big enough for European competition, because traditionally, it has only had one club big enough for European competition. Only Hertha have the money, the squad, the infrastructure to make playing in Europe a legitimate prospect. But it is not they who have made it this far. It is Union.

Union don't make it any further. A misplaced back pass from Timo Baumgartl allows Slavia to take the lead in the second half, and though Max Kruse bundles in an equaliser shortly afterwards, it is too little, too late. A 1–1 draw is not enough, and the European dream dies a slow death of cold in the Advent snow. But even as the disappointment soaks in, the players and coaching staff already start to talk about qualifying for Europe again next season. 'Playing in these competitions makes you want more,' says Urs Fischer at the post-match press conference. He is not the only one who feels there is more to come from this team.

As for the Olympiastadion, Union will be back in just a few weeks' time for a cup tie against Hertha in mid-January. It will be no less cold by then, and Union will be the away team. But after another year in which they have outshone their city rivals even in their own stadium, they will at least be favourites.

When Union reached the Bundesliga in 2019, Dirk Zingler was in the toilet. As the clock ticked down on the promotion play-off, his wife got up from her seat in the VIP box and disappeared into the main stand. With a few minutes to go, Zingler followed her. He later told reporters that when the final whistle went, he was in the gents and she was in the ladies, both shaking with nerves.

'It's true that I didn't see the referee blow the whistle. I just heard the celebration. And then we could finally relax,' he tells me, his eyes flashing at the memory. 'I was here in the 1990s, when there were only 700 or 1,000 people on the terraces. To have gone through that and now to be in the Bundesliga… that was something special.'

Zingler is that rare thing in modern football: a club director who is also a genuine fan. The scarf his grandmother knitted him, the one he hauls out for special occasions, is not just an affectation. There are pictures of him wearing it as a teenager, along with a stripey jumper and a Beatles fringe. Even now, in his comfortable seat in the VIP box, he still swears and sweats his way through games as if he were standing on the terraces. When we meet a few hours before the decisive Conference League game against Slavia Prague, he has the twitchy anticipation of a child on cup final day.

Our interview takes place in the real Alte Försterei, the little forester's cottage which gives the stadium its name. The small detached house looks unremarkable from the main road. Were it not for the signpost outside advertising the next home game and the enormous stadium car park behind it, it could pass for a family home or a village hall. On the outside, the walls are white with neat rows of red-shuttered windows, and the roof is steep and tiled. Inside, the corridors are narrow and the heating is at full blast. Only the fire safety card on the door and the metal grips on the steps indicate that it is an institutional building. In the back yard, an enormous Christmas tree blocks the view of the stadium.

When the stadium expansion finally goes ahead, Zingler may yet move into a more modern, spacious office. But for now, he is here, running a football club from an attic room in a Dickensian cottage with sloping ceilings and low doorways. This is to other club offices what the Alte Försterei is to the modern arenas – cramped and impractical, yet endlessly more fun.

In many ways, the office fits the president. Union have only been headquartered here since the forester moved out in the mid-2000s, but it is still a place drenched in the history of the club, right back to when Union Oberschöneweide first moved next door in the 1920s. Zingler has lived through almost half of that history. He started going not long after Andora in the early 1970s, and he kept coming through the yo-yo years of the 1980s and the financial chaos of the 1990s. He became president in 2004, the same year he helped to bail out the club during the Bleed for Union campaign. When he moved his office into the forester's house a few years later, it was the symbolic start of a process which would culminate with the fans volunteering to renovate the stadium. Zingler's attic room is a product of Union's past, but it is also where he built Union's present.

Now, though, his challenge is the future. If Union's success has given many of their fans altitude sickness, then it is Zingler who has often soothed their stomach. His mixture of business pragmatism and bolshy fan populism has proven remarkably successful over the last two decades, and he is now one of the longest-serving club directors in German football. Yet despite being a seasoned campaigner in league politics, he has also maintained a reputation for being a firebrand rather than an establishment figure. For many fans, his presence is a welcome guarantee that Union are still Union. But it remains a constant balancing act. The higher Union rise, the more their success begins to raise bigger questions about their identity, and how it will change in the coming years.

First, there is a question of supremacy in the city. The European nights in the Olympiastadion and the derby wins in the Alte Försterei were signs that, for the first time ever, Union have a genuine chance of overtaking Hertha as the primary footballing power in Berlin. Even drawing level with their neighbours opens a previously unthinkable question. Typically, the two clubs have drawn from very different milieus at geographically and historically opposite ends of the city. But as their memberships grow and the city continues to merge, that could both redraw the battle lines and open old wounds between East and West.

Even in their own backyard, the club face a changing landscape. The Tesla factory and the new airport are expected to bring new industries and jobs to the south-east of Berlin, and Union will need to find their place in that transformation. A football club which has traditionally fetishised humility and tradition is about to become next-door neighbours with Elon Musk. The dreaded influx of new fans is likely to speed up rather than slow down when they too expand their stadium.

Above all, it is a question about soul. As the city changes, will Union also change beyond recognition? Will they smooth their own edges until they are a pale imitation of what they once were, as some Berlin institutions have? Or will they, like others have managed, keep some of the old spirit alive in a brave new world? Is success worth it, or does going up ultimately just turn everything to *Scheisse*? Sitting in his little office in the Christmas cottage, Dirk Zingler is the man who must answer these questions, one way or another.

* * *

The dream of the Bundesliga had always lingered in the background of Zingler's presidency. When he took the reins in 2004, his fellow directors had just published a new roadmap for the club which, among other things, set the aim of top-flight football by 2010. 'We screwed that up,' he jokes, admitting that in hindsight it was perhaps a little optimistic. 'We were essentially all people who had no idea about football. We were business people and we were fans. We knew that we had to sort out the infrastructure and the finances first, and then start worrying about the football.'

Sorting out the infrastructure also meant consolidating the structures of fan power which are still cherished today. Many of the board members who have served under Zingler are, like him, lifelong Unioners. It was they who ensured fan representation on the supervisory board and brought supporter organisations like the *V.I.R.U.S.* closer into the bosom of the club. 'We're not professional sports administrators who do it for the wages and then go to a different club further down the line. We are club members working in honorary roles. That's why there is still no club in German football where the members have more of a say than they do at Union,' he says.

How long that will last is another matter. A week before our interview, Zingler oversaw a members' AGM with a whiff of acrimony, as some fans accused him of trying to water down the democratic structures of the club. The nub of the issue was a shift in the way proposed changes to the statutes were processed: entirely arcane to the outsider but important enough to get a certain type of German hot under the collar. Critics of the board suggested that the club leadership was becoming monarchical, and that Union was transforming from 'a club led by members' to a 'membership led by the club'.

Perhaps this is simply what happens when your electorate doubles in size over the space of a few years. Zingler admits that success has broadened the gap between the ordinary members and those at the top. 'Obviously there is a certain distance which is going to develop when you are talking about a 100-million-euro organisation with 300 employees,' he protests. As president, he sees his first duty as being to the organisation and the people who work for it, not to individual members or a broader ideology of fan power. 'Most of our 40,000 members understand that. A few hundred don't,' he says.

This is the spikiness which can rub some people up the wrong way. His tongue is certainly sharp, especially towards his critics. You get the feeling he enjoys taking positions which are just slightly at odds with the general mood, which is part of the reason for his often divisive public image. But there is also a lightness to his retorts, a sense of humour which he is sometimes not given credit for. And he is right that, within the club, the majority would follow him to the ends of the earth.

Where there have been hiccups before, Zingler has always ridden them out. The largest of them came in 2011, amid controversy about his relationship to the socialist regime in the GDR. As a young man in the 1980s he had done his military service at the Felix Dzerzhinsky Guards Regiment, a paramilitary wing of the Stasi. At a club with Union's history, that was naturally controversial. Unlike other high-profile East Germans whose past has been pored over in public, Zingler had not been outed as a Stasi operative or even an informer. 'I just stood guard at a government hospital for three years. It was a boring job,' he told *11 Freunde* magazine. But his critics insisted that to be selected for that regiment he would still have had to be considered particularly loyal to the regime.

To be fair, Zingler is frank about having worked within the system. His grandfather had been a high-ranking trade union official in the GDR, and he was a trained metalworker who later became a unionist himself. 'I have always been someone who gets involved wherever I find myself and try to improve things for the people around me. That was true in the GDR, and it is true now,' he says, when I ask about his relationship to the regime. Under socialism, he says, he worked with the authorities to improve workers' conditions. Under capitalism, he started a construction materials business to create jobs for people. 'The political system is irrelevant if you are someone who wants to effect change.'

All of this echoes the debate which historians have been having about East German socialism for decades. Some see the GDR as an illegitimate state, whose people can be put into neat categories of victim, perpetrator, and collaborator. Others argue that, though deeply flawed and oppressive, the relationship between state and people was far more complex than that. 'There were arseholes then and there are arseholes now,' says Zingler. 'Socialism didn't work in Germany. It collapsed. But it is annoying when people conflate the failed system with the actions of the people who lived in it.'

Whatever one thinks of Zingler's past, he is undoubtedly a people person. He only gives face-to-face interviews, is contemptuous of social media, and frequently walks around the ground chatting to fans in the hours before a game. The fact that most Union fans were untroubled by his indirect links to the Stasi is testament to how much trust his hands-on style of leadership has created. The fans know how much they owe him, and he knows how to get them onside.

'People are always at the heart of it for us. That is true of our stadium concept, but it's also a more general thing about humanism: how we get along with each other,' he says. 'Football clubs are reflective of the whole of society. At Union, we have people from the far left to the far right, triple-jabbed people and unvaccinated people. That means we have responsibility, and the one thing we demand from people is to respect basic, humanist values.'

Appealing to humanist values may not be much use when it comes down to a bitter argument over vaccination or the intricacies of the club statutes, but Zingler is relaxed about the internal squabbles. 'The bigger we become, the higher the demands on us will be, and that will create the odd discussion. That is completely normal,' he says. He is adamant that the club is still very much in touch with its base. Nothing has changed since 2004, because Union is still run by people like him, he argues. 'That political stability is really important, and we have had it for many, many years. We come from this region. This is our club. And that makes the club strong. You don't see that very much elsewhere.'

*   *   *

When Zingler says 'this region', he doesn't mean the sandy plains of Brandenburg which divide central Germany from the Polish border. Nor does he really mean Berlin, a city still divided by its own history three decades on from the Wall. He means Köpenick, and at a push, everything geographically east of the Brandenburg Gate. The rest of the city counts as 'elsewhere'. When Union hosted Slavia, Feyenoord and Maccabi Haifa in the Olympiastadion, their fans talked about going on an 'away trip' to Charlottenburg. Hertha's ground is in another district of the same city, but it may as well be in a different town entirely.

'We are an East Berlin club,' says Zingler. He sees that as a geographical fact, but also a social and historical one. 'Everything that happens in Berlin and in Germany happens in the context of the fractures this country and this city have experienced.'

There is an argument that, as Union get more successful and their fanbase grows, they should adapt their identity to reflect the whole of the city. Other Berlin sports clubs have already set a precedent for such a transformation. The Eisbären ice hockey team have moved from the outskirts to the city centre and divorced themselves from their previous identity as EHC Dynamo, a sister club of Union's hated rivals BFC. The city's biggest handball team began life as a branch of a local club in Reinickendorf, north-western Berlin, and now play at a venue in the east under the name of Füchse Berlin. Zingler, though, insists that this is not a path Union should ever go down. 'We always get people suggesting we should do something similar, and most of them have no idea about us or the city,' he says. 'Why would we want to be a club for the whole of Berlin? There are clubs who want that, and you see what happens. They end up without any clear identity at all.'

That is a not-so-subtle dig at their nearest footballing rivals. Unlike Union, Hertha have often tried to position themselves as a club for the whole city, and that approach has only sharpened since Union were promoted. When multi-millionaire investor Lars Windhorst arrived at Hertha in 2019, he declared his intention to transform a chronic underperformer into a 'Big City Club'. The phrase soon became a running joke as Hertha sacked five coaches in the next two years and remained in lower mid-table despite significant investment in their squad.

The gap between expectation and reality seemed to echo Berlin's own hubris. Hertha were the footballing embodiment of a city which had pretensions to being like London or Paris, but was also incapable of building an international airport. When Union cruised to a 2–0 win in the derby in November 2021 and knocked Hertha out of the cup a few months later, it seemed significant: Hertha had spent around 150 million euros on their squad in the previous two years, around six times as much as Union; Hertha had nearly forty years of top-flight experience, Union had just two; Hertha were the club for the whole city,

Union were the upstarts from the suburbs; yet Union were the better team, with the clearer vision both on and off the pitch.

In a city so marked by division and with such distinct districts, Union's strength was perhaps that they avoided spreading themselves too thinly. 'Berlin is such a big city, with four million people in it,' says Zingler. 'Nobody can claim to speak for the whole city. Not even the mayor, because even the mayor has only been voted in by about a third of them. Berlin is diverse, it's colourful, and it's full of fractures and differences. That is what makes it what it is.'

But if nobody can speak for the whole of Berlin, does that still mean the city remains divided? Union's first season in the Bundesliga, the first ever with two top-flight Berlin clubs, coincided with the thirtieth anniversary of the fall of the Wall. But their respective attitudes towards the anniversary could not have been more different. Hertha suggested that, as a symbolic gesture, the first derby should be held on 9 November, the day the Wall was toppled. Union flatly rejected the idea. A derby, Zingler argued, was not about unity, but about differences and 'footballing class war'. Not for the first time, he was accused of stoking the fires of east-west resentment. He disputes this. 'Half of my family grew up in Wedding, in West Berlin. I know exactly what division meant, and I know what reunification meant. But Hertha's suggestion would only have been serious if we were friends with them. And we're not.'

The one-time friendship between Union and Hertha fans had long faded by 2019, and promotion buried it for good. The first derby in the Bundesliga, played a week before the Wall anniversary at the Alte Försterei, was marred by ugly scenes from start to finish. Hertha fans repeatedly fired rockets onto the pitch and into the home crowd, while Union ultras burned blue-and-white flags in their block. When the away fans began to target the dugouts with their fireworks, a group of Union ultras in balaclavas attempted to cross the pitch and confront them and were only stopped by a heroic intervention from the Union players.

But beyond the football rivalry and the excess of testosterone, there was also a more profound divide. When the anniversary of the fall of the Wall did roll around, it was marked very differently in the former East and the former West. While Union let it pass almost without comment, Hertha fell over themselves to mark it at a home game against RB Leipzig. Before kick-off, they played Ronald Reagan's famous Brandenburg Gate speech and David Bowie's 'Heroes' over the tannoy, as fans pushed over a huge replica of the Wall which had been erected on the halfway line. Zingler shakes his head at the memory. 'We live in an ever more superficial society, in which everything is about images and how things look, not how they actually are,' he says.

It is a familiar gripe. The official version of history reduces the fall of the Wall to a symbol, a single moment of joy at the end of division and dictatorship. That is not wrong, but it does tend to overshadow the lived experience of East Germans both before and after the Wall. To his critics, Zingler was a killjoy by talking about difference and class war on the anniversary when he could have been talking about unity and togetherness. He counters that anyone who thinks Germany is no longer divided is deceiving themselves. 'The division is still there because people have been socialised differently,' he says. 'We are still in the phase where the winners are humiliating the losers. It will take three or four generations before the conversation can be had on equal terms.'

Again, the question is less about whether the fall of the Wall was a good thing, and more about how much of a voice East Germans have in the society it created. Many feel that their voices are still worth less and heard only with the caveat that they are from the former East. 'I still get asked in every interview about where I did my military service,' grumbles Zingler, raising the subject without prompting. 'Nobody would ever ask that question to a West German.'

That perceived double standard also influences the way East Germans view both their past and their present. If the fall of the Wall is still remembered as the end of history in the former West, then in the former East, it is merely an example of the fragility of all political systems. Zingler points out that in East Germany, few people believed reunification could happen until it did. Even the dissidents were fighting for a better GDR, not necessarily to destroy it entirely, he says. He doesn't go as far as to directly compare the current struggles of western democracy with the last years of the Soviet Union, but he flirts with the idea. 'In the GDR, we deceived ourselves into thinking we were doing the right thing. A lot of people knew that the system didn't work, but they believed in it anyway. In that sense, we in the East have experience of something which people are only just experiencing now in the West.'

Only someone who has lived through both systems can draw that comparison. But different historical experiences undoubtedly breed different attitudes to the problems of today. And for that reason, says Zingler, it is absurd to assume everyone can get along just by saying they can. 'This city was divided, you have to accept that. There is nothing in this city which has not grown out of or grown up with the fractures. If anyone tries to tell you otherwise, they are the real liars.'

* * *

Accepting the division, and that Union are an East Berlin club, is one thing. But the former East Berlin has changed enormously since the Wall fell, and the years to come could see some of the most dramatic changes yet. The head of Berlin's new Willy Brandt Airport, which finally opened years behind schedule in 2020, has estimated it will create more than 50,000 new jobs in the region by 2035. Tesla's new Gigafactory is aiming to employ between 10,000 and 40,000 people by itself. Even if these predictions prove optimistic, projects like this will still bring change to nearby districts like Köpenick.

In economic terms, that should help Union. More local people equals more stadium-going fans, and major economic players lead to better infrastructure. Union's stadium renovation has already been delayed by a lack of transport options. The expansion of the Köpenick train station into a regional hub was originally planned for 2007 and is now even more overdue than the airport. Without it, Union will struggle to double their matchday capacity. They have good reason to hope that, in the future, the region can change at faster than a snail's pace.

But when I ask Zingler if he sees Union's growth as a part of a wider development, he gives a sceptical sigh. 'I've been to see what they're doing there at Tesla, and I have to say it's not really my world,' he says. With a mischievous twinkle in his eye, he adds: 'They all want to go to Mars with Elon Musk.'

It is no surprise that Zingler is cool on Tesla. He is, after all, a businessman of the German *Mittelstand*, the core of medium-sized businesses which famously power the country's formidable economy. It is a very un-Muskish model of entrepreneurship which prizes substance over style and is built in no small part on the traditional car industry. Perhaps also with a wary eye on Hertha's many false dawns, Zingler is wary of making any bold claims about Union beyond the past and the present. Everything else, as the Germans say, is just 'future music': speculation and dreams about projects yet to be realised.

His scepticism also hints at a cultural conservatism which is never too far from the surface with Union. Beyond the bricks and mortar changes in Berlin, Zingler admits that the club are increasingly going to have to confront wider social questions as they get more popular. 'Society changes and the expectations of us change too. But the question is how do we steer that change? There are some clubs where change is the guiding principle. They always want to be doing the most modern or up-to-date things. Our principle is that we don't change,' says Zingler. 'People move to Berlin and they come to us because we're supposedly sexier than Hertha, but anyone who wants to change us to make us more socially presentable is going to be disappointed.'

Since reaching the Bundesliga, Union have often been criticised for the position they have taken on wider social issues. Their stances on the pandemic divided opinion; during Euro 2020, they decided not to join other German clubs in lighting up their stadium with the colours of the rainbow flag amid a debate over LGBT-discrimination in Hungary; just days before our interview, Zingler riled some fans by laughing off a suggestion that the club should provide vegan sausages on matchday as well as the traditional bratwurst. 'I've got nothing against vegans, but people should know what they're getting with us. And if they think we're all just old, white men, then fine,' he huffs.

Zingler's allergy to symbolism and gesture politics can occasionally frustrate more progressive fans. But even if he plays up to the stereotype, he is not a very convincing reactionary. On issues from homelessness to the refugee crisis, he has also shown concretely that Union take their social responsibilities seriously. He is conservative only in the sense that he believes he has something worth protecting, and the fact that so many new people are flooding into the club is proof of that. 'We are seeing that there is a high demand for what we have to offer,' he says. 'And we're doing pretty well. Our stadium experience is still the same whether we're playing Bayern Munich or Sandhausen. And we still sell mostly bratwurst.'

But his aim is not simply to sit and stew. The old forester's attic in which he is sitting may be one hundred years old, but almost everything around it is new: the car park and the main stand behind it were built in 2013; the rest of the stadium is made of concrete laid in 2009; and the skate park over the road was only opened in 2012. 'I am exaggerating a bit when I say that our principle is that we don't change,' he admits. 'Society is constantly changing and of course we change with it. Whether it's Tesla, Amazon or a new airport, Berlin is constantly changing, and it will keep changing. That's the appeal of this city. But the point is that we have been playing football on this spot for a hundred years.

'The city changes. We are stable.'

*   *   *

For a long time, the only thing that was truly stable about Union was the dedication of their most committed fans. Since 2004, Zingler and his fellow directors have added economic and structural stability, which in turn have led to footballing success. The question now is how Union keep both those aspects – the culture and the cold hard figures – equally stable in the years to come. Most fans trust the current leadership to keep that balance. But almost everyone interviewed in this book at some point asked the same rhetorical question: 'What happens when Dirk Zingler isn't there anymore?'

Zingler's current term runs until 2025, by which time he will have been at the club for more than two decades. He has already been in office longer than any German Chancellor, including Angela Merkel, and has outlasted most of his fellow club presidents in the Bundesliga. There have been directors who have served for even longer, but as top-flight clubs become more professional and internationalised, Zingler may prove to be one of the last of a dying breed. The club patriarch, good for a headline and fiercely loyal to his region and the people in it, was once an archetype in German football. Nowadays, there are fewer of them about.

Often, something does get lost when those figures finally bow out. Some clubs, like Schalke, have descended into full-blown crisis after the departure of a long-serving president. Others, like Mainz or even Bayern Munich, have remained financially stable but struggled with questions of identity. Zingler is determined to make sure that neither happens when he leaves Union. 'I see it as a big responsibility to make sure the club is set up in a sustainable way. When the time comes, that means getting people who can maintain the course we have managed to steer for the last fifteen years or so. When the time comes, we'll have to decide who those people are. But for now we still have a lot to do.'

First and foremost, there is another construction project to oversee. The expansion of the Alte Försterei, which Union hope to begin work on in 2022, will be the next major step in the club's relentless rise. The seating areas will be expanded to comply with Bundesliga and UEFA regulations, meaning that Union can stay in their beloved home regardless of how much more success they enjoy in the future. Unlike most top-flight stadiums, however, it will remain majority standing. Even in success, Union remain a club who insist on doing it their own way. 'We are building a stadium which we think is good for us. We are not measuring it against anyone else's,' says Zingler.

As he sees it, that is an approach borne of common sense rather than ideological zeal. They are not being different for the sake of being different, nor are they attempting to be pioneers of a new kind of football. The stadium, like everything else, is the result of what Zingler calls 'authentic decisions' about how the club should be. In a city which has spent several decades trying to shake off its past with bold visions of the future, Union make a point of being anti-hubristic. They have built slowly, and unlike some of Berlin's more ambitious projects, they have been astonishingly successful.

Union fans were only half-joking when they sang '*Scheisse!* We're going up!' in 2017. They could see the golden age that was looming on the horizon, and it filled them with foreboding as well as joy. Success, after all, had never been in their blood. Being an Unioner had never been about winning trophies, football matches or even local derbies. Even when they revelled in their city rivalries, they had never seriously aspired to overtake BFC or Hertha. Union wasn't about taking over the world, it was about escaping from it. It was about community, family, and protecting what you had. To lose that would be shattering.

When they did go up, many of their fears were realised. Elbows sharpened as the community became more crowded. Unioners had to cope with both the accusing glare of the media spotlight and the cold realities of football commercialism. After a decade of relative comfort, the world had once again moved on. After half a century as rebellious outsiders, Union had now joined the elite.

But it will take more than success alone to kill the Union spirit. In the early 2020s, a few years on from promotion, there is little sign that they have become just another top-flight club. They and their president can still divide opinion like few others can, and they still provoke ferocious loyalty from their own fans, whether old or new. The little stadium in the forest is still one of the loudest and most magical on the continent. The people inside it still come here for something more than just football.

When I ask Zingler about his vision for the future he returns to the idea of people. 'I would be very happy if Union was still a home for people in twenty or thirty years' time,' he says. 'Home means that this place is important to you, that you feel comfortable here, that it's the place of your fathers, your grandfathers and your friends. I would like it to remain that.'

What happens on the pitch, he adds, is almost incidental. 'That's the best thing about it. It can be a home whether we're in the Bundesliga or back in the third division.'

EPILOGUE

At around 5.15pm on May 15th, 2022, the Alte Försterei erupted. On a sunny afternoon on the final day of the season, Union had thrown away a two-goal lead and their hopes of qualifying for the Europa League were hanging by a thread. With two minutes to go, Nigerian striker Taiwo Awoniyi flicked the ball up with his right foot and prodded it into the bottom corner with his left. As he ripped off his shirt in celebration, the stadium roof shook with the noise.

It was the second time in two seasons that Union had qualified for a European competition with a last-minute winner on the final day. When they reached the Conference League in 2021, most people thought a zenith had been reached. Union's first season in Europe for twenty years would surely be a giddy one-off, not to be repeated for at least another decade. But just twelve months later, it was happening again.

The 2021/22 season was arguably the most successful in the history of the club. Union won three derbies against Hertha, beat RB Leipzig at home and away, and came within a whisker of reaching the German Cup final. Awoniyi's dainty finish on the final day secured Europa League qualification in fifth place, their highest ever league finish since reunification.

The party lasted long into the evening. An hour after full-time, the players emerged on the balcony above the stadium car-park to lead the thousands below in a wild celebration. As the sun slowly began to sink over Köpenick, Christian Arbeit announced free beer for everyone.

There was also a note of melancholy. Awoniyi's winner was his last act in an Union shirt. The Nigerian completed a move to Nottingham Forest a month later, and he was not the only key player to leave Berlin that summer. Earlier that afternoon, midfielder Grischa Prömel had wept openly as he bid farewell to the Waldseite.

For a club like Union, this is the reality of modern football. Despite their TV income having soared in the Bundesliga, theirs is still one of the smallest budgets in Germany's top flight. When richer clubs come knocking, even those lower down the table, Union usually end up selling. Very few players, however beloved they may be, stay more than a few years. In the summer of 2022, there were just two players left in the squad from the team that had won promotion three years earlier.

That lack of continuity in the dressing room would unsettle other teams, but it has not halted Union's rise. Every summer, they bring in a host of new faces, and almost every new arrival raves about how easy it is to settle in Köpenick. Union's success has not been fuelled by an injection of cash from a wealthy investor, but by good leadership, teamwork and an immovable sense of community.

That spirit has also endured off the pitch. Like many other Bundesliga clubs, Union joined a wave of solidarity for Ukraine following Russia's invasion in February 2022 and, as in previous crises, their response was driven in large part by active engagement from sponsors and fans. The Union Foundation helped provide apartments for Ukrainian refugees in Berlin, while the club itself teamed up with the Jewish Community of Berlin to provide football camps for orphaned children from Odesa.

They weren't alone. The debate over Germany's role in the first few months of the war naturally tended to focus on energy policy and the country's reliance on Russian gas, but that should not obscure the admirable response of German civil society. According to official figures, Berlin alone welcomed more than 267,000 Ukrainians in the first few months of the war, more than triple the amount which arrived in the UK in the same period. As in the Syrian refugee crisis of 2015, it was ordinary people who organised to welcome them, volunteering in droves to help at arrival centres like the one at Berlin's central train station.

As Union fan Sven Mühle puts it: 'The question is whether you have put something in motion, whether you have helped someone.' At Union, they hope that culture of involvement and community action will continue, even as the club enters a completely new era.

For as Union continue to exceed their wildest expectations on the pitch, it appears more and more as if promotion was not a flash in the pan, but the start of a much bigger process. This is a project which continues to grow, and the club has a clear vision for its own future. In 2022, they released the final plans for the stadium expansion, which they planned to begin the following year.

'Once we're finished, it will still be the Alte Försterei, but it will be different. This is a stadium which will shape the next 40 to 50 years,' said Zingler in an interview with the club's YouTube channel in May 2022. 'This is our last step to becoming a real grown-up club.'

It is not just the stadium which has accelerated that process. Union have also now professionalised their women's team, with a view to gaining promotion to the women's Bundesliga in the next few years. The long-overlooked youth system is also set to be overhauled with the construction of a new academy building. The club's sponsorship deals are also only getting bigger. In 2022, Aroundtown scaled back their partnership with the club, paving the way for a Europe-wide insurance company and a US comedy channel to expand their involvement. Slowly but surely, Union are reaching new levels commercially as well as on the field.

That means an irrevocable shift in the dynamics of football in Berlin. While Union are scaling up to a larger stadium, Hertha are hoping to downsize into a new ground near the old Olympiastadion. The city of Berlin, which long felt lucky to have even one club in the top flight, now has two established, medium-sized powers in the Bundesliga. And that too reflects a wider trend. Berlin is still not the economic capital of Germany, but it has begun to pull level with the traditional hubs in the former West.

There is, as always, much to be lost in that process. And even amid Union's current success, there is still a nostalgia for the harder times of previous decades. But as they swigged free beer in the spring sunshine, there were few Unioners who would truly have wanted to turn back the clock.

They had tasted success, and it didn't taste *Scheisse* at all.

BIBLIOGRAPHY

Biermann, Christoph, *Wir Werden Ewig Leben*, (Kiepenheuer & Witsch, 2020)

Censebrunn-Benz, Angelika, 'Geraubte Kindheit – Jugendhilfe in der DDR' in *Deutschland Archiv*, 30.6.2017, Link: www.bpb. de/251286

Dost, Robert, *Der zivile Club: Die gesellschaftliche Stellung des 1. FC Union Berlin und seine Anhängerschaft in der DDR*, Hochschule-Mittweida (University of Applied Sciences), 2010

Hesse, Uli, *Tor! The Story of German Football*, (WSC Books, 2002)

Karpa, Gerald & Czerwinski, Tino, *1. FC Union Berlin*, (Sutton Verlag, 2005)

Koch, Matthias, *'Immer weiter, ganz nach vorn': Die Geschichte des 1. FC Union Berlin*, (Die Werkstatt, 2013)

Koch, Matthias, *1. FC Union Berlin, Populäre Irrtümer und andere Wahrheiten*, (Klartext Verlag, 2021)

Lesching, Jochen & Gluschke, Dieter, *Stadion an der Alten Försterei: Das Buch zum Bau*, (Edition Else, 2010)

MacGregor, Neil, *Germany: Memories of a Nation*, (Allen Lane/ Penguin, 2014)

Nussbücker, Frank, *111 Gründe, den 1. FC Union Berlin zu lieben*, (Schwarzkopf & Schwarzkopf, 2018)

Rapp, Tobias, *Lost and Sound: Berlin, Techno und der Easyjetset*, ('Suhrkamp Verlag, 2009)

Rabenschlag, Ann-Judith, 'Arbeiten im Bruderland. Arbeitsmigranten in der DDR und ihr Zusammenleben mit der

deutschen Bevölkerung' in *Deutschland Archiv*, 15.9.2016, Link:
www.bpb.de/233678

Sachse, Christian, 'Verschleierte Zwangsarbeit für westliche
Firmen' in *Deutschland Archiv*, 7.10.2016, Link: www.bpb.de/234183

Schneider, Peter, *Berlin Now: The City After the Wall*, (Farrar, Strauss
& Giroux/Penguin, 2014)

Willmann, Frank (Ed.), *Stadionpartisanen: Fans und Hooligans in der
DDR*, (Neues Leben, 2007)

Willmann, Frank & Luther, Jörn, *Eisern Union!*, (BasisDruck, 2010)

Willmann, Frank & Böttcher, Jan, *Alles auf Rot: Der 1. FC Union
Berlin*, (Blumenbär/Aufbau, 2017)

Other sources

Berliner Kurier

Berliner Zeitung

Bundeszentrale für politische Bildung - bpb.de

B.Z.

Der Tagesspiegel

ExBerliner

Frankfurter Allgemeine Zeitung

GQ

Taz

Textilvergehen.de

"Und niemals vergessen" podcast

www.stasi-unterlagen-archiv.de/

www.ddr-im-blick.de/

ZEFYS Zeitungsportal DDR-Presse - Staatsbibliothek zu Berlin